Cornucopia Limited

Cornucopia Limited

Design and Dissent on the Internet

Richard Coyne

The MIT Press
Cambridge, Massachusetts
London, England

MIT Press books may be purchased at special quantity discounts for business or sales
promotional use. For information, please email special_sales@mitpress.mit.edu or write
to Special Sales Department, The MIT Press, 55 Hayward Street, Cambridge, MA 02142.

This book was set in Garamond 3 and Bell Gothic by Graphic Composition, Inc.,
Athens, Georgia. Printed and bound in the United States of America.

Library of Congress Cataloging-in-Publication Data

Coyne, Richard.
Cornucopia limited : design and dissent on the Internet / Richard Coyne.
    p. cm.
Includes bibliographical references and index.
ISBN 0-262-03336-4 (alk. paper)
1. Engineering design. 2. Electronic commerce. 3. Web sites—Design. 4. Internet.
I. Title
TA174.C68   2005
006.7—dc22

                                                                    2005045100

10 9 8 7 6 5 4 3 2 1

To John Lansdown

Contents

Preface

The network economy presents itself in the transactions of electronic commerce, finance, business, and communications. It is also a social condition. Writing at the end of the 1970s, Hiltz and Turoff[1] highlighted the extension of digital networks, satellite communications, and video transmission as a means of forming the world into a total communicative structure, a "global village."[2] More recent scholarship recognizes that the network society is less a unifying entity than a discontinuous matrix of constant change and "organizational fluidity."[3] Commerce in cyberspace presents an enigmatic condition of indefinite limits and in-between spaces.

This book is about thresholds, margins, hybridities, and the gaps between solidities. This is also the inter-territorial precinct of design, where assumptions are challenged, new entities emerge, and monsters lurk. I theorize the liminal (in-between) condition. The interaction between the vital spheres of design and the network economy mark the test site for our investigation.

The theories of liminality[4] I present provide a framework for analyzing the network economy from the point of view of design. I present design less as a precise science of control or problem solving than as an open-ended, disjointed, and transgressive exploration. With its emphasis on intervention, design provides a way of *thinking* about the network economy. Design crosses territorial boundaries, stimulates controversies, polarizes, and often offends. Design is also acquisitive and promiscuous in its use of sources and models. The scope of design extends from cities to Web sites. It also loops back into the reflective process and provides ways of thinking about, and framing, the problem of the network economy.

The reputed origins of the Internet in scientific and academic altruism suggest that trade on the Internet is predicated on the operations of the gift society. Some think that the Internet works well as a social enabler because people contribute to the informational tank for free, ahead of any consideration of making a profit. The elevation of the gift resonates with design, but I show how the gift society is already fraught. It is an awkward standard under which to gather, but one that can usefully be pitched in the region of the threshold, the boundary, the in-between space, the suspect inter-territorial region that is the preserve of the trickster. Vibrant dissonances and resonances happen along the edge between the digital economy and design, and the metaphor of the threshold wins over the gift.

I progress the discussion along five designer metaphors: *household, machine, game, gift,* and *threshold.* Economic theory is grounded in the *household* according to Aristotle. The Romantics and Marx claimed that labor is subjugated under the rampant *machinery* of capitalism. Economics presents as a *game,* and the computer games industry delivers a prominent economic archetype. The *gift* is presented as precursor to commercial exchange. I subject each metaphor to scrutiny in terms of how it deals with the *threshold,* in other words as it is dissected by the cynic or manipulated by the trickster and other liminal dwellers in the network economy.

I am indebted to the insights of colleague Bruce Currey in encouraging some of the themes of this book. Dermott McMeel, Stephen Cairns, Dorian Wiszniewski, Mark Dorrian, and Pedro Rebelo also provided valuable insights. As ever, I am grateful to Adrian Snodgrass for directing me to the theme of interpretation, and the gap.

Introduction: Permeable Portals

The network economy depends on design. Web sites are composed, pages arranged, products and systems configured, planned, organized and marketed. Digital products include electronic documents, computer games, booking systems, databases, corporate Intranets, handheld navigation devices, and security systems. The creation and presentation of this digital abundance has to be accomplished knowingly, integrating diverse media and systems, calling on understandings of social and cultural conditions, history, and user expectations, and following procedures that promote creativity, innovation, and rigor. This is the territory of design. The early days of computing were dominated by a technical agenda, driven by the need to control digital processes, to calculate, and to program. Now design can operate independently of any knowledge of these procedures. The control of digital routines is hierarchically organized to partly obscure their basis in bit processing, leaving the designer to concentrate on images, tools, metaphors, meanings, functions, interactions, usability, and innovation. The designer can also concentrate on media "content," the fashioning of imagery, text, video, and sound through narratives and meaning structures.[1] According to one pioneer game designer, the computer emerged from the back room of the programmer into the creative design realm when graphics and sound enabled developers to exploit the computer as a medium "for emotional communication art."[2] It seems that design embodies human aspirations and puts the spotlight on the experience of the computer user or consumer.

Whether a programmer or not, the digital designer contributes professionalism, usability, and "cool" to the network economy. There is no doubt that design is important economically. Badly designed software, systems, and content do not sell well. Conversely, good design provides a market advantage. Consumers want easy-to-use interfaces, programs that do not crash, smart functionality, clearly articulated graphics, and media content that is up-to-date, informative, entertaining, arresting, and well targeted. But design also sells. That is, a product that asserts conspicuously that it has been designed can promote value. If appropriately targeted, the design label can appeal to a level of refinement beyond the run-of-the-mill, populist or commercial. But design is everywhere, even when the designer label is hidden. Smart designers can even design products to look undesigned or underdesigned to suit the market.

Already the description of design given so far will be irksome to some. The picture I have presented is of design as a manipulative exercise driven by commerce. Design is often disparaged in this role. From a critical perspective, design is complicit in the excesses of the media age. Industries offer a treadmill of perpetual innovation in order to return profit. In their extensive and helpful critique of the computer game industry, Kline, Dyer-Witherspoon, and De Peuter incriminate design in the process of constantly creating and nurturing artificial markets for products—obviously to enhance sales and profits. A computer games company must create its products, then innovate upgrades to keep alive its markets, which are readily exhausted by short-lived consumer and entertainment values. They write: "Moreover, to profit in this circumstance requires cultural intermediaries who are concerned with aesthetics and popular taste, a legion of designers and artists, and advertising and promotional wizards engaged in engineering or orchestrating the incessant changes in demand on which the absorption of perpetual innovation depends."[3] Design perpetuates an excess of production. It is as if we already have more than we need, but design keeps us demanding more. It renders us slaves to fashion, and in turn servants to the power of capitalism. For Kline, Dyer-Witherspoon, and De Peuter, design constitutes "the transmission of meaning from 'producers' to 'consumers' in the context of the power relations of a market society."[4] This manufacture of consumer desire is a commerce in symbols and meaning systems. The practices of digital design are part of "a strategic marketing process"[5] by which symbols are converted to a "mediated experience" for an audience. The same can be said of any commodified object. E-commerce on the Web perpetuates a promotional aesthetic, which deploys deception. For Web theorists Burnett and Marshall, the Web is "a showcase for what it can do and not necessarily what it does."[6] As an offshoot of consumer culture, the Web, and design on the Web, sells promise—and sometimes this promise has a hollow ring. Design makes things appear what they are not.

But does design have to be identified with commercialism? A contrary position holds that design is essentially above commerce. Like art, it is a dignified and altruistic pursuit. Commerce is a corrupting influence, which needs to be resisted. I won't develop this heroic stance further, because it provides the point of departure for the chapter that follows. It is sufficient to point out that a conundrum exists. How is design positioned in relation to commerce? Design seems to occupy an uncomfortable place between commercialism and creativity, economic pragmatism and idealism. However it is cast, the relationship between design and commerce is a troubled one.

We could try to smooth over this troubled association. More contentedly, we could assert that design embraces a spectrum of practices, which bear fluid and variable relationships with commerce. But there is much to be gained by elevating and even exaggerating the differences between design and commerce. In what follows I will show that the in-between condition is a familiar place for designers, a position made even more stark in the network economy. Design is neither subservient to commerce, nor above it, but occupies an uncomfortable position that worries itself with the space between the embrace and the denial of economic considerations.[7]

Edgy Design

Design has a natural affinity with the boundary between regions, the edge condition, the position between polar opposites. For the anthropologist Victor Turner, this region of "betwixt and between" is where "novel configurations of ideas and relations arise."[8] For contemporary architectural theorists, such as Bernard Tschumi, "the ultimate pleasure of architecture lies in the most forbidden parts of the architectural act; where limits are perverted, and prohibitions are *transgressed.* The starting point of architecture is distortion."[9] Design is transgressive. Similarly for Koolhaas, the issue of design is not "meticulous definition, the imposition of limits, but about expanding notions, denying boundaries, not about separating and identifying entities, but about discovering unnameable hybrids."[10] For Hill, liminality is about composing a "montage of gaps."[11] On the subject of relational art, Bourriaud similarly describes the contemporary exhibition in terms of "the interstice," as creating "free areas, and time spans whose rhythm contrasts with those structuring everyday life."[12] Creativity works by way of contrasts with what is expected.

Historically, designers and artists have positioned themselves and their work outside the mainstream. One thinks of the bohemian artist of the nineteenth century, able to move in and out of polite society, sometimes treated as an oddity, indulged, kept at bay, respected for her genius, and who in turn draws on the bourgeoisie for subject matter, and as inspiration. By this reading, the rebel is never entirely in or out, accepted or rejected. The boundary is a creative place to be. It is often at the boundary between countries, where culture, language, and cuisine mingle, producing rich hybrids, or exaggerations of difference. The edge condition receives ample attention in literary studies, linguistics, philosophy, and cultural theory, from which I will draw in this book. In design this identification of the edge actually serves a utilitarian purpose. Focusing on the boundary sets people thinking, and designing, even when the boundary is between two diametrically opposed positions: the high country and the low country, the seafarers and the land bound, the creative and the dull, the economic and the altruistic, the efficient and the wasteful.

As an instance of this creativity at the edge, consider how an architect might deal with the problem of designing a medical clinic in a shopping mall. At first various ideas come to mind: well-being, health, service, the body. Considering the context, the impersonal, commercial non-place of the shopping mall, several oppositions also come into play: well-being and illness, health and wealth, sustaining the body and indulging in excess, the intimate world of the body and the public world of the market. The architect might focus on one idea, such as intimacy, discuss it through, consider its opposite (the public sphere), and develop a design that explores the relationship between the two. The design emerges as a response to this tarrying along the edge condition (between the intimate and the public). The edge tests the designer's thinking. Sometimes it makes the design problem even more difficult, or more interesting. The edge is a site of resistance. Sometimes the way we think of the relationship between the two regions has to be reconfigured. The boundary is changed. Design in this light is not just about a problem, but the configuration and development of a worldview. What I have alluded to here is just the flicker of a process that builds up heat throughout designing. According to this model, the designer starts with an "idea," brings to mind its opposite, then works with what emerges from the friction between the two, as a continuous process. For some, this is how we think in any case, however we sophisticate it with logic and formal analysis.[13]

I posit edgy design in distinction to systematic method, where the designer will identify the problem to be "solved," break it into parts, and attempt to solve the problem piecemeal, an approach common in software engineering.[14] It is also in opposition to a method that requires you to look up a catalogue of solutions (e.g., Web page templates, or standard designs for clinics). Edgy design brings no guarantee of success. The flicker can lead to a bonfire or just smoke. The process is indeterminate, discursive, questioning, playful, and dialogical. The ideas float, there is a chain of associations, certain ideas and oppositions are more productive than others, the negotiation of the middle position is fluid, sometimes brittle, agonistic, fraught, and occasionally incendiary.[15]

To bring edgy design home to the network economy we can consider the design of that ubiquitous digital category, the Web portal, such as Yahoo.com, or a university Web site, with its range of private and public information for customers, students, staff, and the outside community.[16] (Given the ferment and challenges of digital design in the era of global communications, media convergence, mobile devices, robotics, surveillance, and intelligent environments, our imaginary task will hardly tax the resources of edgy design, but its simplicity makes it a useful example.) The task for our imaginary designer is not to design a building, but a Web portal for a service, organization or institution.[17] Let us trace a possible thought process.

The portal prompts the theme of *access,* which readily brings to mind its "opposite," a concern with *security.* And here the designer can draw on a well-established discourse within the network economy: the debates about freedom of access, open-source software, security and cryptography.[18] The origins of the World Wide Web are often attributed to the aspirations of the communities of scientists and researchers freely sharing expertise and information.[19] The literature on hypertext shares a similar ideology. Advocates of hypertext see in the Web an opportunity for nonlinear, democratic, a-centric textual production,[20] and the founders of the Web see it as a medium of "mind to mind" communication.[21] The Web is the main medium for purveying the ideals of open-source[22] and free software (www.gnu.org) and freely distributed creative production (www.creativecommons.org). The portal becomes a virtual clinic with an open-door policy. The life of the street is admitted to the intimate confines of the interior.[23] The adage that "information wants to be free" might inform the designer's thinking about the portal.[24] The use of the World Wide Web is caught between its supposed idealistic origins of open access, and its increasing institutionalization, corporatization, and yielding to encryption procedures.[25]

So the Web portal is an expression of the troubled threshold between the private and the public. What is the character of the Web portal within this problematic? From an institutional point of view, a Web portal is simply a series of Web pages, structured and organized to provide access to the information, facilities, and services available.[26] The "enterprise portal" may also provide relevant links to the rest of the web. It may have an Intranet component, with access restricted to members of the organization or users within its domain. From the perspective of the Web liberalist, the idea of the portal offers potential for access to communities, the exchange of ideas, experimentation, free speech, and support for otherwise marginalized groups. From a more radical point of view, the portal suggests the possibility of a chink in the borders around the restricted areas of corporate networked communications. For the edgy designer, the portal could be the gap in the corporate fence.[27]

The designer of our Web portal may wrestle with the conflict between the open society and the corporate, the seamless and the fractured, the homogeneous and the richly textured and lumpy. In fact the designer may further draw on the nature of the designed and built physical environment, which is already characterized by heterogeneity and discontinuity, and which is yielding increasingly to the presence of ubiquitous digital devices. For the designer, the portal is a granular entity in an imperfect medium, much like an array of gates, fences, bridges, bollards, openings, signs, and obstructions in a physical landscape. While deliberating on the theme of access, a designer might consider that the Web portal involves an ambiguous and risky relationship between open access and security.

So the portal design need not be restricted to the usual type of security solution, which focuses on registration and password access, but by the notion of dynamic and variable security protocols, by permeability.[28] Leaving the door of your house open to the street is hazardous, but less so if there is a stream of active comings and goings, and if trusted neighbors are passing by. Crowds are not always safe places, but active communities where people are watching out for each other are as secure as it can get. Architecture and urbanism have long been suspicious of fortress design, where higher fences and more closed-circuit television (CCTV) cameras are meant to reduce antisocial behavior. The result is barren cityscapes made up of impermeable walls, uninhabitable edges, devoid of people and activity. Where they succeed in barring delinquency at all, they also exclude carers and concerned citizens. Permeability is risky but rendered feasible simply by the fact that a site (a Web site or a physical place) is actively in use.

A Web site's constant use by a community can perhaps maintain security on that site. A stranger would be challenged, which is not to say made unwelcome. Security is most likely to be an issue when the site is barely in use, or if the site simply peters out into disuse and we forget to check it. This is the downtown office precinct on a Sunday, or the holiday camp out of season. There is a temporal dimension. The site could be configured so that it exhibits successive degrees of permeability depending on use. So if there is a period when the site is empty of activity then the gate swings shut, site access is restricted, and you need the password to reopen it. As long as there are signs of life, and there is friendly traffic, then the restrictions diminish: Your password cookie has a longer life, or you don't require a password at all. This is an automated solution to a low-risk problem, but one that could be extended to other corporate and institutional contexts, as one strategy to encourage "permeable portals."

(What I am offering here is an example of a design result: an "enterprise portal" that breaks with the usual provision of blanket password security, but that varies its security protocols depending on the activities taking place on the site. Such systems may already exist, or have been found wanting, or be overtaken by other concerns, techniques, or technologies. I hope the reader will not equate the limitations of the example in our thought experiment with the plausibility of the process by which the result has come about.)

This is the space of thinking an edgy designer might traverse. Rather than take the obvious problematic engendered by issues of security, edgy design distorts the issue of security through the concept of permeability. This is an example of design thinking that is oppositional and agonistic. It is about boundaries. It is also a design thinking that is risky, political, and transgressive, and were we to take the design further then the digital product (the Web portal) might be seen to exhibit these characteristics as well.

The permeable Web portal also provides a further metaphor for understanding design: the convergence of design with the media-rich network economy. On a Web-enabled computer desktop, many digital channels can be open at once, some streaming content, others offering potential, some affording glimpses, others gaping wide. In design the multiplicity of portals and their various conditions demonstrate the value of networked computing, as the computer user integrates, synthesizes, compares, and juxtaposes. These are common processes for designers, who are used to drawing stimulation from a promiscuous range of sources. Now the Internet adds to this profusion.[29] When these images are thrown together, we have a "portal" into something new. Permeability and profusion in design enable this to happen. Permeability also invites inclusion. The usability of computer systems is not finalized through a market survey or user questionnaire, but characterized by an ongoing dialogue, a recognition of the conflicting demands of different constituencies of users and developers, and technological possibilities and constraints.

Design is edgy, and risky, in the same way that breaches in network security and permeable portals are risky. In the rest of this book I will examine the space between regions, the threshold between conditions, exemplified in the boundary between design and commerce. According to this reading, design already contains within it the impetus to transgress.

Design as Theft

Not all design is suggestive of innovation, risk, or the edge condition, but even the production of routine, imitative design originates in transgression, through concepts of theft. Karl Marx began his social philosophy with the proposition that property is theft,[30] so perhaps the design of commodities already implicates theft.[31] Design is already one step from outright thieving.

Theft in the network economy involves the passage of information by breaking and entering, cyber-piracy, a rupture in portal security. But goods and labor can be seized in other ways too, through extracting the form, shape, and genius of an object of production. Here we are dealing with the appropriation of not only the object, or the work that went into its production, but also the "idea." The object is not so much taken from its owner as copied, in some or all of its aspects. One might think of stealing the "idea" of the permeable portal, for example.

We can think of design as beginning with this basic transgression, that of copying. If copying is carried out without recompense or acknowledgement, then it becomes plagiarism and infringement of intellectual property, the restitution of which taxes courts and legislators.[32] Copying is a risky business that has the potential to offend and is perilously close to theft. The simplest design strategy is to copy what someone else has produced, with or without consent. In fact a cursory reading of the history of architecture, engineering, sculpture, basic crafts, and the arts in general reveals the importance of this propensity to extend the world of beautiful and useful objects simply by copying what already exists. Inevitably minor variations creep into this succession, but the skill is faithfully to copy what was there before, or possibly improve on it. This is design as a mimetic art, and an aspect that is amplified, or at least brought vividly to our attention, in the network economy. In the early days of Web design the word on the street was that if you liked the layout of a particular Web site then you only had to copy its source code, substitute your own content, and call it your own. This was an easy route to cool Web design. In fact digital products participate readily in this mimetic practice. There is a confluence between the media of production, representation, transmission, and presentation. The mode of copying is now of negligible cost, compared to the labors that produced the original. Whereas to copy a building or a sculpture constitutes another construction project, with its own contingencies, to copy software or digital sounds and images is nearly instantaneous and free. Digital mimesis is easy.

Copying connects with certain philosophical legacies. For many, the start of this chain of copying resides in an ideal object. For Plato, the chair on which you sit to eat your breakfast, the sculpture people admire in the courtyard, or the bed you sleep in are already copies, of some ideal, the earthly form of which is merely a shadow.[33] Paintings are further copies of things, and poets may write falteringly about chairs and paintings, that is, about copies of copies. The occupations that work closest to the original ideal are the most exalted. Designers readily buy into concepts of an ideal. Designers are often idealists in many senses, imitating the ideal Platonic forms, or Platonic solids (cubes, octahedra, etc.), appealing to ideal social conditions, or claiming access to some transcendent principles of taste, beauty, or equity (open-source software, free software, open access, barrier-free computing) that is to be given expression in the design in some way.[34]

As well as "designing" a door or a chair by making an outright copy of another door or chair though with different materials, we can copy across categories. So a chair can have the form of a building, and certain designs for thrones have backs shaped as battlements and with bulwarked armrests. If this is something that no one has ever produced before, it may have the appearance of originality. This is where design starts to look like an interesting activity. There is some skilled judgment being exercised in selecting what is copied, and translating the chosen elements to a new context. Another way of looking at the edgy design of our permeable portal is to think of it as a hybrid in this way. It is software pretending to be architecture, or a child of mixed parentage: computing and building, an uninviting barrier and a welcoming help desk. Perhaps the Web portal is conceived as crossing two digital categories, the firewall and the help desk, taking characteristics of each.

Design and Metaphorics

If design exhibits the character of copying from one category into another then it can more generally be taken as a manipulation of *metaphor,* giving a thing a name that belongs to something else,[35] that is, treating Web sites as if doorways. Design-by-analogy is more specific, involving the identification of the features of one object (Web site) and their transference to another (door). But with metaphor we may never be sure what the features are. We cannot presume buttons, links, text, and images in the case of Web sites, or hinges, handles, door swings, and openings in the case of entrances. To design metaphorically is more like throwing two concepts together, like *Web site* and *doorway,* or *firewall* and *help desk,* and seeing what emerges, or watching the collision. In our thoughts the Web site becomes somewhat doorlike, and a door assumes something of the character of a Web page; the firewall becomes like a help desk and the help desk like a firewall. But we cannot know in advance what those characteristics are. In some cases it will be the shape of the door, at other times its permeability, or its tendency to exclude. In the context of Web design it is less likely we will think of a door in terms of rebates and draught excluders than of locks and openings. But then anything is possible as a design proposition. In fact, other metaphors may come into play that distort either concept further. To think only of doors while designing Web sites would amount to a kind of fixation (or fetish, which can be no bad thing from the point of view of some Web designers,[36] if pushed to the extreme). In fact designers sometimes prefer not to talk about metaphor, because it suggests they are always designing Web pages to look like doors. But, understood in its most general way, design as the play of metaphor is a very open means of describing what happens when something is designed. Returning to edgy design, there is a space created by two terms, concepts, or objects, whether named or not, and the designer's imagination, and practical skills, are exercised in that space. The process is fluid and indeterminate. Certain metaphors (doors) suggest others (access, flow, permeability) and their obverse (walls, defense, resistance), and design is animated by such associations—or else it takes place in the space between them. Already our topic of design in the network economy has acquired a surfeit of metaphors: portal, door, room, fortress, firewall, house, and theft. Metaphors seem to accrete, get in the way of each other, and grow, in rhizomic fashion.[37] Even if we ditch the idea of metaphor as dealing in naïve associations, there is something going on that is like it. Metaphor provides a reasonable metaphor for whatever it is that edgy designers do.

What is copying then? To resort to metaphor is to take on a more sophisticated form of imitation. By an alternative reading, we could say that copying is just a diminished working of metaphor. It seems that metaphor is a sufficiently rich concept to account for the complexities of design in just about all its aspects.

Design involves rigor to be sure, and is never accomplished just by word associations. Some of this rigor includes a careful examination and questioning of the metaphors being used. In design there is also such a thing as *analysis,* a kind of rigorous research that accompanies the creative process: being sure client needs are met, unpicking a set of requirements, fulfilling a contract, user testing, and evaluation. But if metaphor is to maintain its sovereignty as an explanation of edgy design, then we should be able to sustain the metaphor theme as an account of every aspect of designing. This can be done, but to pursue that here would take us from our allotted course (to use a metaphor).[38]

Some designers prefer an analytical approach and are not particularly interested in the metaphoricity of what they do. But others celebrate the creative aspects of design and enjoy looking at the world sideways, that is, in unusual ways, almost out of habit, identifying, mixing and distorting words, definitions, themes, and metaphors.[39] They see familiarity in strange things, and they are excited when they see familiar things in a strange way. This is one of the great contributions of design to intellectual endeavor—a sideways look at the world, and a thieving mindset, the mettle to pillage any discipline for its metaphors.

Designing Sideways

Another way of acknowledging the role of metaphor in edgy design is simply to note that many designers enjoy the unusual brief (set of requirements for a design), or make a conventional brief unusual by rewording it in a strange way. What would a portal be like that is both secure and permeable? What is a thieving portal? Can a Web site assume the character of a chair? Can a chair be a portal? Though the end product may be orthodox, such questioning may leave traces in the final designed product, more as a nuance than an innovation. Such questions and their metaphors may also simply add grease to the design process, speed things along, help the designer come to terms with the nature of the task ahead, aid communication among the participants, or help the designer out of certain limiting preconceptions. They may also instill resistance to the design process, make design harder in ways that also make it more interesting.

A designer working in the network economy might pursue similar techniques of inquiry, in sideways fashion, from an unusual perspective. If there is something about commerce that suggests the market, then a designer might be interested in where the concept of the market derives. What is a marketplace like? There might be an aspect of the market that is at the margins and that can provoke something new and interesting, such as the market as a colonnaded place for philosophers, a counterpoint to the home, a place of perimeters and thresholds, or a place for dogs (or the cynics, to be discussed later). The market may also be a ground for thieves, consumption machines, vain bodies, or the society of the spectacle.[40]

Designers don't only need word association lists to provoke design, but narratives linking such terms. History is important to a designer, for many reasons, not least is that the history of a term such as "market" indicates something of its authority, legacies, and the privilege that we ascribe to it. Histories are also constructed to accommodate and validate the artifacts that populate the world, and there is now a profusion of rival histories to account for the character of digital media in the network economy.[41]

That design might have its origins in a kind of theft (copying) is of potential interest to a designer, as a provocation. "Appropriation" might be a more common term than theft, but is less vivid, controversial, and suggestive of other metaphors. Design as theft is perhaps an activity that subverts the market, since thieving distorts the fair trade of the marketplace. It perhaps provides a different way of looking at what design is, and its relationship to economics. The fact that theft has provided a starting point for a critique of economics (Marx) provides a common origin in something risky and transgressive, as does thieving's relationship with the gift.

Non-designers can also benefit from a designerly, edgy, way of looking at the world of commerce. We may suppose that one of the "functions," of art, if it needs one, is to challenge preconceptions and help us look at the world with fresh eyes. This purpose is certainly served by designers in the instrumental worlds with which they deal. The chief medium of this communication and challenge is of course the designed artifacts themselves. A really good Web site can take us aback and reveal something new about the network economy (as can a work of architecture, a poster, a computer game, a painting).

This book does not present examples of designed artifacts that contribute to an understanding of the network economy, but is concerned with effecting a conversation between some of the thinking that designers find stimulating and the thoughts of businesspeople, economists, managers, and social theorists (who by no means form a homogeneous group). The artifacts of design can challenge, but so can the reflections and thoughts of designers, including the way they can appropriate, misappropriate, contort, and pillage the familiar terms of economics.

This "commerce" between design and economics is not necessarily a happy communion of minds, a harmonious sharing of metaphors. Edgy design does not crave union. In fact the enmity between the thief and the trader provides a useful metaphor here, or at least the metaphor of antagonism is useful. The two terms of a metaphor can be seen as battling it out in some way, appropriating each other's attributes, or each trying to cancel out the other. If Web sites and doors, or firewalls and chat rooms, can be brought into antagonistic play, a battle fought on the basis of similarity and difference, then design and commerce can also be brought into collision. Each is trying to gain the upper hand, or to take something from the other, or to appropriate the other's terminology.

Design as Service

In the spirit of the thief, what does the network economy take from design? It can take labor. Design is easily presented as a grudging servant of commerce. Computer systems that support digital commerce could be expected to take account of user needs and requirements, and fitness for work, leisure, and domestic contexts. There are artifacts to be designed to interface with and house the electronic environments, the hardware, automated teller machines, headsets, video conferencing studios, and mobile electronic devices. One hopes that the service of design is willingly offered, though for some, design seen only as a service saps it of its potency. Edgy design has more going for it when allowed scope to act as a force for social transformation, a mode of communication, a language game, and when seen as a totality that is more than the sum of a number of design commissions.[42]

Under the metaphor of theft, design can also assume the role of the lesser of two antagonists, in that the network economy has an impact on design. Digital commerce carries implications for engineering, architecture, urban design, and planning. Design has to address the fact that the concept of the commercial center and the suburb are transformed in the light of distributed computing, as is the home as a place for tele-working. Accepted building and institutional typologies—the school, the bank, the clinic—undergo change and evolution under these pressures, which further require new information technology systems and infrastructures.[43] In this subservient position, design is called on to respond to these needs.

Designers also have to operate in the network economy, and they have diminishing choice in the matter. It seems that designers have to participate in business-to-business digital commerce, with other designers, consultants, and suppliers. They have to market and deliver their services online. Designers design electronic environments. They are also users (willingly or not) of digital commerce, participants in the network economy.

Designers are also being called on to translate their familiar, material worlds of chairs, sculptures, and beds into virtual spaces, and to design virtual market spaces. According to the cyberspace/cybermarket metaphor, computer networks constitute a kind of space invoking concepts of containment, movement, navigation, boundary, and structure. It is also possible to generate spatial imagery from geometric models, further suggesting that computer networks constitute inhabitable spaces. Computer networks enable people to communicate with one another, as if meeting in rooms. So cyberspaces can be populated by avatars, representations of individuals, conversing and transacting. In the same way that designers envision objects to populate physical space and architects divide and apportion material space to facilitate meetings and transactions, so some think that cyberspace designers will design cyberspaces[44] including the electronic marketplaces, their objects, and environments. So under the metaphor of theft, design is at the service of the electronic market and arguably loses its edge.

Design as Plunder

Of course, were we to move to another set of metaphors, embracing the giddy language of free-market economics, then we might see the preceding in terms of a cornucopia of opportunities, and in this design might loot from the market. Design could be said to plunder the language of the market, the language of merchandise, value, exchange, money, payment, and transaction. In enthusiastic mode it might embrace free exchange, entrepreneurship, competition, and opportunity. Perhaps these terms already belong in the realm of design and are being wrested back from economics, or they may belong with economics and are being foisted onto the world of design. In either case, the exchange suggests antagonism.

And design does appear at times to be at odds with commerce, with which it forms only an unwilling alliance. Creation has been posited as an altruistic activity, the nobility of which is sapped (stolen) when we express the motivation for invention in monetary terms. Commerce seems to suggest a reduction of every endeavor to a single dimension, that of monetary value. The worth of a painting is summed up by what it can fetch at auction. Designers and artists have never been entirely happy with the necessity to commodify their creative production, and thereby abrogate its potency as gift. I will examine further the antagonism between creation and commerce in the chapters that follow.

But designers can counter commercial metaphors with their own. Historically the market is set in opposition to the *household* (chapter 1) (which is in fact Aristotle's first site in his treatise on economics), and the household conjures up the values of community and care, with which, arguably, the creative impetus finds greatest resonance. The private world of the household has an interesting relationship with the public world of the street, mediated by various portals and thresholds. The home is also in an interesting, oppositional relationship with the metaphor of the *machine* (chapter 2). Insofar as computers and systems arrest the attention of the designer, they do so as machines. Creativity has long wrestled with the machine, which in some respects has come to represent so much of what art is against: automation, control, reproduction, mindless copying, predictability, and of course capitalist production. Machines also steal jobs. But there are also machines that are out of control, runaway devices, malfunctions, breakdowns, glitches, that provide metaphors for edgy design. If the thieving metaphor is too agonistic, then there is always the concept of *play* (chapter 3), in which design and creation find a happier residence. Play has a competitive aspect, but it is a kind of controlled and benign thieving: taking the opponent's pieces, status, or victory, all in the spirit of a simulation. We have suggested that design might be theft, but it is also more benignly about the *gift* (chapter 4), a further opposition to the machinery of commerce, and borrowing the mood of giving that is characteristic of the household. The domestic boundary, defining the domain of the gift, across which commerce is conducted, or across which the thief intrudes, constitutes a *threshold* (chapter 5). The threshold condition is the site of edgy design, risk, hybridity, the problematic, and a portal into the new. In what follows I argue that the metaphor of the threshold proves the most potent metaphor of all in accounting for design and innovation in the network economy. The threshold has a history and a legacy that points toward a theory of transgression. Not only is the portal permeable, the portal also permeates the network economy.

We examine in some detail what the household, the machine, the game, the gift, and the threshold have to contribute to understanding the digital economy. Throughout we hear echoed the pragmatic concern with metaphor and language. At the threshold we wrestle with trickiness and cynicism, issues to do with words, but issues not far removed from the network economy and at the leading edge of the impulse to create.

Home Economics

The network economy provides a giant laboratory for experimenting with new ideas for selling products. The e-commerce machine is undergoing evolution and design even while it is in use. For the enthusiast, this is democratic design: Everyone can participate in shaping the digital economy.

The opportunities for e-commerce put the spotlight on the household. The Internet brings the market into the home, the site of mass consumption.[1] Furthermore, the home can be the source of economic production. Apparently, just about anyone can be a cottage entrepreneur. Furthermore, the personal computer is reputedly a home-based invention, with its origin as the covert creation of the back room, the garage, and the workshop, and a significant threshold in the personal computer market was reached when the industry started to regard the computer as a household appliance.[2]

The domestic orbit of the Internet supports a model of democratic and decentralized free computer software, as in the cooperative, open-source development of the Linux operating system.[3] Here software is developed by programmers spread around the globe, with no apparent organization or management. The democratic production of software presents an ideal for the design and development of computer systems. It also bolsters concepts of the free market. According to one commentator, "The Linux world behaves in many respects like a free market or an ecology, a collection of selfish agents attempting to maximize utility which in the process produces a self-correcting spontaneous order more elaborate and efficient than any amount of central planning could have achieved."[4] I will examine the relationships among concepts of the "selfish agent," utility, and design subsequently. Here it is sufficient to point out that the model presented is a domestic one. It appeals to modesty of scale, autonomy, and humble origins, and is against big business.

If the Internet encourages a communal, familial aspect to the design of software, then the Internet, and e-commerce, are also "designing" us. As e-commerce infiltrates every aspect of business and home life, it shapes attitudes, preparing the world for its own growth and expansion. The purpose of this chapter is to align e-commerce with the language of design, and to do so with reference to the sources on which theories of creation draw, as well as the economic literature. The main message of this chapter is that economics, as it is for design and the Internet, is best understood from a pragmatic point of view. That is, we draw on the language of social and interpretive (hermeneutical) inquiry.[5] It seems that a practical orientation to e-commerce favors metaphors of the household above those of the marketplace, though it also concerns the threshold between the two.

Design versus Economics

The impetus to create is not always in harmony with economics. Digital commerce sometimes engenders distaste among designers. Magazines, self- help manuals, and Web guides advising on how to succeed in business constitute the latest assault.[6] E-commerce as a discipline and a practice becomes infected with populist overstatement.

The language of the economic crusader proves a very blunt instrument for grasping the subtleties of moral decision making. The economic language of the campaigner does not support the subtleties of moral inquiry. Considerations of ethical consequences appear as an addendum to the economic theories under discussion and are not integral to them. In one e-commerce self-help book the business person is exhorted: "If you don't use it, embrace it, and immerse your business in it, then the Internet will one day take your customers away from you and your business will die. It may already be doing this."[7] As in the earlier passage about the Linux operating system, there is an immediate appeal to self-interest ("selfish agents"). For the enthusiast, there is really no time to question whether this new aspect of the information revolution is a good thing for other people, within the orbit of one's own business or globally. The important issue is whether or not the business will thrive economically.

On the other hand, the history of design reveals an automatic privileging of the ethical among designers. The simplest claim of design is that designs meet people's needs. To create is to serve people, and in so doing enter the moral sphere of needs, wants, desires, appropriateness, and justice. When the created object enters the economic sphere, when it is traded, bartered, or sold, then the economic system enters the frame, sidelining issues of justice, which have to be forced back into the picture. Putting it crudely, from the point of view of dominant design narratives, creation is noble; making money is vulgar.

I will later dismantle this distinction, but it is worth examining it here as a means of opening up further understandings of design in the network economy. As outlined in the introductory chapter, such oppositions provoke inquiry.

The idea of self-interest as the primary motivation for commercial activity is generally attributed to Adam Smith, the eighteenth-century Scottish philosopher and political economist. In *The Wealth of Nations,* Smith explains how we need each other's help in society, but we cannot expect it by appealing to good will. We have to interest our potential collaborators, benefactors, and providers by appealing to their own interest and show them that it is to their advantage to do for us what we require of them.[8] For Smith, we need to "address ourselves, not to their humanity but to their self-love, and never talk to them of our own necessities but of their advantages."[9] So we pay for what we need, and we encourage the provision of goods and services by ensuring that the providers can make a profit by it.

But Smith's model of economics has its antagonists, particularly among the Romantic writers of the nineteenth century who claim territory in the realm of design. It is the elevation of self-interest as the motivation for commerce that seemed to offended the romantics the most. In "Unto This Last," a polemical essay against the nineteenth-century industrial order, John Ruskin claims of Smith's model that it presents people as "actuated by no other moral influences than those which affect rats or swine."[10] The economist inverts the natural ordering of the human virtues by assuming that the socially beneficial qualities, such as altruism and honor, "are accidental and disturbing elements of human nature; but avarice and the desire of progress are constant elements."[11] In a mocking tone, Ruskin suggests the association of free-market economics with particular personality types: "In a community regulated only by laws of demand and supply, . . . the persons who become rich are, generally speaking, industrious, resolute, proud, covetous, prompt, methodical, sensible, unimaginative, insensitive, and ignorant. The persons who remain poor are the entirely foolish, the entirely wise, the idle, the reckless, the humble, the thoughtful, the dull, the imaginative, the sensitive, the well-informed, the improvident, the irregularly and impulsively wicked, the clumsy knave, the open thief, and the entirely merciful, just, and godly person."[12] Under Smith's regime those of a temperate nature tend toward riches. The interesting and creative people are prone to extremes and to poverty. As I will examine in chapter 5, such people are also aligned with trickery. The creatives are the liminal dwellers, the edgy designers who occupy the threshold between social order and confusion.

The derogatory conflation of economics as a study with the actual practices of dealing with money matches Thomas Carlyle's identification of economics as the "dismal science." In advocating "letting men alone," Smith's philosophy of laissez-faire holds the promise of a "gay science." On the contrary, for Carlyle economics offers "a dreary, desolate, and indeed quite abject and distressing one."[13] It is not only that the study of economics is dull, but it has dispiriting consequences, particularly if seen as a way of justifying slavery, or validating the grim misery of working conditions in industrial England: "In the midst of plethoric plenty, the people perish,"[14] a claim no less relevant under the charge of inequality promoted by unfair trade agreements, the policies of the World Bank, and the domination of small nation states by the powerful.

So in the formative years of the industrial revolution, the battle line is already drawn between the science of economics and the promotion of art. It is a war between self-interest and altruism. It is also perhaps a battle between those claiming authority through an appeal to hard-nosed empiricism (Smith was associated with the Empiricist philosopher David Hume) and those grounded in a first-person idealism. The battle is a variation of the conflict between the objectivism of the Enlightenment and the subjectivism of the Romantics. These polarities define a space in which other oppositions are acted out: popular culture and art, entertainment and education, Hollywood and film house, New Ageism and philosophy, manga and fine art, cyberpunk and civil society, and the transgression of one into the territory of the other. It is also a battle between the Stoics and the Platonists.

The Market Edge

The marketplace features as a major metaphor for the network economy, and is already characterized by an edge, or perimeter condition. In addition to *The Wealth of Nations,* Adam Smith is known for his important book *The Theory of Moral Sentiments,* in which he surveys the contribution of the ancients to an understanding of morality, calling substantially on the authority of the Stoics for his justification of a life of "self-command."[15]

The market connection is obvious. The Stoics took their name from the *stoa,* the colonnade that surrounded the marketplace, or agora, of ancient Athens, where Zeno of Citium (ca. 300 BC), the founder of the movement, would instruct his students.[16] This architectural association between Stoicism and the physical place of exchange may have escaped Smith's analysis, but it furthers his case. Stoicism appears as an early theory of the market and, for Smith, of the free market. The network economy trades in market metaphors. Appeals to ancient Greece, the electronic agora, suggest democracy, people power, a noisy commerce in both goods and ideas, an electronic b@zaar.[17]

Like many metaphysical systems, Stoicism appealed to the power of a divine unity. For Plato (to be considered subsequently), the unity abides beyond earthly existence, but for the Stoics this unity is in the world around us. This Stoic pantheism presents the world as a unitary system. The Roman emperor Marcus Aurelius, one of the Stoic writers on whom Smith draws, describes this unity in terms of a single organism: "Always think of the universe as one living organism, with a single substance and a single soul; and observe how all things are submitted to the single perceptivity of this one whole, all are moved by this single impulse, and all play their part in the causation of every event that happens. Remark the intricacy of the skein, the complexity of the web."[18] This proposition is echoed in much New Age populism and is ever present as a common description of the network society.[19]

Occasionally Smith describes this unity as "the whole machine of the world,"[20] which comes close to a premonition of "the capitalist machine," to be examined in chapter 2. But the appeal to a world unity is to exhort us to know our place, and therefore to be content with our lot. A stoical attitude to losing a job, hardware failure, or corrupted files is one of forbearance. If we elect to complain about our current condition, then we breach the moral order. To complain shows lack of wisdom in two ways. First, it appears as an attempt to deny the natural pattern of interconnections, the pre-ordained order of the universe. Second, it suggests that, if I complain, then as one recalcitrant fragment I am denying my place in the universal scheme of things. It is easy to see how stoic naturalism led to Smith's advocacy of laissez-faire and the primacy of self-interest. For Smith, Stoic doctrine explains that "every animal was by nature recommended to its own care, and was endowed with the principle of self-love."[21] For Smith, though we are motivated by self-interest, it is "our own final interest considered as a part of that whole, of which the prosperity ought to be, not only the principal, but the sole object of our desire."[22] So self-interest should be characterized not as a disregard for others but as our primary contribution in caring for the whole. It follows therefore that we should be stoic in the face of economic failure, as well as success, in light of a consideration of the bigger picture. Smith describes the Stoic attitude as follows:

A wise man never complains of the destiny of Providence, nor thinks the universe in confusion when he is out of order. He does not look upon himself as a whole, separated and detached from every other part of nature, to be taken care of by itself and for itself. He regards himself in the light in which he imagines the great genius of human nature, and of the world, regards him. He enters, if I may say so, into the sentiments of that divine Being, and considers himself as an atom, a particle, of an immense and infinite system, which must and ought to be disposed of, according to the conveniency of the whole. Assured of the wisdom which directs all the events of human life, whatever lot befalls him, he accepts it with joy, satisfied that, if he had known all the connections and dependencies of the different parts of the universe, it is the very lot which he himself would have wished for.[23]

The consolation to economic hardship is that if only you knew how your misery fits within the complex ordering of the universe, you would not have wished it to be otherwise. Insofar as Stoic free marketeers promote the care of the underprivileged, they encourage the poor to participate in a regime of "self-command," to enable them to enter the free market, which is the foundation of many "back to work" schemes to wean people off state welfare.[24] The stoical attitude also emerges in accounts of the inflation of the dot-com "bubble" and its subsequent implosion. With a mind to the bigger picture, the network economy promotes entrepreneurial and investment risk. After the event, it reflects that the bigger picture was not so rational after all: "behaviour that seems rational at the individual level can lead to collective insanity."[25]

There is an element of Stoicism in the bureaucratization often perpetrated through network communications. Though he does not make direct reference to the Stoic connection, the resigned attitude becomes the cornerstone of Max Weber's account of Protestant asceticism as the basis of capitalism. The acquisition of wealth under early capitalism presented as an opportunity to be a wise steward of God's riches rather than a means to greater comfort, luxury, or display. The spirit of capitalism is revealed in the stoic industry of the studious bookkeeper rather than indulgence in conspicuous consumption. For Weber, this asceticism has subsequently lost its religious basis, and capitalism becomes hollow and meaningless in the industrial age. As identified by Ruskin, advocacy of self-interested free enterprise does not necessarily accompany profligacy, an excessive enthusiasm for the good things of life, but indicates a drear, miserly, and perhaps hollow attitude. It seems that those most able to acquire wealth by this means are least equipped to enjoy it. Whether or not this is empirically the case, market critics gain satisfaction from identifying the mediocrity of the vulgar nouveau riche and the popularizers, including the profiteers of the information revolution, entrepreneurs who benefit from free-market opportunism.

If Stoicism bolsters bureaucracy, it also provides theoretical support for empire. Stoicism in various guises was the dominant philosophy of Rome at its height. The Roman philosopher, Seneca, also despised the show of wealth: "We have enslaved our souls to pleasure, indulgence in which is the beginning of all evils; we have betrayed them to ambition and public opinion, and everything else which is equally empty and vain."[26] Even contempt for luxuries is not enough: "What virtue lies in despising superfluities? You can admire yourself when you have come to despise essentials."[27]

Vitruvius, the Roman theorist of art and design (before design was recognized as such), operated within the Stoic tradition, counting the Stoic emperor Marcus Aurelius among his patrons. Vitruvius asserts: "I have never been eager to make money by my art, but have gone on the principle that slender means and a good reputation are preferable to wealth and disrepute."[28] This apparent disregard for riches is consistent with the Stoic view that the wise person must bear up and do without.[29] In keeping with the Stoic enthusiasm for the interconnection of all things, the architect is to be educated in drawing, geometry, history, philosophy, music, medicine, law, and astronomy.[30] The unity of nature is to provide the model for the unity of architecture. As the parts of the human body are proportioned with regard to the whole frame, the parts of buildings are to be harmoniously ordered,[31] and the classical orders derive from the "truth of Nature."[32] Vitruvius's account of the art of making is dour: a practical architecture devoid of excess or even poetry.[33] Knowing your place in the universe apparently provides little scope for flights of fancy, or design at the edge.

Smith's few accounts of the act of creation are also utilitarian, focusing on the successive substitutions of menial tasks by machine, the expansion of the division of labor. Smith gives the apocryphal account of the boy whose job it was to manually open and close the valves that regulated the power for a steam turbine.[34] It occurs to the boy that a machinic intervention could do the job just as well. By tying a piece of string to the valve, the operation of another part of the machine could be used to open and shut it. It seems that as we become more specialized, our work becomes more machine-like and a machine substitution becomes a possibility. As extensively catalogued in Rifkin's *The End of Work,* it is the production-line workers, those whose labors are at the lowest level of the division of labor, who are most under threat from this process.[35] Their labors are the most easily substituted by the labors of others, and by increasingly sophisticated machines. Computer automation now provides further substitutions, this time at the level of the intellectual worker. As I will show in chapter 2, this implicit model of invention as the successive division of labor resonates with the models of those theorists of the 1950s and 1960s (the design methodologists) who tried to show that design could be treated as an ordered and even scientific process, the subsumption of all invention under the rule of the machine, first material and now electronic.

The Stoic legacy is also evident in contemporary concepts of the e-entrepreneur. In the manner of the Vitruvian architect, the entrepreneur dabbles in many disciplines, seeing them as potentials to be mined for ideas and opportunities. Though there is no despising of riches, the e-entrepreneur also operates in a climate of risk taking, where failure has to be taken on the chin.

Against Grime: The Academy

Debates about network economics and the impulse to create already involve various positions commonly described as idealistic, which are apparently removed from practicalities. If the Stoics had their place at the perimeter of the marketplace, the students of Plato (429–347 BC) are associated with the rarefied world of the academy, away from the confused and sensual delights of the bazaar.[36] There is a crucial difference between the theories of the Stoics and the Platonists. For the Stoics, we are participants in a natural unity. The universe that we see and experience is the unity. But for Plato, the unity resides beyond our universe, in the realm of ideas, designated as the realm of the Intelligible.[37] For Plato, we inhabit the fickle and transient world of the senses, where we are presented with things as they appear rather than as they are in their essence; and appearances can deceive. Of course we can aspire to transcendence above the world of the senses, and it is the task of the wise to advance to the source of illumination, the emanation of the Intelligible. The Romantics, such as Coleridge, Wordsworth, and Ruskin, were Platonists, and idealists, insofar as they appealed to the high ideals of honor and sacrifice, as essential human characteristics, over and above the incidental or even aberrant property of self-interest, the latter being associated with the (instant) gratification of the senses. The idealist, or Platonist, is therefore happy to associate the earthly realm where the bodily senses are in full operation ("the sensible"), with the crass world of base pleasures, commerce, and self-interest. The higher plain of ultimate reality and transcendent unity is home to nobler instincts such as honor, duty, self-sacrifice, and creativity.

Plato provides an early injunction against the rule of the mass market in these terms. The taste of the masses is governed by the immediate concerns of self-interest and gratification. No one would submit to the judgment of the multitude "a poem, or a work of art or some other service he would render to the state, thus going out of his way to make the public his masters, without falling under the fateful necessity to give them whatever they like and do whatever they approve."[38] The public cannot recognize essence, that is, what is really beautiful or really good. The majority will never be philosophers, who are the ones best equipped to contemplate the beautiful and the good. Ideas are always corrupted by the sensible, which is to say by contingency. The closest ancient Greece came to participating in popular music, television, and computer games was the enjoyment by the multitude of dramatic poetry, which, according to Plato, appeals to the emotions, the lower aspects of the soul. The higher aspects of the soul relate to reason.[39] Poetry that appeals to the emotions is deceptive and the furthest removed from reality. Poetry is also removed, as is art, from reality in that it constitutes a mere representation of a representation. The skilled craftsman, the carpenter who makes a bed, or the craftsman who makes a horse's bridle is closest to the reality. What each one makes is a copy of the archetype, the one true bed or bridle resident in the realm of the ideal. The painter merely copies the crafted object, or the poet describes it. Plato had no time for poets and less for those who played on the emotions, what for us today constitutes the appeal of mass media sensationalism and sentimentality. The hyperbolae of e-commerce evangelism offends the contemporary Platonist insofar as it appeals to emotive argumentation: anxiety at not keeping up, lust for ostentatious pleasures, fear of losing customers, the desire for control. For the same reasons, contemporary idealists also have difficulty coming to terms with the fact that they may be designing for a mass market, whether in bricks and stones[40] or bits and bytes.

Contemporary theorists of popular culture identify the complex relationship between high and low culture, the received taste of the elite and the marginalized preferences of the masses, who ostensibly have less power, though some scholars have identified pockets of populism that are driven by an impetus to appropriate what is offered by literature and the mass media, to adapt it to one's immediate concerns, as a means of empowerment.[41] This is exemplified in the fan cultures surrounding various television programs and movies. On a similar theme, Penly writes of fans appropriating and adapting products of the popular media for their own uses, such as turning the *Star Trek* stories into erotic novels.[42] By this reading, power is exercised and undermined by negotiation through the categories of high and low, a process increasingly abetted by the Internet, which encourages cultural pillage and appropriation.

Leaving aside these edgy incursions, Platonic idealism finds many instantiations in the history of art and design, including in the appeal to idealized forms. For the modernist architect and painter Le Corbusier, architecture is a matter of exploring forms in light, a philosophy exemplified in much modernist design: "the masterly, correct and magnificent play of masses brought together in light . . . cubes, cones, spheres, cylinders or pyramids are the great primary forms which light reveals to advantage."[43] The appeal here is to the truthfulness of the forms, and their illumination, as opposed to the kind of design that panders to "brutal instincts" through the whims of mere style and ornament.[44] Product design, from sewing machines to laptop computers, is no less inclined toward this formal idealism.

Le Corbusier was a champion of mass production, but idealism is also manifested in the anti-industrial argumentation and aesthetic of his restless forebears, the Romantics, those who sought to counter the forces of mechanization, to rehabilitate the emotions and bring them into the game of transcendence, through ornament as much as form. For Ruskin, the "function of ornament is to make you happy."[45] This pleasure resides not in human creation, the supposed classical perfection[46] of the Doric, Ionic, and Corinthian orders, as outlined by Vitruvius, but in representing nature's order. Ruskin delighted in ornamentation based on humans and animals, progressing to the increasingly abstract shapes of nature, then to ornamentation based on the simple line,[47] the purest of formal elements, but grounded in nature. Ruskin's aesthetic brings to mind pre-Raphaelite paintings, the subsequent stylistic flourish known as "art nouveau," and the sinuous curves and folds of contemporary digital organicism, sometimes referred to disparagingly as "blob" architecture.[48] Ruskin's philosophy accords with the romantic version of idealism, with human subjectivity as the motive force to transcendence. We transcend this world by giving rein to feelings, particularly those that ennoble us by drawing us toward the beautiful and the sublime. Plato's realm of the supra-individual Intellect becomes the site of intense subjectivity, a glorified state of mind.

Ruskin's much vaunted "naturalism" is less a pantheistic celebration of the oneness of nature (as expounded by the Stoics) than a means to defining the hierarchical territory of an emotional grand tour, a pilgrimage of the passions. So Ruskin's description of St. Mark's in Venice is a play on the emotions at the same time that it is an exercise in ecstatic release from the constraints of earthly and sensible grounding. We progress from the narrow alleyways of the city "resonant with the cries of itinerant salesmen" to the transcendence of glittering pinnacles and confusion of delight: "until at last, as if in ecstasy, the crests of the arches break into a marble foam, and toss themselves far into the blue skies in flashes and wreaths of sculptured spray."[49] Ruskin's celebration of hybridity, a sensibility to the chaos of the bazaar, the conjunctions of disparate trades, also takes on a transcendent aspect. The façade of St. Mark's is a "shrine at which to dedicate the splendour of miscellaneous spoil."[50]

Apart from his quest to rise above the grime of the market, Ruskin's Platonism comes through most strongly in his final appeal to honor. Contrary to Smith's appeal to self-interest is Ruskin's demand that we do good because it is morally right and honorable, absolutely. It is our highest calling. In this the Romantics are at further odds with Stoicism.

The idealist position comes under attack from Marx. I will reserve an account of the Marxist critique of idealism and ideology for chapter 2. The Platonic legacy in the realm of computer systems design is palpable in many ways, not least in the quest for a transcendent cyberreality, where enthusiasts make claims toward a brighter digital future while ignoring the current failings of technology. Technological optimism places a high premium on concepts of the future as fulfilling all that is deficient in the present. I labor this point elsewhere.[51] It is also a theme taken up with ambiguous endorsement by Wertheim in her aptly named book *The Pearly Gates of Cyberspace*,[52] with Dante's *Inferno* as its defining narrative. Dante's narrative is of a hierarchical universe, and Neoplatonic progression to a divine reality, comparable in some ways to the quest for cyberspace. The move into cyberspace is seen by some as a release from the body to a transcendent unity beyond our current existence.[53] It is a release to the world above the grime of the marketplace, even beyond the sculptured spray of spires and finials.

Lifestyle and the Garden

The network economy aspires to "the good life." The promise of "lifestyle" improvement sells furniture, clothing, grooming, and health products. In this the network economy draws on aspects of the Epicurean legacy. Our exploration of the architecture of economics needs to be extended to a consideration of the garden. If the Stoics inhabited the fringes of the marketplace, and the idealists the rarefied world of the academy, then the Epicureans were the Philosophers of the Garden, so named after the garden that formed the center of the school founded by Epicurus (341–270 BC). The name accords with the school's interest in the cultivation of refined taste, the subtle predilections of the connoisseur. We commonly associate Epicureanism with advocacy of the good life, as portrayed in lifestyle magazines, television programs, designer furniture, advertising, the leisured aspects of Internet culture, and self-help guides to health, fashion, home decoration, and dating. This pedagogy in sophistication and enjoyment is not far from the grounding of the Philosophy of the Garden in materialism.

An acknowledged source for concepts in modern physics, the Philosophers of the Garden developed the conviction that all things are made of microscopic particles, atoms, which have known propensities. When we die our bodies dissolve back to these particles. For the Epicurean there is no realm other than the sensible, the earthly realm that is perceived by the senses. For the Epicurean, wisdom comes through appreciating that there is no appeal to "higher ideals," eternal reward or punishment. After death we are in the same state as before, which is that of non-being. But far from instilling a mood of pessimism, or denying all meaning and hope, the Epicureans set their sights on enjoying the here and now. Since there is nothing other than the material world, we need not fear death or the retribution of the gods: "The man who has truly comprehended that there is nothing terrible in ceasing to live, has nothing terrible to fear in life."[54] Without recourse to the ideal realm, we fall into considerations of the senses. We decide the good from what is around us. The quest is to maximize pleasure and to diminish pain, "taking the feeling of pleasure as our guide."[55] We may as well party while we can.

Apart from any injunction to recklessness, Epicureanism also engenders a sober keeping of accounts. The social philosopher Jeremy Bentham at the start of the nineteenth century was content to attribute his concepts of utility to Epicureanism.[56] Pleasure and pain exist on a continuum, as if on scales. We always strive to weight the scales in favor of pleasure. There is no injunction to unrestrained indulgence. Excesses do not give pleasure in the long run. Nothing is wrong in itself, but we must think of the consequences. The Epicureans extolled the virtues of a simple life, with few possessions, and moderation. Unlike the followers of Plato, who thought there was some ideal state transcending current circumstances and to which they could aspire, there was little incentive among Epicureans to be involved in civic affairs. They were enjoined to live unnoticed, a position easily taken for apathy.

The network economy enjoys three major inheritances from the Epicureans: materialism, utilitarianism, and concepts of leisure. Materialism maintains that there is no divinity or spirit, and it finds ready expression in arguments that seek to subordinate concepts of mind, thought, spirit, and soul to considerations of matter, exemplified in Dennett's accounts of the mind as software running on the hardware of the brain, and from which it may possibly be extricated.[57] Economic materialism ostensibly places value on material possessions and the comforts they provide, above meaning or ethical value, and arguably finds support in Epicurean materialism. But utilitarianism also introduces the prospect that issues of morals can be decided on the utility of certain actions. Epicureanism has also become synonymous with a lifestyle built on pleasure and hence leisure, and it has an affinity with the idea of simplicity and sophisticated taste. The latter involves tranquility of mind, where we do "not have to wander as if in search of something missing, nor look for anything to complete the good of mind and body."[58] In the network economy, tranquility readily gives way to frenzy. Such is the state of the vexed Epicurean mindset in the contemporary network economy.

The economics of Smith and Bentham, and by implication Stoicism and Epicureanism, have weight in modern economic theory, each owing much of its elaboration to the writings of the nineteenth-century libertarian philosopher John Stuart Mill.[59] Discourses on electronic commerce seem to draw on both Stoicism and Epicureanism, and both fit comfortably within a frame of reference that could be construed as rationalist: the extremes of the so-called economic rationalism of the twentieth-century economist Milton Friedman[60] and contemporary advocates of unregulated markets; so too the celebration of the Internet as the ultimate free-market environment. Of course Benthamite utilitarianism has given the world of design the grim legacy of the Panopticon, a naïve form of architecture apparently configured on the grounds of pure utility, which offers a kind of social control.[61] By contrast the word "design" now finds ready association with the apparent converse of dreary conformity, a simple and subtle architecture of the connoisseur. The modernist legacy of design presents itself to mass media strategists, including those of the network economy, in terms of free-market Epicureanism: simplicity, utility, and sophistication. This is a kind of cool that, in the network economy dominated by sensationalism, public inquisition, Big Brother evictions, and personal improvement, is more like a fever.

The Household

Mainstream broadcasting promotes a thirst for the living space of the other, encouraged by surveillance cameras and supplemented by audience feedback on the Internet, Web diaries, and webcams. But the network economy arguably originates from the home.

The Romantics advanced resistance to early economic rationalism in much the same way that Platonic idealism resisted the Stoics and Epicureans. But the academy offers resistance on another front, through Plato's student Aristotle, whose philosophy it is accurate to attribute not to the bustle of the marketplace, the isolation of the academy, or the pleasures of the garden, but to the complex familial relations of the household.[62] Whereas Platonism presents the world as a pale shadow of the inaccessible divine unity, the Intelligible, for Aristotle the divine order is attainable. Things are moving toward their full completeness, and human beings may after all attain the good life.

In a famous passage of the *Nicomachean Ethics,* Aristotle outlines the chief intellectual virtues. *Episteme* is scientific knowledge, which, in keeping with the tenets of idealism, is eternal and unchanging. *Techne* is artistic or technical skill, bringing something into being, arguably the preserve of invention and design. At the highest end of the chain of virtue lies wisdom, *sophia,* the apprehension of all the virtues, with *nous,* raw intelligence or intuition as "the state of mind that apprehends first principles."[63] But the pivotal virtue is *phronesis,* practical wisdom, the exercise of prudence, the ability to balance rules, the ability to apply the right rule to the right situation. Aristotle identifies prudent people as "those who understand the management of households or estates."[64] So it is fitting to identify the household as the site at which prudence is best exemplified. Prudence resides between art and science, "reasoned and capable of action in the sphere of human good."[65] Prudence is acquired by experience and is the chief estate of political science. Aristotle's account of the city, the *polis,* begins with an understanding of the relationships within the household,[66] those of husband and wife, parents and children, masters and slaves. In fact "economic science" and "household management" provide alternative translations of the Greek word for economics, *oikonomia.*[67] *Oikos* means house; *nemein* is "to manage." By this reading, the network economy derives from the home, and is not entirely alien to it, though the economic tradition draws away from its origins in husbandry and habitation.

In his survey of the legacies of the ancients, Adam Smith gives an account of Aristotelian prudence but diminishes its importance by describing it as "the habit of mediocrity according to right reason,"[68] and demonstrating its subservience to the Stoic virtue of "self-command." Under Smith, economics seems to lose its association with domesticity.

The theory of prudence has been adopted and elaborated by the hermeneutical writers such as Hans-Georg Gadamer and Martin Heidegger before him.[69] It is also a common theme in contemporary writing in sociology and in social economics.[70] Prudence, interpretation, practice, and application point to the rule-resistant spheres of the human sciences, the realms of human action. It is appropriate to think of prudence in the case of the management of a household, as it is in the home that the complex of social relations is most resistant to an understanding in terms purely of self-interest, and hence free-market economics.[71] The web of relationships within the family, kinship ties, and interactions are more complicated than suggested by monetary transactions (exchange) and legal contracts. The point is made well by certain social economists. According to Godolier: "Whether in the sphere of kinship or politics, there is always, in every human activity if it is to become constituted, something that precedes exchange and in which exchange takes root, something that exchange both alters and preserves, extends and renews at the same time."[72] So develops the concept of the "economy" of the gift, a primordial mode of interaction between people that economic exchange depends upon, and with which it is in a dialectical relationship. The establishment of a science of economics is inevitably frustrated by that which falls outside the economic system: the black market, bribery, theft, scalping, piracy, and systems of transaction that do not seem to require a determination of monetary value, or more benignly systems where things are given away for nothing. There is a conflict between giving and selling. Each system disturbs the other.

As indicated earlier, the Internet demonstrates the intriguing property of encouraging some individuals to give goods and services for free. In terms of Smith's free market, the gift appears as yet another kind of economic transaction. Gifts act as inducements to buy. We use gifts to develop a clientele. If we give then we expect to receive in return. But the giving of gifts also seems to work outside economic systems. It provides a bond within a family and a community. It is a way of gaining admission and developing trust. The gift fits within a complex of social relations. The gift works against regulation and contract; if there are rules then they are unwritten.

From Ruskin's point of view, the Internet gift economy is perhaps analogous to the conduct of a team of artisans. The claim to participation in the gift economy is a variant of the general claim that the Internet represents a return to a craft culture, tribal life, a holistic, authentic mode of being. For the romantic the gift also invokes concepts of sacrifice. Of Ruskin's "seven lamps" of architecture, the first is sacrifice, "the offering of precious things, merely because they are precious, not because they are useful or necessary."[73] Sacrifice is "the opposite of the prevalent feeling of modern times, which desires to produce the largest result at the least cost."[74] Ruskin writes about the self-sacrifice of the soldier, who in the face of battle has only his death and duty in front of him. He will "die daily."[75] For Ruskin, similar commitments to duty above personal interest apply to lawyers, physicians, and clergy. From this commitment to duty, it follows that workers should receive equal wages irrespective of the quality of their work. Their reward is to be employed and to be chosen for their work. This assumes the operation of a kind of "economy" of mutuality and honor. Smith's economics assumes the merchant or manufacturer is only after profits. According to Ruskin, these professions need to be rehabilitated. Merchants provide sustenance. This is their higher calling, but what will they die for?

Of course, Ruskin's idealism carries many of the errors of the economic rationalists in ignoring the complex of social relations that provides the context of our exercise of prudence. The practice of gift giving is not captured only in the lofty ideals of sacrifice, with its appeal to intrinsic value. The appeal to sacrifice seems quaint in the digital age and appears in only diminished form in Internet gift culture. The concept of sacrifice suggests the operation of an isolated individual and perhaps bears the sign of a grievance: I sacrificed my time and energy developing this software, and now someone else is making a profit from it. The gift in the network economy seems driven by a sense of community formation rather than sacrifice.

Design makes ready claim on Aristotelian prudence. Any invention occupies the unsteady position between the rule and its application, ideas advanced in the area of design by theorists such as Schön.[76] But design is not only the preserve of a Ruskinian idealism. In the grand spectrum of exchange for money versus the exchange of gifts, or economic rationalism versus situated action, in an Aristotelian sense, design belongs on the side of the gift.[77] It is also grounded in the philosophy of the household. I will examine the gift in greater detail in chapter 4.

Conclusion: Four Positions

The discussion in this chapter has focused on four sites in which design and the network economy are in play. The stoa (marketplace or agora), the academy, the garden, and the household are material places, but they are also spaces in which various theoretical positions materialize.

The electronic agora promotes conceptions of the network economy, in its traditional and pioneering aspects. E-commerce claims several innovations in the way we make commercial transactions.[78] The environment in which we buy and sell is integrated into the same workstation where we communicate (email), type our reports, browse, and recreate. The agora comes to the consumer. There is the promise of the customization of goods and services. Through smart online software, it is becoming relatively inexpensive to customize the design of a product and link this to manufacture and supply. There is the much-touted "pull" phenomenon. You can make the advance to potential suppliers rather than waiting to be told what is available, or waiting to have them "pushed" to you. Consumers can be put in touch with one another to exchange goods with little mediation. The e-commerce marketplace is inexpensive to access and is relatively unregulated at the moment, which means that it is a fairly simple matter to experiment with marketing ventures and strategies.[79] The Internet marketplace stretches across the globe, so it is possible to see what goods are available at sites otherwise inaccessible, to compare prices, and even to make purchases independent of import and export controls. This suggests a further globalization of commerce. In turn the economic aspects of the Internet seem to be challenged by the persistence of free software and data and the willingness of people to provide certain data, goods, and services without considering payment. These and other developments have been explained by some as an elaboration of the ideal of unregulated free enterprise, the language of the ever-expanding marketplace, the philosophy of the stoa.

The academy also furnishes us with metaphors that find elaboration in the network economy, including basic prejudices about popular culture.[80] The academy's investment in a unity beyond our current condition motivates the enthusiasm for the Internet as a medium for transcendence, a means to a better society.

The metaphors of the Epicurean garden are also suggestive and perhaps give an account of aspects of advertising and the mass consumption of the good life. Along with other aspects of the mass media, the World Wide Web provides ample opportunity to promote consumption as a means to pleasure, health, and well-being. The Internet also supports Epicureanism's utilitarian dark side, that of social control, relentless surveillance, and scrutiny via CCTV and web-cams, though both come together in popular voyeuristic TV programs that fuse surveillance with lifestyle.

The metaphor of the household already has a stronghold in digital narrative: the Internet as cottage industry, the origins of personal computing, home working, the practices of noncommercial collaborations. The household also supports the practical virtue of phronesis, the prudent exercise of the faculties of interpretation, which have ready application in a critique of digital commerce.

If the Stoics were of the marketplace, the idealists of the academy, the Epicureans of the garden, and the Aristotelians of the household, then the school of philosophers known as the Cynics were the vagabonds on the street, the itinerants, the beggars, the homeless, the dispossessed, the peripatetic philosophers against home-bound metaphysical systems. In terms of the gift the cynic is dependent on the handout. Narratives validating the Internet also trade in metaphors of the wanderer, leading me in chapter 5 to consider the bricoleur, trickster, or thief and her relationship to edgy design and the digital economy.

This chapter has served as a polemic on the theme of the household as a basis for understanding the network economy. I exaggerated the problem of the relationship of design to economics as a starting point. We have aligned e-commerce with the language of design by indicating their common legacies. The main message of this chapter is that economics, as it is for design and the Internet, is best understood from a pragmatic point of view, with recourse to the language of interpretive or hermeneutical inquiry. A practical orientation to the network economy favors metaphors of the household above those of the marketplace.

Rampant Machines

E-commerce enthusiasts have proposed that digital communications and the Internet pave the way for perfect market conditions.[1] On the Internet consumers are presented with near-complete information about products, they can compare quality and price, and competition can flourish. E-commerce presents "friction-free capitalism."[2] The metaphor is that of the well-functioning machine. If the e-marketplace can function as a machine in this way, then why not the home? After all, according to the modernist architect Le Corbusier, "the house is a machine for living."[3]

Though we are now largely inured to its sentiment, Le Corbusier's aphorism provoked on several counts. It was an exhortation to functionality, simplicity, rationality, and design for a household to be what it wants to be unencumbered by the friction of drudgery, waste, grime, and ornament.[4] For the high modern designers, the house should be created as a machine suitable for its purpose in the same way that a ship, airplane, or racing car is an efficient, self-contained, mechanically serviced and propelled vessel, well-suited to supporting the activities of its occupants and designed for speed. Updating this analogy, we can add the model of instantaneous data transfer and digital communications: the slick machinery of electronic commerce. This is the inconspicuous machinery of the Internet,[5] delivering the market directly into the home.

If we allow that the house and its infrastructures may be machine-like, the lives and interactions of its occupants, the constitution of the household, or the home, surely are not. In some cases the home and the machine constitute a suitable opposition. The factory, the office, utilities, and the market may succumb to descriptions in organizational terms that appeal to the workings of a machine: flow, components, connections, inputs, speed, predictable and calculable outcomes. But the relationships of the home are surely resistant to such descriptions. Whatever a house as a functional structure might be, a *home* is not a machine. It is also the case that a house has other ascriptions that are excluded from the machine metaphor, such as providing shelter, serving as a place of gathering and repose, and being a repository of memories,[6] and there is Le Corbusier's lesser-known metaphor: the house as a temple.[7]

In this chapter I will examine the metaphor of the machine, and its implications for design in the network economy. In order to do this, I will examine metaphor itself, and its linguistic cousin, metonymy. Readers have already seen that design draws substantially on the power of metaphor. Those familiar with metaphor may prefer to advance to the section that follows on causality, though in this section I introduce metaphor and metonymy as machine.

Metonymy: More on Metaphor

Metaphor provokes by the interaction of opposites (a house is or is not a machine, the Internet is or is not an ocean, commerce is or is not subject to frictional forces), or technically by the attribution of an object to an unlikely category. Prosaically, a house is not a machine at all, but an artifact, a construction, a building, or an essential component of urban living. The deliberate "category error" of assigning the house to the group of things normally including racing cars, ships, washing machines, disk drives, and cash registers provokes us into thinking of ways that this assertion is true or not. The phrase "a house is a building" does not attract attention or animate as much discussion.

Metonymy is a close cousin to metaphor, or even another way of looking at metaphor.[8] In metonymy a part is used to signify the whole, as when we offer to lend a *hand* but mean to assist in ways involving more than a single body part. We use metonymy when we refer to working *online,* where the line (the connecting cable) is only a part of the network infrastructure, or we elect to pay with *plastic,* which is only one property of a credit card, which is in turn only one aspect of our capacity to pay, and only one small part of the complex financial system that makes credit possible. Language has this atomistic character. A word momentarily, at least, singles out a part from the whole, with the rest receding into the background, and the part never quite captures everything that is meant. We understand what others say and write thanks to language conventions, tacit understandings of contexts of use, and the constant interplay of multiple meanings.

On analysis, insofar as language is metonymic, the identification of what constitutes the part or the whole may be contested. The assertion that a house is a machine is metonymic to the extent that it purveys one *part* of the house's functioning or assemblage as standing in for the *whole* house. The modern house is equipped with machinery: washing machines, plumbing, heating, refrigeration, distributed home entertainment, and digital communications. The machine description just singles out one aspect, or component, of the whole. A house contains services, systems, and devices that are mechanical, and these machine components are being used to signify the whole that is the house. So it is not just that the house is misclassified as a machine (metaphor), but it is "mistaken" for its parts (metonymy), its machinery.

The assertion that a house is a machine is also metonymic in that the machine is just one part of modern life: the modern social, cultural, and technological condition.[9] The machine stands in for modernity. The house is also inevitably a part of the modern condition. The metonym therefore employs one part to signify another part (machine for house), with the whole (modernity) implied, or subject to speculation and dispute. It is an absent whole. The metonym involves a complex of part-whole associations. It would be possible to spend several pages unpacking the many and varied relationships implied. Suffice it to say that any metonym is only a part of a bigger linguistic construction, and any explanation of a particular construction is but a part of all that could be said. Any metonym is itself subject to the constraint of metonymy, of only being dealt with in part.

There is no avoiding metaphor and metonymy, but the formulation of the metonym, the choice of components in the metonymic part-whole relationship, is not innocent. The architects of high modernism had an agenda in latching onto the machine. The metonym buys into the whole cultural condition of improvement, progress, and science that is modernity. Using the machine to stand in for the house attempts to situate the modern house as a full participant in the modern condition. In general terms the moderns, who embraced the machine metonym, participated in a long-standing "ideology," a belief in an ideal or utopian technological condition or aspiration. The machine was marshaled to stand in for progress, to validate industrialization, mass production, rationalization, and efficiency.

Whether or not we choose to identify that our assertions are subject to the workings of metonymy is also implicated in ideological battles. The high modernist would claim not to be dealing in metaphor, but to be asserting fact, or at least provide very little reflection on the metonymic character of their assertions.[10] The assertion provokes by declaring something as true, a truth perhaps not previously recognized. Not only might ideologists be identified by the particular choice of parts and wholes in the metonymic relations of their narratives (machine, system, speed), but they may never acknowledge that they are using metonymy. According to Barthes, a critic of consumer culture, this is an example of language's potential for imposing and propagating an ideology, of purveying stories and assertions as if innocuous fact, whereas they actually reinforce a particular ideological position. Such bogus "facts" might assert the rightful dominance of the moneyed classes over the laboring classes, the bourgeoisie over the masses, the information rich over the information poor: in short, the dominance of capitalism.[11]

Barthes identifies the insidious character of statements his contemporaries took for granted: the indigenous population of the conquered country are indolent; old-age pensioners are irascible; money makes the world go round; economic growth is the key to a high standard of living; e-commerce is frictionless. These statements are metonymic, in that one part, a component (money, growth, friction) or attribute (indolence, irascibility), assumes privilege over the whole (nations, peoples, lives, the world, commerce). For Barthes and others, the concealment of the contested nature of such assertions proves the insidious character of capitalism.[12] Among other errors, taking such assertions for granted engenders a yet more compliant consumer culture. To the extent that the high modernists fail to reflect on the controversial nature of their choice of part and whole, they participate in the ethical neglect of the capitalists, or the bourgeoisie. Machinery forms just a part of our world, and yet it is accorded great privilege, such that the attribution of a phenomenon to being machine-like goes uncontested. Barthes and his fellow critics assert that it serves well the capitalist system to associate society and production so strongly with the machine, and also to suppress the contingent and contested nature of language.

Metonymy also provides an account of the resistance of the Romantics to what they saw as the evils of industrialization and modern economics. Whether or not the machine is the main component in the metonymic relation, metonymy is always a reduction, and so has the capacity to offend our sensibility to appreciate things in their wholeness. Romanticism positioned itself against the reductionism of modern science and sought to reinstate an appreciation of the whole that is nature. According to Ruskin, no matter how much you dissect and magnify "oaks, roses and daisies," you discover no more than that they are each made of fiber and bubbles, of charcoal and water: "for all their peeping and probing, nobody knows how."[13] In metonymy the whole is reduced to a mere part, and the more ignoble the part the more pronounced the reduction. If we share Carlyle's and Ruskin's suspicion of the machine and the trappings of industrialization, then the metonym of the machine may well provoke disapproval.

On the other hand, not all parts are ignoble and the Romantic may well affirm the appropriateness of "a house as hearth," "bricks and mortar," "a threshold," or "a stone ornament." In fact Ruskin's partiality to stone ornamentation suggests that stone is metonymic for architecture. He could also see the whole of nature in a mere rock covered in lichen.[14] But in focusing on the part as opposed to the whole, metonymy inevitably attributes a diminished aspect for the full aspect.

As we have seen, language always has a metonymic aspect. We can never find quite the right word. We single out particular aspects of a thing to stand for the whole picture that we are trying to understand. There are many examples from the world of information technology and digital media where the whole proves elusive, and many pages are expended on explaining that to which the inadequate terms might refer: the Internet, the World Wide Web, cyberspace, digital culture. So it is with the network economy, the scope of its territory having yet to be fully charted. This is not simply an embarrassing feature of language or of information technology. Language has this character. The meaning is settled by use, and use is established in context.

But from the point of view of the consumer critic, it is in the interest of those who wish to conserve a particular ideology to treat certain words and meanings as if fixed, and to deny the metaphorical or metonymic nature of language.[15] The antidote to concealed metonymy is to apprehend language as multivalent, situated, and performative.[16]

A further antidote is to resort to the trope of irony. Irony is commonly taken as an attempt to use words in a way contrary to their common usage: to describe bankruptcy as a minor inconvenience, or an empty toner cartridge as a national disaster. For the philosopher Richard Rorty, "the opposite of irony is common sense."[17] In connection with Socrates, irony is taken as a pretense at ignorance to provoke a critical response, which is to say to reveal the inconsistencies in an opponent's argument. It might be in mock ignorance that we take the part to stand in for the whole. A metonym is ironic insofar as we deliberately use an ignoble, incidental, or diminutive part as a sign for the ineffable, respected, or powerful whole: "No. 10" for "the Government," or "plastic" for "credit card." To refer to a credit card transaction as "paying with plastic" is perhaps a trivialization of a complex and powerful system on which one is in fact dependent. One of the credit system's most incidental aspects, the material constitution of the identification card, and a material recognized as inexpensive to produce, becomes an ironic sign for the whole. "A house is a machine" perhaps strikes us as ironic, considering the incomprehension many people face with the frustration wrought by dependence on ubiquitous machines and their breakdown: the idiosyncrasies of the computer, home video recorder, or digital camera. For some, the perpetration of irony is one of the characteristics of the modern age.[18] In the current cultural condition of irony, we take it for granted that any assertion entails its opposite. It may be that the high modernist valorization of the machine and speed can be taken in an ironical way. Contemporary advertising and graphic design are capable of harnessing the power of irony. One thinks of cigarette advertisements that almost make a virtue of the health warning they are forced to contain. Of course a metonym may have its origins in irony, only to become tamed, or rendered innocuous by frequent use.

Design that is at the edge, provocative, and innovative draws irony into its repertoire. Ironies are always multiplied to the nth power. According to Kline, Dyer-Witheford, and de Peuter, the double irony for design is that the economic imperative always wins. When a computer game's promotion of violence, stereotypes, and negative prejudices is brought to the attention of game designers, they can always resort to the claim that the game is in fact an attempt to expose the futility of the behavior and values it depicts, that the reductive substitution of the part for the whole is a joke. The designer can claim that the game uses exaggerated, sophisticated, and multilevel ironic commentary to expose contemporary social mores. Irony excuses everything and keeps everyone happy. The designer has the satisfaction of indulging in a kind of transgressive play where everything is the opposite of what it seems, and the teenager gets to shoot up bad guys.[19]

But the concept of "making money" has a metonymic aspect that seems to have escaped the influence of irony in some quarters. The early days of a technology suggest opportunities to accrue money quickly. The metaphor of the moneymaking machine is apt. Coin and paper money come out of machines. Handles turn, metals are pressed, ink is conveyed to paper, and the product is purveyed through the economic system. The money machine, the machinery for the manufacture of coin, is a metonym. One small part of the system is used to signify the whole. The production of coin and paper money becomes representative of the whole complex economic system. Wealth can be achieved with the instantaneity of turning a handle on a press, a metonym that seems to underlie much of the populist business literature, including that which purveys instant success and wealth through digital commerce. The difficulty and complexity of accruing wealth is masked by the apparent simplicity of operating just one small mechanical part of the economic system as metonym.

The four sections that follow advance a critical position on causality, the systems view of design, bureaucracy, and ideology, under the machine metaphor. Readers already familiar with such critique may prefer to skim these sections before advancing to the more controversial sections on monstrosity, uselessness, and the romance with the machine.

Causal Machines: Modernity and Mechanism

The machine features as a metonym for things outside its instrumental sphere, including the elusive concept of modernity. Dealing in parts, the trope of metonymy also has properties in common with the machine. One of the distinguishing features of a machine is that it is constructed of interrelated parts. For Vitruvius, "A machine is a combination of timbers fastened together, chiefly efficacious in moving great weights."[20] The parts of a machine have to be identifiable because each has its own movement: axles, sheaves, blocks, and windlasses. Other artifacts, such as sculpture and buildings, do not require such clear articulation. Contrary to the makeup of the machine, beauty and function are conflated in the work of architecture and rely on the whole configuration. Contrary to machines, architecture depends on order and symmetry, "a proper agreement between the members of the work itself, and the relation between the different parts and the whole general scheme."[21] For the ancients, the machine seems not to be caught up in this requirement for unity. The machine exists only for "practical necessity."[22] It is a means to an end, a means to achieving a unified whole in the architecture. As such, the machine promotes a particular theory of causality.

Metonymy invokes various connections between parts: house and machine as components of modernity; plastic, card, transaction, and credit rating as components of a credit system. The linking of parts and of parts to whole informs the issue of causes. For Aristotle, one of the ways that "cause" is used is "for that from which a thing is made and continues to be made."[23] So bronze is a cause of a statue, and silver of a bowl.[24] The relationship of the parts to the whole is a relationship of mutual dependence. This is no less the case with the machine. For Vitruvius, "When one end of the rope is fastened to the windlass, and the latter is turned round by working the handspikes, the rope winds round the windlass, gets taut, and thus it raises the load to the proper height and to its place in the work."[25] If you take away one part of a machine, it is likely that it will cease to work. It then becomes apparent from the successive removal and replacement of parts that the machine can be understood as a causal system, with certain parts depending on others. The chains of relationships that we refer to as causes and their effects are clear. Furthermore, the machine is a component within a chain of causes, the end result being the construction of buildings.[26]

The idea of the machine as a system of causally connected parts informs conceptions of nature: that which is other than what we have made, the non-artificial. For Vitruvius, the machine is copied from nature. A machine is a model of the universe: "All machinery is derived from nature, and is founded on the teaching and instruction of the revolution of the firmament."[27] But this is already a mechanical interpretation of the whole. We could equally assert that our identification of nature and our understanding of it are informed by our machines. Furthermore, that one might have provided the blueprint, the template or the model for the other is already a commitment to causes of the mechanical kind. The machine as part serves metonymically to account for the world. The power of the metonym is that it supports our thinking of the world in terms of parts: nature as an identifiable component of the world in distinction to people and things that people make, the categories of the natural and the artificial. It also directs us to think in terms of causes, or at least to think of causation in a mechanical way. This is one of the twentieth-century philosopher Heidegger's laments about the way we think in the age of technology. We operate under this imperative to see the world in mechanical, or technological, terms, where everything has a mechanical cause.[28]

Whatever Vitruvius's view, the early moderns clearly saw the natural order as a machine. As with the house, the metaphor is of nature as machine. Descartes applied the machine metaphor to the body, which having been made by God "is incomparably better ordered, and has in it more admirable movements than any of those which can be invented by men."[29] He describes the body as consisting of tubes, valves, and pumps, with the heart as the generator of heat to give the blood its energy. The body is a machine with life, the soul being resident in the machine of the body. The soul or life force inhabits the body. Similarly, Newton's conception of the universe is as a giant clockwork, with the parts following calculable paths depending on their relationships. Gravity causes moving objects to follow orbits, heat causes gases to expand, and an external force causes a moving object to change its momentum.

Machine interpretations trade in causes, but as a language game metonymy also participates in causality by reversing it. According to certain language theorists, a common case of metonymic use is where an end effect is offered as a substitute for a complex of causes.[30] A part of a phenomenon, one of its side effects, is used to signify the whole, a symptom is taken for the complex of causes. For example, getting hot under the collar (a well-worn example of metonymy) is merely a symptom of getting angry and barely accounts for the psychology of the condition. To talk of the cause of the anger might involve us in a contested field of interconnected factors, involving human psychology, background, circumstance and relationships. We circumvent this complexity by going straight to the effect. Smith's appeal to the foundational status of self-interest can be construed as metonymic. Following Smith's early critics, self-interest is a symptom of the complex of attitudes and social conditions that go to make up the commercial ethos, not a founding cause. As we will see subsequently, it could be the case that we are motivated to give (altruistically), with nonmonetary giving as a "cause." Commercial transactions follow from this propensity and are a way of dealing with the conflicts inherent in the gift. The behavior we construe as "self-interest" follows as a symptom, a by-product of the predisposition to give, perhaps in response to frustrations in our tendency toward communal sharing. Similarly, machines may only be a by-product or symptom of the world and not a cause (as if nature is a machine), and yet machines are used to signify the world. Insofar as metonymy is a play on the part and the whole, it is also a play on causes.

Of course, the network economy is prone to complexes of relationships in which the issue of causes is often occluded. Computer systems, the Internet, economic systems, present as complex networks. Network theorists identify several key features of complex networks.[31] In a complex network there may be structural complexity, where the network is an intricate nonplanar tangle. We can sometimes draw diagrams of local area computer networks (LANs), but the geographically dispersed Internet, with its hubs, WiFi, servers, and clients becomes too difficult to draw other than in greatly simplified form. A complex network may change over time. In the case of the World Wide Web, pages and links are being constantly created and lost. The links between nodes can also have widely different values, directions, and effects. In fact in the case of the

Internet, there is a substrate of electrical signals being passed from one node to the next, but in accounting for this activity we sometimes think of files, sound bytes, images, streamed video, email messages, and the media of transmission including landlines and wireless transmissions of various frequencies and modalities. Complex networks can also exhibit dynamical complexity, where the nodes form nonlinear dynamical systems, where the congestion at a junction is related to the flow of traffic in a nonlinear, discontinuous, or even noncalculable way. There could be many different kinds of nodes. For the Internet there are servers, client computers, mobile devices, household appliances, and other myriad invisible hubs and connections. These various factors can also influence each other. Strogatz gives the example of the electrical power grid, which depends on time, in terms of how it has grown over the years. This is a case where evolution over time affects topology (the configuration of connections). As a further example, in the case of neural systems, when neurons "fire" together repeatedly in certain patterns, the connection between them is either strengthened or diminished. Here nodal dynamics affect connection values.

These characterizations of complex networks point to a problem with machine causality. In the case of the failure within the complex system that led to the boom and bust of the dot-coms, there was an inevitable search for a "scapegoat," but history shows that such a search is often driven by a political and ideological agenda rather than a scientific search for causes.[32] Different factors may alternate in their roles as either symptoms or causes: the Internet, Wall Street, the press, the e-entrepreneurs, the greed of the investing public. In the network economy causality is not machinic, but social.

Design Machines: Method and the Division of Labor

The machine metonym is reinforced in Smith's account of economics.[33] For Smith the economic system has three parts: land, labor, and capital. To set up a business you need to locate on land, which you must buy or rent. You also need laborers to do the work. The cash for paying laborers, maintaining buildings and machinery, and buying materials is circulating capital. The buildings and machinery are fixed capital. Machinery has a special place in contributing to the productivity of the business. Even if the appropriate machines are expensive they can enable laborers to produce more and increase the company's profits.[34]

For Smith wealth is created primarily by labor, but in keeping with the powerful metonym of the machine, he presents the whole system, labor included, in a machine-like way. Labor succumbs to the compartmentalized, part-whole, causal structure of the machine. According to Smith, no one can produce all that they need on an individual basis. Individuals inevitably lack all the necessary skills and access to all the resources. It also wastes time if an individual is constantly moving from one task to the next and preparing for each task afresh. Dividing the work makes the whole process more productive. The factory is the prime example of the division of labor. Like a machine, it has specialized interconnected components (specialist individuals, teams, and machines) to enable the passage from raw materials to finished product. For the anthropologist Sahlins, the primitive home provides the prototype for the system of divided labor that later became factory production. The man is engaged in the hunt while the woman prepares the meal.[35] Of course, as with the mechanical view of nature, to see kinship and sociality in such terms is already to grant credence to the machine ethos. Smith's prime example of the division of labor is of eighteenth-century pin manufacture, where there is a precise articulation among those who prepare, forge, and sharpen the steel, paint the head, and package the product.[36]

Smith's account of the division of labor also provides an account of invention in machine terms. His example of the boy who manually opened and closed the valves that regulated the power for a steam turbine shows a highly specialized labor.[37] By tying a piece of string to the valve, the operation of another part of the machine was used to open and shut it. The boy thereby had more time to play with his friends. It seems that as we become more specialized, our work becomes more machine-like and a machine substitution becomes a possibility. By this reading, invention derives from human labor, through substitution. There is also the suggestion that this kind of labor-saving machinery allows more time for leisure.

Increasing specialization leads to increasing automation. For the social critic Marx, the invention of machinery comes about by less auspicious means, by "a process of analysis—by subdivisions of labor, which transforms the worker's operations more and more into mechanical operations, so that, at a certain point, the mechanism can step into his place."[38] The production-line workers, and now data entry clerks and digital operatives, are at the lowest levels in the division of labor.[39] Their labors are the most easily replaced by the labors of others and by increasingly sophisticated machines.

This implicit model of invention resonates with the early models of the design methodologists, those heirs to the optimism of the modernist tradition in the 1950s and 1960s, who sought to put design on a scientific footing and saw design as a mechanical process. Design methodologists attempted to system-atize the design process in a manner analogous to the treatment of production as the organization of increasingly specialized labor. One such theorist, Alexan-der, proposed that design operates as a process of analysis, whereby a design problem is broken down into sub-problems to such an extent that the lowest level of sub-problem can easily be met by a simple, predefined solution.[40] The next stage is to synthesize a complete solution from all those ready-made sub-solutions, that is, to work back to the whole. So the design of a small town can be dealt with by considering the need for food to be grown, goods to be ex-changed, and people to reside. Each of these sub-problems can be further di-vided. So the exchange of goods needs areas for display, storage, keeping money safe, and making purchases. Eventually, each sub-problem presents with a known sub-solution in terms of banks, vaults, cash registers, supermarket shelves, and parking lots. As any designer of retail facilities knows, the assembly and configuration of the big solution from these components requires repeated iteration and evaluation. The design method is commonly summarized in terms of analysis, synthesis and evaluation. We break a whole problem into its parts (analysis), we synthesize a provisional whole solution, and we evaluate the prod-uct, and the process is repeated.

This model gives one account of computer systems design.[41] With modular programming it is possible to break the design of a system into components. So the design of a system for electronic purchase might involve storage of product, customer, and transaction data, an interface that presents products to potential purchasers, a means of facilitating payment, confirmation, delivery, and then stocktaking and inventory. There are off-the-shelf "solutions" to each "sub-problem," in the form of database systems, browser plug-ins, and Web page templates. Synthesis involves configuring these components and adapting them to the specifics of the problem. Evaluation is an iterative process taking place re-peatedly throughout the design, but most evidently during the phase of user testing.

Criticism of this approach comes from many quarters. The Romantic would counter that a design method is a case of rampant metonymy, a machine out of control. The part is given undue significance as standing for the whole, as if di-viding the whole into parts provides access to the whole. A design method is metonymy multiplied. From a pragmatic point of view the reductive model has limited applicability in understanding the operations of invention, creation and design, including the subsequent writings of Alexander, Ishikawa, and Silverstein.[42] Problems that lend themselves to the reductive treatment are already "solved," in that the appropriate reduction is already known, as in the identification of the components of a factory process, a town layout, or a supermarket plan. Reducible problems are not necessarily the kind of problems that pose a challenge for designers, or at least it is the reducible aspects that provide the least challenge. Interesting design tasks present interconnections between levels in the problem hierarchy, and there are often many ways to divide an interesting problem into sub-problems, parts into sub-parts. These complexities are not easily addressed by simply iterating the process. Criteria for evaluation also fail us. A problem space expands and contracts depending on how we define it in relationship to its context. In fact the challenge of Web site design might be not only to select and organize the components, but to convey a message, react against the usual user expectations, develop a visual and interactive language, and adopt and adapt a metaphor, processes resistant to the workings of method.[43]

The shortcomings of design method also cast doubt on the sovereignty of the division of labor as a model of commerce, making us skeptical of any thought that the division of labor generates a "grand design," a better society or even simply a better system. If retail, by this model, is to benefit from increasing specialization, then all retail would conform to the model posed by the supermarket, where labor is divided into delivery reception, forklift operators, shelf stackers, checkouts, complaints personnel, accounts, supervisors, managers, security, and so forth. Increasingly we find that these tasks are being automated: Checkout is handled through mobile bar code readers, mail-order systems substitute catalogues for sales personnel, and customer loyalty is promoted through financial incentives, the awarding of points, and bonus schemes. The substitution continues with online retail, with the complete automation of the customer interface. Not only does the piecemeal substitution of work tasks by yet simpler tasks, and their eventual replacement by automated machines fall under the charge of being uncaring, treating individuals as machine components waiting to be replaced, but clearly the division of labor has its limits.

Design methods commonly borrowed from models of language that assumed the fixity of meanings, the view that in language we are constantly trying to establish the truth status of propositions and that truth can be understood atomically. If the parts of a statement are true, then the whole statement is true. It was also an attempt to get down to clear unambiguous language, devoid of metaphor. It is as if language, as for design, can be understood reductively. If we follow the neo-Marxist critic Marcuse, whatever the political ideologies of the promoters of the reductive view of language (logical positivism) and of design methods, they unwittingly bolster the capitalist ideology.[44] It is in the interest of those who wish to conserve a particular ideology to treat certain words and meanings as if fixed and to deny the metaphorical or metonymic nature of language. It is in the interest of those who wish to diminish the power of troublesome labor by rendering their work more machine-like and to formulate atomic design solutions that are rational, inevitable, and efficient. If the antidote to concealed metonymy is to apprehend language as multivalent, situated, and performative, then the antidote to design methods is similarly to apprehend design as complex, situated, social, and indeterminate. As for design, there are other models of making things that are counter to those of the production line. For example, contemporary management theory commonly presents the importance of the team in setting production goals, and setting and solving problems, and the importance of diversification among the labor force.[45]

If, as we have already examined, irony provides an "antidote" to concealed metonymy, then irony also provides an alternative view of design: design as the play of opposites, the indeterminate workings of metaphor and metonymy, and an exploration into the surreality of incongruous juxtaposition, themes that I will develop further in subsequent chapters.

The Bureaucratic Machine: Organization and the Network Economy

As an object of reflection, an efficacious metonym opens the discussion to indeterminate connections, a vigorous configuring and reconfiguring of meanings mediated by contingency, context, and opinion. Machine connections do not have this character.

Contrary to a linguistic trope, a machine is made up of components with relationships of dependence, commonly interpreted in terms of causes. The parts are organized, with certain parts apparently under the governance of other parts. The computer provides an obvious example. For Turing there are three parts to a mechanical computer: the store, the executive unit, and the control.[46] The store equates to the paper on which the human functionary writes things down, but also the books of rules, tables of instructions, and the human functionary's memory. The executive unit is the part that carries out the individual calculations: adding numbers together and making deductions. The control executes the book of rules or table of instructions correctly and in the right order.

Turing's metaphor is that of the human functionary, and the functionary in turn operating not just as part of an organization but *as* a human organization, with her own internal and hierarchical division of labor. Human organization becomes a metaphor for the machine, but in turn the machine informs the understanding of human organization.

Understandably, as it is brought into service to explain the workings of the machine, human organization is described in a divided, reductive, and machine-like way.[47] There is no consideration of the more personable aspects of human organization, such as meting out justice, the exercise of duty, building trust, or even prosaic functions such as collecting revenues. Turing's account is metonymic in several ways. Machines are a part of an organization, but here they stand in for the whole organization. The functionary is one part of an organization, but here the individual is discussed as if the activities of an individual explain the whole. Furthermore, insofar as we think of human organization in machine terms, there is also a propensity to focus on bookkeeping, just one part of an organization's operations. The record keeping and accounts department stands in for the whole organization. For Turing, the functionary is in fact called a "computer," the common term for those people whose job it was to perform calculations. The metonymic origin of the electronic computer is completed in its appropriation of the title of the person in the organization who does the calculations.

Under Turing's account, the computer is a bureaucratic machine. An organization is often termed bureaucratic when it is centralized, hierarchical, and formal, that is, when it assumes the character of a machine: compartmentalized and causally connected, with little room to maneuver outside those constraints. So conceived, bureaucracy is a product of the industrial age and inevitably bears a pejorative cast.

For the Romantic critic, insofar as human organization is machine-like, it diminishes the freedom that makes us human, by dividing us into so many components. The division of labor is also the bureaucratization of the workplace and the diminution of the individual's autonomy. For Ruskin, "It is not, truly speaking, the labor that is divided; but the men:— Divided into mere segments of men—broken into small fragments and crumbs of life; so that all the little piece of intelligence that is left in a man is not enough to make a pin, or a nail, but exhausts itself in making the point of a pin or the head of a nail."[48] The laborer in the system is only permitted to know enough to perform her allotted task.

Work relations under the division of labor are based less on kinship and trust than on disinterest. Individuals are not stakeholders in the overall operation. One laborer or bureaucratic functionary can be substituted for another.

For the social theorist Max Weber (1864–1920), in a similar vein, bureaucracy presents as the mere husk, the remnant, the wake of productive endeavors, and in turn of creativity. It is what you are left with when the original motivation for productivity has receded.[49] Human organization becomes self-sustaining but with no substance. The lost substance for Weber is religious motivation, formerly expressed through the Calvinist endorsement of frugality and hard work, faithful stewardship as a dutiful return for God's provision. The appeal to religion is also the appeal to the bigger picture, the source of perfection and completeness. According to Weber, the religious motivation for hard work and enterprise gave way to *necessity* brought about by industrialization. Now we need charismatic leadership to rescue us from the imperative of soulless industry. Borrowing from the romantic legacy, for Weber the charismatic leader is the artist, the visionary, the gifted. Giddens describes the charisma Weber seeks as that "quality of leadership which appeals to non-rational motives."[50] For Weber the religious basis of commerce has been lost, we are without charismatic leadership, and we are trapped within a gray world, the iron cage of bureaucracy.[51] Of course there are any number of candidates for charismatic leadership, not only the twentieth-century ideological dictator, but also the designer, the entrepreneur, the source of genius, the "new blood" of the network economy.

Bureaucracy is human sociality reduced to parts. It restricts freedom, it becomes self-generating, and it can get out of control. It becomes self perpetuating, with no checks, no humanizing or ameliorating influences. The organization is like a machine in that it is anonymous and faceless. As such bureaucracy features prominently in narratives of dystopia.[52] There are two popular images of dystopia. The first is dystopia with agency: misery produced by intentional villainy, greed, oppression, the stock in trade of the popular Hollywood dystopia, imposed through the agency of personified evil. But the most potent dystopian scenario is of insidious helplessness engendered by industrialization and bureaucracy. Here there is no identifiable villain. This is the dystopia of Orwell's *1984*[53] or Gilliam's film *Brazil.* Bureaucracy becomes associated with "group-think" and the mediocrity of committee decision making, to be contrasted with the charisma and vision of the creative individual, as also brought into relief in Rand's heroic novel *The Fountainhead.*[54]

For all its putative freedoms and opportunities, the Internet has the potential to mask the face of an organization and to render it more bureaucratic and machine-like. Access to persons seems even more distant, as when confronted with a "closed" sign at the complaints desk. When the Internet transaction does not go through, the computer screen is maddeningly mute.

As we have seen, an antidote to the undesirable by-products of the bureaucratic machine is to listen to those who present the importance of the business team and of diversification among labor. Equally potent is irony, a dose of satire that never tires of exposing the shortcomings of the faceless bureaucrat, and the contradictions of any organizational strategy. Bureaucracy is a metonym for organization, which in turn stands in for institutions. Derrida provides an ironic account of institutions, such as universities, and suggests that the edification of the student is rightly a building up of knowledge and expertise, establishing a place in the great professional institutions (economics, law, architecture).[55] It is also a tearing down, an undermining of their credibility. The social philosophers Deleuze and Guattari posit the rhizome as a parasite on bureaucratic structures. The rhizome grows from within to subvert the edifice. The trappings of bureaucracy and the keeping of accounts draw on the operations of a tree-like growth, but creative subversion "can begin to burgeon nonetheless, throwing out rhizome stems, as in a Kafka novel."[56] Institutions are prone to disturbances to their own operations and authority, from within. An ironic response to the bureaucratic machine might be just that: leaping between the positive and negative, allowing the frictional sparks of the runaway machine to ignite change.

The Universal Machine: Marx's Critique of Ideology

Metonymy uses the part to signify the whole, but is there a transcendent whole to which all parts may refer? Smith transforms the Stoic confidence in "the universe as one living organism, with a single substance and a single soul"[57] into the abstraction of "the whole machine of the world."[58] As well as a machine standing in for the universe, the machine can present *as* the universe: hence we have the concept of the universal machine. Following Plato, the universal is the immutable, the abiding, the enduring category, always applicable, covering all cases. It is closely associated with the ideal, that which transcends the contingencies of the world we apprehend with the senses. A universal machine is an idealized machine.[59] Turing had such a machine in mind when he broached the concept of the Oracle, the universal machine that could carry out any calculation, including "uncomputable" operations. Mathematicians harbor the concept of the ideal machine, the mathematical and logical construct that is theoretically interesting, but not necessarily practical to build and use.

The computer and the Internet are frequently presented in idealized form in any case. The computer world is caught up in anticipations and utopian images, and it seems to matter less to the promoters of the technology what computers can accomplish now than what they will or should accomplish in their idealized form in the future. So much of the promise of electronic commerce, the democratization of the marketplace and seamless transactions (friction-free capitalism), assume a technology and a design cunning that do not yet exist.

Ideology appeals to concepts of the universal. As we have seen, an ideology claims to give an over-arching account of the world, with everything and everyone in their place. Plato's idealism suggests such a social order: the sovereign, the philosopher, the craftsman, the artist, the poet.[60] In dystopian accounts of the bureaucratized, industrialized world, this order is transformed into a condition where everyone is placed in "the whole machine of the world." We are cogs in a machine. The social order takes on the character of the machine. From the pen of critics such as Marx, the ideology of the industrialized world in turn assumes the character of a relentless, all-consuming, universalizing machine, rendering everything in its path subject to its own machinic operations.

The Enlightenment defined itself as anti-ideological. For the Enlightenment mind, the Platonic appeal to transcendence is ideological, the appeal to some state of being beyond the current condition, where we are better off. Ideology can be used as a method of subjugation, maintaining the status quo, a source of prejudice. Smith pitted his free-market philosophy against the ideology of mercantilism, in a way analogous to Descartes' veiled critique of tradition and the church. The Enlightenment was against ideology of this kind, promoting instead notions of free inquiry into the nature of things, the growth of science, democracy, equality of opportunity, public office by merit rather than birth, and the free market.

Ideology of the kind the Enlightenment opposed has resurfaced in various guises: the maintenance of an old order under modern conditions. This is an order that can only be maintained by force, coercion, and censorship: usually as an overt nationalism, fascism, xenophobia, and empire. Of course the mass media and the free market have been marshaled in opposition to ideological regimes. For Friedman, one of the twentieth century's foremost proponents of free enterprise, "the market works to preserve political freedom."[61] In championing elec-

tronic commerce that putatively crosses social, regional, and national boundaries, the Internet claims no small part in providing an instrument for subverting
restrictions on liberties. The Internet is touted as an anti-ideological palliative.
Democracy, capitalism, and the free market are pitted against ideology.

Commentators often position the Internet against ideology. For cultural
critic Sady Plant, the Internet developed from a particular, militaristic ideology,
but then became an intellectual medium, then a people's medium.[62] The latter
somehow subverts its original ideological purpose. The Internet is also contrasted with hierarchical and restricted network systems and practices. It has an
anarchic character. It is also presented as a means of subverting ideologies. The
old market system has been likened by some to the construction of a gothic
cathedral, apparently requiring hierarchical organization, and resulting in a
single, huge, static edifice.[63] On the other hand the Internet is supposed to be
more like a bazaar, chaotic, dynamic, and opportunistic in its organization.

The argument here is a diminished form of the neo-Marxist critique of ideological systems in architecture and art. Under such critique ideological art shows
the correct order of things, often created under duress in the modern age.[64] Art
against ideology attempts to depict a breaking up of that order. The architectural theorist Tafuri examines ideology in the design of cities. The pre-ideological
condition recognizes the complexity and conflict of the city. Tafuri quotes M. A.
Laugier on the design of a park in 1765: "There must be regularity and fantasy,
relationships and oppositions, and casual, unexpected elements that vary the
scene; great order in the details, confusion, uproar, and tumult in the whole."[65]
Ideology attempts to submit that chaos to order. Everything is supposed to be
in its place. The order of governance is well represented in the configuration of
civic buildings and the radiating avenues of the baroque, and in the neoclassical
city, but it is also present in the organic layouts of the Garden City movement,
and the ideal, regular city plans of Le Corbusier and the moderns.

Of course, any city eventually succumbs to the chaos of contingency. As is
evident in the vibrancy of many cities where there was once an attempt at grand
order, such as Paris and New York, the city develops in the space between order
and contingency. It is in the forces that presume to think they are ordering
people's lives wherein ideology resides, not in the attempt to create ordered
space, though there are many attempts at non-ideological planning, such as
Tschumi's famous Parc de la Villette on the outskirts of Paris. Tschumi describes
his grand plan in terms of overlays of conflicting schemas, which provide inter-
stices for unpredictable events to happen.[66] Similarly, the Internet is not

anarchic in its design or without structure. In the manner of the city, its usage has turned it into something that allows certain things to happen and restricts other opportunities.

Ideology functions as a metanarrative. By the philosopher Lyotard's account, metanarrative is a way of stifling debate.[67] It purports to provide the ultimate authority, or court of appeal, on matters. But one form of ideology can replace another. The Enlightenment replaced the ideology of institutionalized authority with its own ideology of progress. The Enlightenment promoted the vision of a better world, in which history is on an inexorable march of improvement, like a machine transforming the world to its own form.[68] Marx sought to critique the ideology of the Enlightenment project, particularly its teleological, or causal, accounts of history.[69] History is replete with stories of conquest, and the conquerors are inevitably the custodians of the record. The identification of success and failure in history is an ideological pursuit insofar as it seeks to justify the domination of the bourgeoisie over the laboring masses. The Enlightenment's ideology is of progress through industrialization, and mechanization, a narrative that puts the conquerors, the bourgeoisie, as the main actors in the plot.[70]

Against ideology, Marx posits "dialectical materialism." Contrary to Epicureanism and the scientific materialism that derives from it, Marx posits a nondeterminate materialism that is unresolved, unsettled, and conflictual.[71] Marx borrows both from Hegel's concept of the dialectic and from the primacy of sense experience as explored by Locke and the empiricists.[72] Contrary to ideology, dialectical materialism relies on the senses as the source of all knowledge, and it acknowledges that we are informed by common sense, the power vested in the social sphere rather than the individual: "If man is social by nature, he will develop his true nature only in society, and the power of his nature must be measured not by the power of separate individuals but by the power of society."[73]

The concept of the division of labor is ideological to the extent that it gains its impetus from a belief in the inexorable march of improvement through yet greater efficiencies, which bring about invention and further improvement. The ideology of improvement valorizes the market as the arbiter of what is appropriate in the control of labor. Belief in the sovereignty of the market constitutes a metanarrative. We let the market decide, as the final court of appeal, as the "invisible hand." For Marx, capitalism is under the charge of ideology. As we have seen, ideology is also insidious in that it does not recognize itself as ideological.

For Marx ideology is dismantled through various transformations, which involve exposing ideology for what it is. When an ideology is recognized as a metanarrative, there is the chance of its dismantling, or the positing of alternative narratives. Marx also advocates social revolution as the ultimate transformation. In practice, the socialist revolutions foretold by Marx have not brought about the transformations expected. But advocates of Marxism since Marx seem to deal with revolution more vigorously through the trope of irony, particularly as developed by Deleuze and Guattari.[74]

Transformation: Dismembering the Capitalist Machine

The causal connections that make up the machine work together to bring about transformation. Hoisting machines transform the movement of the body into the movement of a vertical rope to lift heavy objects.[75] In a mill the movement of water is transformed into the rotation of a wheel, which in turn is transformed into a motion that grinds corn. Technically, one state of the machine is transformed into another state, or one form of energy is translated into another. In the process raw materials are transformed into useful products. Turing's definition of an information-processing machine entails the concept of a paper tape with symbols that can be read and rewritten according to a program of instructions. States of the machine, described in terms of symbols, are transformed into other states, depending on a program. Design has been so described as a transformation of states in a machine-like way, as though design involves programs or rules for transforming one state of the design into another: transforming a rudimentary sketch plan into a configuration of walls, a computer program outline into a list of commands, a specification for a Web site into a working online system.[76]

Concepts of transformation are ubiquitous in language, from concepts of the transformational rewrite rule in grammar[77] to Austin's performative language theory.[78] Metaphor and metonymy transform our thinking: A house becomes a machine, the credit system becomes a piece of plastic, human organization becomes an iron cage, society becomes a marketplace. To the degree that we let the metaphor do its work, we become attuned to certain ways of thinking and acting revealed by the metaphor.

Insofar as we see the world through the metaphor of the marketplace, it presents as a means of promoting freedom. By all accounts, one of Smith's great innovations was to bring the laborer as consumer into his explanation of the production process. Laborers compete in the labor market and are paid a fair wage for their labors. Laborers need to be paid fairly in order to consume in the market for the goods that they and their co-workers produce. Unregulated markets and free competition are concomitant with free individuals. Free exchange, free trade, freedom to set prices, and freedom to choose become the quintessential expressions of liberty. According to Friedman, the free market is an indispensable means toward political freedom.[79] As a privileged metaphor, the capitalist machine is licensed to claim this transformative function.

Marx disputes this equation of a free market with human liberty, the power of the market to transform us into free individuals. For Marx, competition in a free market did not abolish all boundaries, but only those boundaries that were obstacles to free markets.[80] It is not labor that is liberated or served by free enterprise, but "capital that establishes itself freely in free competition."[81] It is only when capital has established itself in the dominant position that we are free to move around, but on its terms: "The domination of capital is the prerequisite of free competition."[82] So we only enjoy freedom "on a limited foundation— that of the dominion of capital."[83]

For Marx the transformation of capitalism is not to make us more free, but to make us more like machines. Marx develops the criticism outlined previously that under the free-market system labor becomes subservient to the machine, in that labor is eventually replaced by the machine. Labor gets subsumed within capital: "But once absorbed into the production process of capital, the means of labor undergoes various metamorphoses, of which the last is the machine, or rather an automatic system of machinery."[84] The metonymic transformation to parts is extended as laborers become so many machine components: the "automaton consists of a number of mechanical and intellectual organs, so that the workers themselves can be no more than the conscious limbs of the automaton."[85] It is no longer the worker in whom reside skill and virtuosity, but the machine "which possesses skill and force in the worker's place, is itself the virtuoso, with a spirit of its own in the mechanical laws that take effect in it."[86] Because the virtuosity resides in the machine, the laborer serves the machine rather than the other way round. The work task is transformed into machinery, and the living worker is transformed "into a mere living accessory of the machine."[87] The worker becomes the means whereby the action of the machine can take place. For Marx it is only "in the imagination of economists" that the machine comes "to the aid of the individual worker."[88] The laborer is transformed not only into a machine, but into a machine accessory. The business of call centers, telephone marketing, and home working has come under scrutiny as an example of such a transformation in the network economy.[89] Information laborers are garnered from areas where labor is relatively inexpensive, they do not need to be relocated, training is minimal, their performance is monitored electronically, particularly against the clock, and they can be replaced easily.

The recovery from this transformation into the machine is for labor to heed the call to bring about its own transformation. Marx had urged his followers not to interpret the world, but to change it.[90] Marx borrows and adapts Hegel's concept of the dialectic, the historic movement of one social force in opposition to another (thesis and antithesis), and their temporary resolution in a third condition (synthesis).[91] For Marx the movement involves the struggle between the bourgeoisie and the proletariat.[92] The ultimate outcome of this dialectic is total revolution: "brutal contradiction, the shock of body against body, as its final *dénouement.*"[93] At times Marx's thought takes an ironic turn. He also supports the imperatives of capitalism, which has within it the seeds of its own destruction. Displaced labor will inevitably generate unrest.[94] Capitalism needs to be allowed to run its course in order for the revolution to socialism to take place.

The Monstrous Machine: Net Hybrids

As we have seen, the transformations wrought by the machine are not always for the good, and one person's assessment of the outcome of any machine operation may be contrary to another's. Machines can build up and destroy. For Smith the money machine produces liberty; for Marx it destroys by making us more like the machine. Vitruvius's account of the machine seems also to focus on destruction. A builder needs to know the construction appropriate to what a machine is capable of accomplishing: the work of cranes, pulleys, wheels, aqueducts and viaducts. Vitruvius also identifies the machines of destruction: catapults, ballistae, ram-tortoises, movable towers, ditch-filling tortoises, tortoise diggers, and siege engines. Before building a city one must consider the machines for its destruction. We may surmise that between the operations of the machines of construction and of destruction lies the opportunity to develop an intimate knowledge of the city. For Vitruvius, "not by machines but in opposition to the principle of machines, has the freedom of states been preserved by the cunning of architects."[95]

Computers have also been designed for and against destruction. Turing's early encounter with machines was as encryption machines, strategic instruments of war, the precursors of contemporary network cryptography. Military operations were only effective if internal communications could go undetected. The encryption machine exploited the weakness in enemy communications by decoding messages passed between enemy U-boats.[96] The invention and development of the Internet (and its predecessors) seems to have been informed by the exigencies of destruction, as a distributed and redundant, rather than a centralized, system to counter the possibility of it becoming incapacitated through a nuclear strike.[97] Generalizing Vitruvius's tribute to architects, we design artifacts (cities, buildings, computer systems) to withstand the ravages of whatever subverts their functioning. The potency of this play between construction and destruction is exemplified in the computer world through the perpetration of computer "viruses," a subversive movement within computer programming culture that is not entirely destructive. The constructive/destructive game of the computer hacker places security, robustness, and automated agency on the agenda. As part of an industry of moves and countermoves, it informs the development of operating systems, networks, and programming practices. Encryption practices for digital media are also caught in a bind between the desire to keep systems secure and the desire to curtail the means of concealing criminal activity, drawing on a collection of techniques: strong and weak encryption, escrowed encryption (strong encryption with an emergency decryption capability), authentication, firewalls, auditing.[98] Providing a legal means of crossing security barriers and preventing illegal hacking constitute conflicting requirements.

Machines of destruction can also serve "as a defence against danger, and in the interest of self preservation."[99] But from the point of view of the citizens under threat, or the city under siege, the capacity of a machine for destruction appears monstrous. For Vitruvius, machines are a means to an end, a component in a causal chain, a means to the production of a final work, which is symmetrical, ordered, and whole. Under the destructive machine, that which is supposed to effect positive transformation assumes the character of something that contributes to decay and ruin. Machines are meant to counteract the ravages of time, the weathering of the elements, the dissipation of energies. Instead, the monstrous machine hastens the process. It seeks to shatter the whole, to destroy symmetry and order. Our machines are turned against us. Monstrosity does not pertain to destruction per se, but the denial of the assumed characteristics of a category, the hybrid product of an inappropriate union between categories. The machine's monstrosity comes from the denial of its capacity to be positively productive. This is a classical definition of monstrosity. A monster is an entity, the parts of which belong to an entity of an opposing category.[100] The workings of metaphor and metonymy are also monstrous.

The house-machine hybrid is a monster in that the parts are not in the right place. Metonymy presents the part as the whole. It may also offer the wrong part for the whole. The machine is a part of the category of the artificial, and yet in the metaphor of nature as a machine, it stands in for nature, which is a different category. This swapping of parts brings us closer to the popular depiction of monstrosity. Shelley's Dr. Frankenstein creates a monster composed of parts from different bodies, some from the bodies of criminals and outcasts.[101] The seams in this artificial body attest to the mismatch of parts. The body is outside its category. Instead of being born and subject to growth and development, it is manufactured and passes through a ludicrously short period of self-education. The creature's pretense at gentlemanly manners only exaggerates its mispositioning in the world of humanity. The creature has some human characteristics, but these are distorted and betrayed by its origins in the mortuary and the laboratory. The machine-human hybrid, the current obsession of advocates of "cyborg ontologies," provides a variation on Shelley's monster, as does the putative artificial life generated within computer systems.

Monsters can be tamed or destroyed. They can also be let loose to do their work, if we dare. The metonym as monster can be set against the world as machine. The outcome may be a dismantling of the status of the machine metaphor, or perhaps further hybridity.

The Useless Machine

Machines can be useless and dysfunctional, in the same way that metaphors and metonyms can fail to spark a productive association or provoke a profitable understanding. One metaphor can subvert or overwhelm another, as can machines. Turing's Colossus was the undoing of the German Enigma machine, rendering its coding strategies dysfunctional. The metaphor of house as machine eclipses Le Corbusier's "house as temple" metaphor. The world as machine gives way only reluctantly to other models, less catchy, less validating of the industrial imperative: the world as construct, the world as a term in language, the world as primordial condition, the world as common sense.

A typology of dysfunction would include machines that are rendered inoperative by other machines, machines that do not do what they are supposed to, machines with unexpected behaviors, obsolete and incapacitated machines, imaginary machines that could never work, machines as amusement, machines conceived in ignorance of machinic operations, machines pushed beyond the limits of their effective functioning, and sterile or stillborn machine hybrids.[102] The digital world is populated with such dysfunctional machines, not only in museums, in storerooms, and as landfill, but in research laboratories, sci-fi novels, films, and computer games, and in the collective imagination of enthusiasts and skeptics of digital media: the CAD system with the seamless interface, the truly intelligent expert system, the cyborg, the holodeck, the teleporter, the flying car, the time machine, athletic performance-enhancing prosthetics, the virtual vacation machine, the unmediated virtual store, the true labor-saving device, the foolproof encryption/decryption method, the frictionless capitalist machine. Dysfunction is not necessarily the same as "no function." On the one hand, such devices serve to fuel the capitalist imperative of hope in a better product, always just beyond our grasp, making us more compliant as ever-expectant consumers. They can also be turned to the task of provoking by their absurdity or impossibility.

One of the means by which the oppositions of a metaphor are set in play is through the exchange of terms. So a house as a machine encourages us to reflect on the house-like qualities of machines. What is it that dwells in a machine? For Descartes, the soul dwells in the machine of the body. There is also an ancient legacy that puts a god in the machine. The term *deus ex machina* (god out of the machine) has some currency in the network economy.[103] It further invests the machine with importance, but it is also a term of skepticism. Greek and Roman plays would often invoke a divine character who would arrive on stage to sort out the difficulties of the plot, the complex of problems the other characters had created. The god would emerge from a contraption above the stage. The arrival of the deity would provide an element of surprise, but it was regarded as a cheap trick by some playwrights and critics. It is an admission of the need for an unlikely and unconvincing character or event that resolves the complexity of inter-related story lines.[104] Some of the useless machines mentioned previously serve this purpose of yielding an unlikely solution to a difficult problem, but at the same time remind us of the absurdity of the condition that made it necessary. It is as if the modern condition is so fraught with difficulties and convolutions that we need to write the unlikely scenarios of telepresence, digital transcendence, artificial life, and friction-free capitalism into the script, as gods from the machine.

Diogenes the Cynic is also instructive on the subject of the useless machine. There is an account that his city was under siege. The other inhabitants were busy rushing around arming their machines of defense, barricading the gates, and stockpiling food. He was equally busy pushing his barrel up a hill and letting it roll down again. He repeated the process for hours on end. When challenged as to what he was doing, he declared that as everyone else was busy doing something, he thought he had better be busy as well. His useless labor with a simple machine served a rhetorical purpose that has not been lost on the commentary of time. Diogenes is reputed to have lived in his barrel. Perhaps this useless machine is the original machine for living, or the house as machine is in fact a dwelling that is not a home, or the home is not stable but on the move, unrestrained by the earth's friction. Perhaps the one who emerges from the machine is not a god after all, but the cynic.

The Romance with the Machine

As we have seen, if the home is resistant to the machine the same cannot be said of the market. Vitruvius devotes the last of his ten books on architecture to the machine, paying particular attention to devices for constructing buildings and for warfare. But he introduces his account through familiar examples, and these connect with prosperity and commerce, such as yokes and plows for oxen to supply an abundance of food, and carts, wagons, and ships for transporting goods. In commerce there are methods of testing weights by steelyards and balances, which "saves us from fraud, by introducing honest practices into life."[105] For Vitruvius, these machines "are habitually used as general conveniences."[106] So prosperity relies on machines, and by implication the market is enabled by them. For Smith and Marx, for good or ill, the machine becomes the main constituent of capital, and labor is defined by it.

Against Smith's optimism, the Romantic critic is not necessarily opposed to the machine in total but participates in a cyclical movement of fascination and repulsion.[107] As an advocate of the whole, the Romantic is against the individuation suggested by the machine. But that which is anathema is also a source of sublime fascination. The Romantic stands before the terror from a safe position and enjoys being at the boundary between the beautiful and the grotesque, the sacred and the profane, the mechanical and the crafted. Ruskin would stand thus before the locomotive: "I cannot express the amazed awe, the crushed humility, with which I sometimes watch a locomotive take its breath at a railway station, and think what work there is in its bars and wheels, and what manner of men they must be who dig brown iron-stone out of the ground, and forge it into THAT!"[108] There is humility and respect for the machine of "active steel" and the triumphant labors that brought it about. The machine is monstrous, in its scale, in what it can do, but also in its hybridity, its similarity to, and its difference from, the animal skeletal frame. Frankenstein's creature is similarly in the company of the grandeur of nature, the sublime spectacle of the glaciers of the Swiss Alps. As nature offers us its inhospitable terrors we also have the dread and wonder of the mechanical contraptions by which an assembly of dead components is brought to life.

But the hybridity of the machine also threatens its functioning. The parts start to work against one another and the machine runs amok. Not only is this the case as the machine breaks down, but in the way the locomotive destroys the pleasure of the journey, transmuting the traveler into a "living parcel,"[109] the machine pollutes and desecrates the mountain air, lakes, and slopes,[110] and the industrial machine destroys all sense of dignity in labor and turns workers into machine accessories. Our helplessness before the machine is further amplified by incomprehension. As helpless components in the machine of capitalist labor, we lack the view of the whole. It is not only the locomotive that causes disquiet, but the reach of the railway system and its influence, the all-embracing network, the capitalist edifice, that we are helpless to comprehend and control. No less is this incomprehension amplified than with the mechanisms and the reach of contemporary high-speed digital networks.

To escape the rampaging machine, the Romantic allows his imagination to revert to a pre-industrial state, the time when machines were just tools, labor was not so organized and care, skill and sacrifice were the motivations for creation, above self-interest. The nostalgia is for craft, which is a product not entirely innocent of the machine age. For Ruskin, the worth of handcrafted stone or wood is in "its being the work of poor, clumsy, toilsome man,"[111] as opposed to the product of the machine. Craft acquires its definition by virtue of its contrast with the machine.

But it seems we cannot do without machines. Considering the necessity of their evil, we find that the machines of preference are those that are conspicuous, comprehensible, whose qualities can be appreciated in terms of craft: Ruskin's steam locomotive with "Titanian hammer-strokes beating . . . glittering cylinders . . . fine ribbed rods . . . omnipotence of grasp."[112] We revert to Vitruvius's hoists, waterwheels, and catapults to explain the machine age. These objects are metonymic for the machine world, comprehensible, imaginable objects that stand in for something much less easily grasped, such as ubiquitous, interconnected network systems and microscopic solid-state circuitry, the invisible world of modern-day technology. In conjuring up such devices, we note that the tangible term "machine" also serves as metonym for the whole complex of the technological system in which we find ourselves.

Pleasure and optimism, as the contemporary Romantic contemplates the simple machine, readily turns to an exaggerated belief in its capabilities. Where the machine is isolated from the complex technological and social field of which it is a part, then it indeed inspires awe. The steam locomotive has transformed the countryside, the electric light globe has illuminated the world, the microchip has revolutionized the way we work. Given the romantic propensity toward unification, it is but a simple step to invoke the machine as a means of uniting disparate parts: the railways unite the world, electric current brings life to dead matter, the god emerges from the machine and unites the plot. No more is the imperative toward unity more evident than in the enthusiasm for cyberspace, artificial intelligence, artificial life, and frictionless commerce. It seems the computer is capable of bringing about the unity of all things, of nature and artifice, human and machine, production and consumption.

If we (as technoromantics) believe it, this extreme optimism in turn takes us back to our appreciation of the machine as sublime. In turn this attitude turns to anxiety over the downfall of the machine and those in its path, and to a nostalgia for craft, the idealized reconstruction of the machine as craft object, and the machine as the engine of an unsettled unity. The cycle continues.

This is the machine of romantic fiction and film. It is also standard fare in those other objects of mass consumption, computerized adventure games: Lara Croft before the lethal, spinning blades of an item of archaic military hardware, the exquisite mechanics of the telescopes, elevators, spinning domes, and swing bridges of the *Myst* games. Like so much modern fantasy, the quest is for a unification, technologically mediated and ultimately frustrated.

The cycle of the romantic machine also implicates metonymy, which furnishes us with several exit points. The machine is not in isolation. The locomotive is a part of a technological system, implicating social values, norms, systems of design and management. The artist-critic is not alone before the machine, but is a participant in a social and cultural milieu, with a history. From the time of Kant and Burke,[113] the concept of the sublime assumes the existence of the individual, selectively isolated from the social sphere. The individual, the precipice, and the machine are contingent and temporary reference points on the larger canvas, which, as with all of language, can never be grasped but through the shifting play of metonymy.

To lack comprehension of the whole is not a failing brought about by industrialization. Any failing is in the expectation that we ever could or should comprehend everything. The machine age seems to offer this promise but lets us down. The machine pollutes and turns us into machines, but *only* metonymically, which is to say contingently, and in a field of contestation. The machine as causal agent stands in for the complex of political and social forces. For Marx it is capitalism that has this agency, understood at times as the machine and through the machine. If capitalism turns laborers into machines during working hours, then it also turns them into leisured aristocrats on weekends. Our role as machine part is the result of only one metonymic transformation in a cast of emerging roles and identities.

On craft, the machine-made brought the handmade into existence. In the manner of a play of metonymy, they each have the capacity to animate the other. The house and the machine are perhaps diametrically opposed, but the positing of one against the other leads us to question and develop reflections on both. That the machine should be posited as a means to unity is metonymy magnified. The machine reflects back on the whole from which it is derived and, through dint of its privileging, assumes responsibility for the whole.

On analysis, the device of metonymy serves to locate the machine, to explain something of its elevated status, to show why it incurred such ambiguous opposition, and to suggest antidotes to the excesses it provokes. Metonymy also positions the machine in pro- and anti-capitalist discourses in a way that implicates design and invention. Metonymy is a form of metaphor, which provides models of design and invention.[114] Design is a play in metaphor, as the valorization of the machine is a play in metonymy. The network economy appears dependent on the rule of metonymy. As an ill-defined whole it is a prime example of our dependence on some part or other to bring it to account. Finally, metonymy is a close cousin to irony. Diogenes the homeless miscreant is never far away, challenging any system we set in place, ready to emerge in the god's stead from the machine in the last act.

This chapter has served as a polemic on the theme of the machine. For readers already familiar with the literature on political economy, it may have helped to gather, or carve up, concerns and misgivings about the network economy in a new way, as issues of metaphor and metonymy, and as issues of the machine: as a system of causal connections, a machine for designing, the bureaucratic machine, the universal machine, machine transformations, monstrous machines, useless machines, and romantic machines. We commonly think of machines as objects needing to be designed. So perhaps the chapter serves as a way of introducing designers to the themes of political economy, but using the familiar devices of metaphor and the unusual perspective, the sideways look, edgy design. In sum, my ambition has been to further the project of Deleuze and Guattari, and others, in writing in a way that might disrupt ordinary assumptions about the network economy and its critique. Continuing the theme of the introductory chapter, this is an attempt to encourage the designer to look at the network economy in ways that can inform the design process. What if, instead of attempting to design well-oiled interactive computer systems, designers were to acknowledge that systems can be frictional and resistant, dysfunctional and disconnected? Perhaps this is the reality of the design situation in the network economy. In this respect the chapter is also a polemic against the illusion of the smooth, or in Deleuze and Guattari's terms, the striated, the hierarchical, and the politely ordered.[115]

The Lost Game

Work brings to mind its converse, leisure, and leisure's manifestation in play. The boy who invented the automated steam valve did so in order that he might play.[1] The common object of play is the game, which is in the company of the machine in explaining the economic system, if not the workings of the universe! Under play, the "whole machine of the world"[2] gives way to its converse, the fictional "glass bead game,"[3] the *unio mystica,* the mystery of one, the game of games. Play also offers an account of such invention and of design as a game. At a more prosaic level, the computer game and its conspicuous consumption[4] provide the latest instantiation of the invasion of the home by electronic commerce, a further commodification of leisure.

By most contemporary accounts, the idea of play is integral to the most profound thinking about the human condition.[5] The hermeneutical philosopher Hans-Georg Gadamer describes the act of interpretation in terms of play.[6] At its most typical, the interpretation of a text involves us in an absorbing fusion between the textual material and the reader. There is a to-and-fro movement[7] as if a ball is being passed from one player to the other, or in the exchange of moves and countermoves in chess. The idea of the game recalls the child engaged in apparently arbitrary, aimless, but absorbing play on the kitchen floor, arranging saucepan lids, or unraveling a ball of string. At its most typical, one relaxes into play, immune from fears or threats, cocooned in a happy state of immersion.[8] For the child it is the realm in which trust is first rehearsed.[9] This is the state of the reader at her most receptive, open and "thoughtful." The reader is immersed in the narrative play of the text, letting it do its work in transforming expectations,

so that she emerges from the text renewed and can return to it with fresh anticipations. The game is never really over. The child returns to the saucepan lids and
the tangle of string, we play yet another round of tennis, we advance Lara Croft
through yet another spike and trap-infested cavern.

For Gadamer, who or what performs the backward and forward movement is
less important for understanding the nature of play than the movement itself.
There are many ways of describing any particular game thus, in terms of repeated movement between the components of the game: the ball and the players, the player and the pieces, the opponents, the player and the situation, the
player and her expectations, the parts of the game and the whole. The idea of
play is captured just as well in the play of light, the play of forces, the play of
waves on the seashore, as it is in the idea of the game. Play need not presume
competing elements, or even a player.[10]

Of course, there is a strong motivation among philosophers in elevating unreflective play as the point of departure for addressing the character of human
being. The valorization of play serves as a foil for the long-held tenets of a rationalist, or machinic, disposition. For the followers of Descartes, it is self-
evident that the point from which we start to deal with the world is the thinking
being, the highly self-conscious individual aware of self: the deliberative, con-
templative, self-aware homo sapiens (wise man) able to declare "I think therefore I am." From this premise all understandings of reason are meant to follow:
the objective world outside the subject, the derivation of knowledge by intro-
spection and logic, and methods and procedures for determining facts.[11]

In keeping with the phenomenological tradition, Gadamer positioned himself against such subjectivist assertions. His philosophy is anti-rationalist (in
the Cartesian sense), and against method. The fusion between subject and object of which Gadamer writes (as in the absorption of the players in a game and
its objects) is not meant as an advanced psychological state, a trance, where we
forget for a while that we are individuals, nor is it to give rein to an unconscious
world of instinct, repressed memories, or interiorized practice, but this state of
being is the primary condition. The idea of self, or identity, emerges out of this
condition in the event of breakdown (in the language of Heidegger[12]). Something jars us from the realm of unreflective involvement into a different realization, perhaps a different game, where self emerges as an entity to be reckoned
with: Who am I? Why am I reading this? How does this text apply to me? Why
am I losing the game? "I," "me," and "we" take on particular meanings depending on context, and their meanings may be contested. In keeping with the

familiar postmodern assertion, the self is not fixed but contingent. In this sense all of life is a game,[13] all of our experience is subject to the contest between various emerging and receding elements, continually "in play." At times, in Cartesian mode, we play a kind of meta-game, where we pretend we are outside of things, observing ourselves as if subjects and objects, as if moving from playing football to the game of managing a team, trading players, and in other ways "objectifying" aspects of the game.

Wittgenstein, in his later, anti-Cartesian phase, used the game as an example par excellence of how meaning in language operates.[14] As we explored in the case of metonymy, there really is no sufficient definition of what constitutes the meaning of particular words. "Game," for example, defies neat definition.[15] At times it is sufficient to think of it in terms of competition, rules, goals, moves, freedom, constraint, artificiality, and rehearsal, but the saucepan lid game seems very different from tennis or rehearsing a battle strategy in a war room. For Wittgenstein language does not operate through the determination of categories by lists of what things (like games) have in common, the drawing of boundaries around sets of objects, but by the human capacity for determining resemblance, itself a game of social negotiation in contexts of the usage of such words as "child's play," "tennis," and "war game."

Resemblance can be explained through the related concept of "typicality,"[16] where we cluster together activities, such as hitting a ball with a racket, dressing dolls, and pressing buttons on a Dreamcaster or X-Box console. For a moment, some activities seem closer together than others (when thinking of birthday presents, playing with dolls is perhaps closer to playing a computer game than it is to war games), with certain activities positioned at the center of a cluster. These might be the games that emerge in a particular context of discussion: dolls on birthdays, the egg-and-spoon race when talking about the village fair, the marathon at the Olympics, chess when referring to calculation and reason, and video games when attempting to describe the character of play in our highly technologized consumer culture. The "typical game" shifts its location, as does the identification of its particular characteristics, the features we choose to extract to make a point about game playing. Contrary to the authoritative claim of various game typologies, such as that offered by the social theorist Roger Caillois,[17] categories and genres of games reconfigure themselves. To suggest that categories shift is not to say that meaning is personal, vague, or relative, but that meaning is dependent on the maintenance (and subtle breach) of the shifting fields of social convention and context.

What are we to make of the claim that we are most at play, in play at its most typical, when unreflectively engaged? Absorptive engagement may not feature in the way chess is described in a book on chess strategies. Clearly many games demonstrate the reverse and celebrate deliberation. The assertion that games are characterized by a lack of awareness of self and identity may be obscured in the language of the dress-up games of children, role games, and the so-called first-person computer game. And clearly a sense of fusion and absorption apply to other activities as well, such as the carpenter caught up in working with the equipment of the workshop (Heidegger's example). The assertion of such typical traits as immersion and abrogation of self awareness are open to the vagaries of context and have their greatest force in the context of a kind of oppositional, agonistic polemic, to which I will return.

What of calculative reason in games? Much has been written about chess in the context of cognition.[18] Although it situates itself in a culture of calculation and logic, and there are computer programs that play champion-beating chess, it seems that advanced human chess playing involves the recognition of patterns, the recollection of previous games and situations, and the reading of the style of play of the opponent, the total of which is barely accessible as a calculative process subject to analytic reflection. On the theme of self-awareness, dress-up games focus on the self but are also games of changed identity, getting absorbed in a role, being someone else. To identify this absorptive capacity of games also asserts something about the world outside the game. It too is a game. In saying something about everything, the game narrative must answer to the charge that it is saying nothing at all.[19]

The proposition we are exploring, of the ubiquity of play, operates by way of reversal. Under the Cartesian tradition, play is a diversion from the proper object of human endeavor, which is to reason, deliberatively and self-consciously, readily associated with the rational and serious business of work. In a culture that places considerable store on the distinction between work and play, and a culture that privileges work, the proposition that *homo ludens* (playing man) has priority over *homo faber* (working man) may strike us as provocative. Whereas the typical Marxist position is that humankind needs to work before we can engage in leisure (labor precedes play),[20] Huizinga asserts, citing evidence from the play behavior of animals, that play precedes all culture and provides the meaningful underpinning of work.[21] This does not mean that life is more about playing computer games than it is about earning a living, but that earning a living is already imbued with the concept of the game. It is parasitic upon it in several ways. Among other motivations, we work hard so that we might have more time and resources to expend on leisure. We work so that we might play. Some people are fortunate enough to have jobs that they enjoy as much as they enjoy playing, and perhaps this is a model or some ideal of what constitutes work. More important, from our point of view here, work is already imbued with that which we normally characterize as play: the carpenter engaged in the unreflective task of making something. We are at our jobs the most when we are engaged in a play-like way. In fact, the attribution of work and play to various activities does not point to different "cognitive faculties" or "states of mind," but, in Wittgenstein's terms, it is a matter of the usage of the words "work" and "play" in different social contexts, even given expression in certain contractual relationships. To play is to be doing something for ourselves on company time, as when an employee might be accused of returning late from a lunchtime game of squash, or surreptitiously playing computer games: "We employed you to work, not to play games." So, to play the game of reversing the priority of work and play is not an attempt to obscure an important distinction, but to sharpen its edge, by appealing to the contingency of language.

Play and reality constitute another distinction. By some accounts, play is a preparation for encounters with reality. We commonly think of the game as a rehearsal for the real thing, a low-risk preparation for high-risk encounters.[22] So play may come before the "real" encounter in terms of childhood development, but we may also revert to play in certain life contexts, such as in preparing for a design task, through exercises. Play has obvious uses in educational contexts. We may also revert to play as a nostalgic diversion back to a risk-free world. Again, the appeal to a reversal problematizes this distinction. Reality is the play. In terms of the radical psychoanalytic theorist Jacques Lacan, the real is already imbued with the imaginary. The imaginary is neither just inside nor outside. The real is not the reality assumed to yield to scientific analysis, but the world resistant to the advances of language.[23]

The reversals of which I have written so far in this book, and which are of the kind that stimulate design, constitute a kind of intellectual game, played in all seriousness, of tarrying with the preposterous notion, the proposition that is counter to "common sense." Huizinga provides an interesting account of the play element of myth in these terms, which might also apply to his own grandiose valorization of play as accounting for law, politics, art, philosophy, war, and all of civilization. To claim as much of play is similar to the case he cites of a small child who declares he has just seen a carrot "as big as God": "The desire to make an idea as enormous and stupefying as possible is . . . a typical play-function and is common both in child-life and in certain mental diseases."[24] The most ambitious ideas speak of play though they may be delivered in all seriousness.

Design and Play

There is little difficulty in associating the serious, work-oriented activity of designing something (a building, product, structure, or computer program) with play. As I suggested in the introduction, designers are not necessarily averse to the preposterous idea as a stimulus to creativity, the tortured metaphor, playing with the sacred. In terms of the work-play distinction, designers are sometimes pleased to ascribe a frivolous, play aspect to their work. In terms of the reality-play distinction, they often like to see the design process as a series of successive rehearsals and revisions, through drawings, models and computer simulations, leading to a final product.

But designing also succumbs to the hermeneutical account of interpretation, with which I began this chapter. Like reading a text, design involves coming to a design situation, always with some expectation of what the final product might be, and engaging in a to-and-fro dialogical game.[25] In the process the designer's expectations undergo revision and transformation. Such expectations may present in the guise of metaphor. At one time the Web designer sees the Web site as an information store, at another time as a portal to other worlds, or an animated billboard, a supermarket, or a meeting place. Such metaphors are in play, with one another and with their negations. At its most typical the game of design is absorbing and engaging, with objects coming into and receding from view in the event of ruptures in the fabric of unselfconscious involvement, and according to the entailments of the various metaphors in play. So a Web site as a portal brings to light the URL link as an object. The billboard metaphor reveals advertising banners, and the supermarket metaphor suggests shopping carts and checkout procedures. Design as play implicates metaphors, materials, tools, the social context of the designer's studio, the brief, the clients, regulatory authorities, and a corpus of precedents, a whole contextual field. The elements are in play. Design so described as play has been explored by theorists such as Schön,[26] and Ehn,[27] and examined in the context of hermeneutics by Snodgrass.[28] It also informs the generalized view of design adopted in this book, and is one that is set in contradistinction to the reductive, machinic, methodological approach considered in chapter 2.

Learning from Computer Games

It is against this background of the ubiquity of play, and an eye for the prepos-terous, that we are in a position to examine computer games and what they might contribute to a further understanding of design. Sober educators often structure student learning assignments around the concept of the game, in-cluding specialized computer games for learning about architectural form.[29] The dour mathematical game theory of John von Neumann aimed to account for competition in economic systems in terms of the game, establishing the properties of games that constitute a "zero-sum game" (where there is a fixed re-source to be shared between two players), and where one player minimizes the maximum loss that can be imposed by another player, the goal of the so-called minimax solution.[30] The influence of Neumann and game theory in the field of computation in general, and artificial intelligence (AI) in particular, is well known.

Even applied to design, AI has for a long time drawn on concepts of the game, and used games and puzzles as test sites of its methods.[31] The idea of problem solving as defined by paths, goals, and decision points draws on concepts of the exploration of a maze, or searching through a series of branching possibilities, in the manner of a game of chess. The difficulties of creating artificial intelli-gence programs have also been explained in terms of the game. The character of the problems amenable to AI techniques is that of a puzzle, whereas supposed real-world problems, such as those encountered by a designer, are much less well defined, more like a game where the rules and objectives are undergoing change as you play. Of course, computerized adventure games now boast characters with artificial intelligence, who act as adversaries in the game plan: dangerous animals, henchmen, supernatural beings, robots, and hybrids who respond to the movements and tactics of the player. Critics of AI have also used the game as a means of demonstrating AI's fundamental shortcomings. For Dreyfus, chess does not rely on the mental manipulation of symbols, as suggested by the tenets of symbolic processing, but on the holistic recognition of patterns in a situation, a process that does not readily lend itself to formal calculation.[32]

Without exploring all these issues in detail we simply indicate here that there is a tradition of thinking about and learning from the game in relation to computers and design. From here I wish to explore what a metaphorical, phe-nomenological, and linguistic orientation to the game contributes to our un-derstanding. Here the emphasis is less on symbols, algorithms, and methods than on the way the game and play feature in our language. In the process we find that computer games at once reveal what was there all along about design and invention, reinforcing well-established assertions, but also opening design to the consideration of new possibilities in the network economy.[33]

Repetition and the Eternal Return

Computer games bring into relief the issue of repetition. According to Marx, labor in the industrialized age succumbs to the dictates of the machine. The successive division of labor reduces work to the repetition of ever more menial tasks. We may refine this observation to the suggestion that attempts at humane forms of work practice, or the move toward professional, managerial, and team-based modes of working have constantly had to resist the repetitive aspects of the industrialized workplace. Following Marx, Stallabras implicates computer games in the tyranny of repetition, which induces consumers to emulate the characteristics of the machine. In *Space Invaders*, for example, "there is an unceasing flow of monsters, as though from a production line."[34] But repetition is a key aspect of play in any case. According to Huizinga: "In this faculty of repetition lies one of the most essential qualities of play. It holds good not only of play as a whole but also of its inner structure. In nearly all the higher forms of play the elements of repetition and alternation (as in the *refrain*), are like the warp and woof of a fabric."[35] For Gadamer the "movement which is play has no goal which brings it to an end; rather it renews itself in constant repetition."[36] Speculation about how play deals with repetition can assist in understanding work and design.

One of the obvious characteristics of computerized arcade games is their reliance on fast responses to a rapid succession of intimidating challenges, as in having to aim and shoot at an invasion of moving targets (as in the *Space Invaders* game).[37] The more abstract challenge of positioning randomly descending shapes so that they form interlocking patterns, as in *Tetris*, also has this characteristic. Action games, such as *Doom* and *Quake*,[38] provide the illusion of racing around in circles in interconnected spaces, collecting ammunition and energy boosts while shooting and being shot at. But then the gentler genres of tactical and adventure games also have this repetitive aspect. Spaces are repeatedly visited and revisited. In *Myst III*[39] the game player finds herself in repeated examination of spaces and objects in order to solve a puzzle or find a way out of one world into another. The puzzles themselves often require the testing of permutations. The solution may involve the discovery of a procedure that requires the repetition of certain operations. So in the introductory environment of *Myst III* (a craggy volcanic island strewn with structures and mechanical devices in various states of repair), the players soon discover that they must journey around the island to rotate and align a series of optical devices, an exercise in simple repetition. Similarly, in *Tomb Raider,*[40] there are micro-challenges, where the player must repeat a jump to grab a rope. There are also more strategic repetitive tasks such as visiting a succession of symmetrically arranged spaces to solve discrete puzzles. The reward for solving each puzzle is a token or its fragment. After each recovery, the player returns to a central room to position the pieces, the sum of which unlocks access to another complex of spaces. The computer game *The Sims* requires the player to "train" the residents of a fictitious household by encouraging them to perform certain acts, such as taking out the garbage, hugging, going to the bathroom, and looking for a job. The game play takes place over the speeded-up cycle of the daily routine.

We commonly think of repetition as a means to an end. In algorithmic or AI terms, repetition is a means of searching through an array of possibilities. Operations are repeated to explore permutations. In fact the goal might be to minimize the repetition of tasks. Trying every single ordering of digits on a combination lock involves us in mindless mechanical repetition, and may be intractable anyway. (At 1 second a try, it takes 10^6 seconds to explore all combinations of a 6-digit combination lock, that is, nearly 2 years working 24 hours a day.) The task is to look elsewhere for the combination to avoid the repetition. It may also be the case that the opportunity to get out of a repetitive loop constitutes a reward. Visiting and revisiting the same places seeking the combination lock, the key, or the talisman proves extremely frustrating, and the game player is much relieved when the repetition is ended.

But there is also evidence that the game play is precisely to ensure that we repeat, and if we are tired of one particular repetition, then the game plan ensures that repetition continues, though perhaps in a different setting. By this reading repetition is the end, not the means. Support for this view comes from Freud's account of the nature of repetition and compulsion in psychology. His famous example is that of the child with a cotton reel tied to a piece of string.[41] The child throws the reel out of his cot only to haul it back in again, and he does so repeatedly, as if gaining comfort from the action. The child punctuates the to-and-fro movement with the words "fort" and "da." For Freud the game is a response to the child's despair at losing sight of his mother as she periodically enters and leaves the room. For Freud, this is the condition of us all, coming to terms with the loss of comfort and the loss of security of the mother's presence.

(If we want to take this further it also invokes recollections of the threat of castration by the father.) In certain cases Freud would identify such repetitive behavior as pathologically obsessive. But most of the time such enactments or encounters with repetition are simply reminders of this primal conflict: the presence and loss of the mother, and all she symbolizes, including oneness, nurture, and so on. For Freud such reminders, through repetition, invoke a sense of the uncanny.[42] It strikes us as strange when some event, such as a repetition, reminds us of our childhood condition, as if to reconfirm or reinforce that which we thought we had grown out of. Repetition represents a kind of reversion to early adolescence. In this it is both a comfort and a source of disquiet. Here resides the sense of the uncanny, the unhomely. We are at home with the repetition, but there is no one home.[43] We do not really belong with this condition.

By this Freudian reading, computer games are capable of causing disturbance in many ways, not least in the way they require us to repeat. The theatrical, painterly and architectural invention behind the spaces created in computer adventure games are certainly capable of invoking a sense of eeriness and the uncanny, no less so for being relatively devoid of inhabitants. The islands of Myst and Riven[44] submit to the description of being uncanny in that they are relatively unpopulated. The player seems to arrive at a place after the population has left. There are the trappings of home, but no one is around. Once she has dispatched the machine gun–toting henchmen, Lara Croft explores the Moorish City of the Dead. The market squares, shops, and alleyways are empty. This emptiness undoubtedly invites a sense of the uncanny, but for Freud, it is in the necessity to repeat that we should look for the uncanny, not merely vacancy. Freud's personal account of being lost in the streets of a town in Italy could well be describing the state of a computer game player: "I hastened to leave the narrow street at the next turning. But after having wandered for a time without inquiring my way, I suddenly found myself back in the same street, where my presence was now beginning to excite attention. I hurried away once more, only to arrive by another detour at the same place yet a third time. Now however a feeling overcame me which I can only describe as uncanny."[45] Empty spaces, combined with the mechanical imperative of striking keyboards and game pads, invite repetition. Without human encounters to arrest our movement, we are free to continue the circulation. Spaces become circuits on which to run rampant, in furious search, and where is there to go, but around and around in unimpeded repetition. By this reading it is the repetition, or its prospect, that disturbs and fascinates, a feature of vacant space made all the more obvious in computer games.

Repetition has gained prominence as a philosophical theme since Nietzsche's account of the "eternal return" or the "eternal recurrence of the same," the heroic propensity within human experience to draw on the hope of renewal, a return after death, a mythology of cycles and restitutions.[46] Philosophical discourses invoking repetition take on a peculiar turn. Taking his lead from Freud's provocation about the uncanny, Derrida maintains that we should not be surprised by repetition so much as by the idea of a first time.[47] Repetition is the norm. We are always caught up in an endless stream of repetitions. For Derrida this is how language operates. There is no original referent of a language utterance, such as an actual game, a psychosis, a first move in a computer game. Every utterance invokes reference to former referents, which in turn have their referents. In referring to a particular computer game, we are also referring to the concept of a game, to writing about the game, to Wittgenstein and to Freud, which have their own referents, and the particular game is also a reference to other games, from which it derives. For Derrida, Freud's repetition of the story of repetition in his voluminous writing is but a repeating of Freud himself. What does Freud uncover in the unconscious of the patient but Freud. Whether or not this discourse advances the study of psychology, it certainly signals the ubiquity of repetition as a philosophical and cultural concern. It also suggests that in the computer game it is not just a repetition of moves and countermoves, but a repetition in a lineage of gaming. As in most examples from the mass media, art, and design under the influence of mechanical and digital reproduction, there is a repetition among game designers, which is to say a direct copying in whole or in part of game plans, weaponry, characters, styles, and genres. And the game player repeats the playing experience, with the same game, with the continuous stream of successor games, and now game players are invited to design their own game levels (with level editors provided by the game companies), to participate in a frenzy of derivative gaming.

Whether or not we accept Freud's psychological account of repetition, the provocation is that our propensity to participate in repetition, to tantalize ourselves with the uncanny, is a primordial condition, or at least it is as entitled to this claim as the Cartesian claim of the primacy of calculative reason, or self-awareness. The game relies substantially on repetition for its impetus, and this repetition is an end in itself.

Whatever the goals or quests of the game, these work to enable us to keep on repeating. If this is true of play, then it also applies to design. Design is already imbued with the repetitive impetus, through historical reference, copying, mimicry, and the workings of the play of meaning, right through to the labor of drawing and drafting, the repetition of elements, computer-aided design (CAD) operations, and the seemingly endless rendering of line and color. The end of design is to keep on repeating. For economics, repetition is translated into "circulation." The end of economics is to keep circulation in play, the means being money, or information about money. As I will examine subsequently, the idea of repetition needs modification if it is to bring us closer to the hermeneutical account of the game with which I began this chapter.

Levels

We have mentioned the subservience of goals to the act of repetition but said nothing yet about variation across repetitive operations. Computer games rely substantially on the concept of levels: degrees of difficulty and increasing levels of challenge.[48] In *Space Invaders,* targets and return fire from the computerized opponent are calculated to arrive with increasing frequency, and once one level of encounter is completed the player progresses to another level of difficulty. In *Tomb Raider,* movement from one environment, a sequence of connected spaces, to the next, is accompanied by greater challenge. Progression to the next level comes as a reward. The task seems to be to escape from one level and to enter the next. A game level is also regarded as discrete. It is a way of organizing computer files into manageable chunks for loading into the computer's RAM. Levels are also progressive. It is usually outside the game plan to revert to an earlier level. Levels may also be arranged in a linear fashion, where there is one exit and entry point between any two levels, and players may only be able to pass through the levels in a predefined sequence. The presence of levels is more obscure in games such as *Myst, Riven,* and *The Sims.* There are discrete environments, increasing degrees of challenge, and the idea of access to environments as an incentive and a reward, but here the idea of levels is overtaken by the more obvious unfolding of a narrative. The aspects of progression and variation in computer games can inform us about the nature of repetition in all genres of computer games and leads us to consider further the hermeneutics of the game.

If repetition stakes a claim in a psychological and linguistic legacy, then the concept of levels makes a similar cultural claim. Homer gave expression to the ancient religious legacy that after earthly existence one enters a netherworld of specters and shadows, the insubstantial world of the dead.[49] Plato reversed this priority by attributing our earthly existence to the shadow lands, while what exists beyond is a greater and higher reality. His positing of a world of ideas, the Intelligible, to be contrasted with the sensible realm solved all kinds of philosophical difficulties (and created others) about universals, perfection, generalization, identity, mind, and memory, which we do not need to revisit here. Plotinus, the successor to Plato, did the most to advance this dualism. He gave elaborate expression to the dual divide as a series of levels, through which we progress to achieve enlightenment. The soul wends its way heavenward through successively unfolding spheres of existence. This powerful sense of hierarchy and of a successive layering of transcendent states informs much of the Romanticism of the eighteenth century, and much fantasy narrative. The quest is for enlightenment, the progress to a realm where the mysteries of being will be revealed.[50]

In his novel *The Glass Bead Game,* Herman Hesse exploits this propensity to seek after a higher mystery by inventing the history of a timeless and mysterious game that captures the essence of all knowledge.[51] The Neoplatonic cults that have supposedly gathered around this game of games enjoy access to hidden truths. It seems that the idea of the game lends itself to such concepts, and indeed many have taken Hesse's story to be an actual history.[52] Computer games readily trade on the mystery of the game, the lost game, and game fragments, in their narratives, to which we shall return later. It should come as no surprise that computer games exploit the fascination with mystery, progression, and layers, in both the form of the games and in their narrative content.[53]

The idea of layers also appeals to the empiricist orientation of contemporary culture. If one can transcend the current level of partial knowledge to achieve higher understanding, one is getting closer to the truth, an understanding of the way things really are. By a simple metaphorical reversal, this is also an uncovering. The truth is buried down there if only you can strip back the layers of obfuscation and ambiguous evidence to find it, as if working through layers in an archaeological dig. Freud's presentation of the unconscious also accords with this account. The unconscious is the site of buried and repressed memories, the traumas of separation from the mother and threat from the father, manifested in such phenomena as disquiet at the specter of repetition. Like a benign tomb raider, it is the job of the analyst to uncover the unconscious, a cathartic and liberating process.

The propensity for computer games to invoke transitions through levels also resonates with Freudian concepts of the rite of passage. What has been said of

Lewis Carroll's *Alice in Wonderland* and *Through the Looking Glass*[54] can be said of *Tomb Raider* in this regard. Both offer male accounts (as does Freud) of what might constitute self-assured female ambition and self-discovery in cultural contexts where such assertiveness is unexpected. Freud weaves a complex narrative of the unresolved need for the young girl to regain erotic attachment following estrangement from her mother. This is accomplished through the offering of gifts to the father, or father substitutes, the ultimate gift of which is a baby. In the meantime, various symbolic substitutes suffice. Alice's polite offerings of congeniality (and a baby turned into a pig) to the various male figures she encounters are nothing to Lara's obsessive offering to male deities of found trinkets (keys that move her to the next level). The rite of passage is chiefly a matter of the young woman maturing past the trauma of believing her mother responsible for her castration (and not being a boy). The passage is from a state of anger with the mother to a relationship of giving to her surrogate father. Alice moves through the worlds of Wonderland or across the looking glass chess board in successive stages that mark her coming of age. Lara moves inexorably through game levels. It does not matter for this reading that the rite of passage is repeated; such is the psychology of repetition. In fact, as noted earlier, it is not the fact of repetition that should cause us disquiet. We should take it for granted that events in our experience repeat. What is strange is that we think there should be a defining moment, a first time, an original trauma to be uncovered and resolved, a single rite of passage to be negotiated.

Irrespective of our view of Freud's account of what motivates men and women to action, there are alternative interpretations of what Freud describes as an uncovering of the unconscious. Paul Ricoeur argues that psychological analysis need not presume the uncovering of a "deeper level" of psychic reality.[55] It is rather the case that the analyst and the patient are engaged in the work of transforming one narrative into another, perhaps transforming a narrative of always being "hard done by" to a narrative of failing to pass through the Oedipal stage. The transition from one narrative to another is never friction-free. There is resistance, work to be done in affecting the transformation, as in a game. This is in the nature of all interpretation, and offers an alternative account to that in which the analyst appears to be uncovering the truth of what the patient actually means, the unconscious motivations behind the words, or to seeing the interpretation of a text as discovering the original intention of the author.

Within historical study, Foucault speaks eloquently against the proposition that intellectual endeavor involves uncovering brute facts, origins, and themes of continuity. In its place he posits an "archaeology of knowledge," which is "precisely such an abandonment of the history of ideas, a systematic rejection of its postulates and procedures, an attempt to practice quite a different history of what men have said."[56] Under the archaeological metaphor of stratification and accretion, history gives way to a consideration of the conditions that enable particular forms of knowledge to flourish. Foucault's is an archaeology without shovels, an analysis of the shifting sands of competing discourses, a field of transforming interpretations. Interpretation presents as a transformation of narratives, a variation on the earlier formulation of interpretation as an encounter between one's expectations and the text. Interpretation is an ongoing dialogical process.

Computer games of the narrative kind more obviously resemble the interpretation of a text. As in the case of a detective story, one of the intrigues of the *Myst* games is to try to discover the canonical story created by the authors from the clues and the fragments of text left around the worlds. Whether or not the player wishes to uncover the story is not essential to the game play, though it does make sense of the puzzles to understand, or perhaps suspect, that the vengeful character in *Myst III* has destroyed the simple ball puzzles on the island where the sons were meant to have had their lessons. Though ostensibly motivated by a desire to uncover the true story, a detective story also gains its allure by the interaction between the evidence and the array of possible stories. It is never just the uncovering of a true narrative, and where the truth is supposedly revealed the story loses its allure, as when one scrutinizes magazines and Web sites that offer to reveal the computer game's story in all its completeness.

The story behind *Myst* is after all a retelling of the Oedipal story of a stern father and wayward sons, with the sons ultimately castrated and estranged from all that symbolizes motherhood: a joyous union, primal bliss, union with nature, and so on. If we thought this narrative worthy, like all stories, it is open to interrogation and analysis. (Precisely how is the writing of books supposed to make worlds that can be inhabited?[57]) Though the story line appears fixed, any story is open to reinterpretation and retelling. Each visit to the game presents a new edge to the narrative, enhanced by the varying meta-narratives of how the clues provide or fail to provide sufficient evidence for the canonical story, not to mention the relationship between the various endings being offered. Repeated encounters with the game also provide opportunities for reinterpretation. Having examined the mechanical island perhaps the organic world of the tree island presents as even more startling. The encounter with one "level" informs our encounter with another, by contrast, by playing on our expectations, and conditioning and modifying them.

But then the same process applies to our encounters in any game. *Tomb Raider* depends less on a story line, but invokes variation on each encounter. The player's encounter with a succession of similar spaces plays on variation. What strikes us as a stable platform in one space is a trap in another. The game is repetitive certainly, but each encounter provides an opportunity for reinterpretation. Repetition can lull us into a particular mode of expectation, only to have that expectation broken or contested by a breach in the series. *Myst* plays on this idea of a discontinuity in a sequence. There is an optical device missing from the configuration on the island described earlier, which turns the task of their alignment into more of a challenge. All of the islands in *Riven* are within view of each other except one, the discovery of which takes the player into a new "level" of engagement with the game. Other parts of the game world start to make sense.

Design too succumbs not just to repetition but to variation across repetitive operations. The design methods movement asserted that a design progresses through layers of sophistication, from abstract to concrete.[58] But a hermeneutics of design would suggest that we are always dealing with successive interpretations, the transformation of narratives, perhaps from a story about the design in terms of shapes, maps, and metaphors to one of systems, walls and uses, with lapses from one narrative to another. Each encounter with a design situation is accompanied by variation, whether for the designer revisiting the plans, the building user walking into the building yet again, or the architectural critic looking for something new to say.

So, too, the economic system trades in narratives. As in the layering of a game, economic systems ostensibly progress through stages from underdeveloped to developed, dependent to self-sufficient, feudal to free-market, ideas captured in games such as *Civilization, Sim City,* and even Monopoly. It is not just that money circulates, but that circulation is transformative. It produces wealth. Alternatively, a hermeneutics of commerce suggests that each repetition of a consumer's monetary transaction provides an occasion for a reinterpretation, not least of one's status, sense of freedom, participation in the good life, access to global capitalism. Furthermore, each "economic cycle" of a corporation or state invites narrative invention on a grand scale: the apologetic of the business report or national budget statement. The game is one of demonstrable progress, the self-justifications of global capitalism and consumer society.

So the concepts of repetition, and of the level, submit to the operations of interpretation, sometimes described in terms of the hermeneutical circle, a to-and-fro movement between the whole picture and part of the picture, the context and the particular, a game of shifting expectations, whether in the computer game, design, or economics.

The Reality Quest

The Neoplatonic legacy suggests progression to higher levels of reality. We transcend the deceptive realm of the senses to encounter the real in its ever-unfolding detail and clarity. Any particular game may embody a narrative of progression through enlightenment, but the history of computer game development in total also participates in this progression. Poole describes the development of the computer game in spatial terms as an extension of the game board (*SpaceWars* and *Pong*) to ever-closer proximity to perspectival realism (*Quake* and *Tomb Raider*).[59] It is as though the game board is a simulation.

The narrative of progressive realism in computer games suggests that instead of making do with a sheet of cardboard with rectangles marking out parcels of London real estate (Monopoly), we really prefer a model of London that we can actually move around in a computer simulation: the more real the better.[60] This trajectory of geometrical improvement takes on strange dimensions in Janet Murray's account of narrative in the context of digital media. She begins with an account of being able to actually live the story of the characters in Emily Brontë's *Jane Eyre,* as constructed on the "holodeck" of the *Star Trek* fantasies. Leaving aside the technical implausibility of this scenario, there is the assumption that narrative is a simulated form of life experience, perhaps making up for deficiencies in experiences otherwise available to us. For Murray, digital narratives, of the kind one encounters in an immersive computer world, offer us the opportunity to "enact stories rather than to merely witness them."[61] We can't go back in time so we read a book about some events in the past. We don't have the time and money to have an adventure in Africa, so we watch a film about Africa. The progression to reality advances from reading a book, watching a film of the book, playing a computer game of the film, and entering into a fully immersive 3-D simulation of the world of the narrative. The trajectory of Murray's account leads one to think of narrative as a representation of life experience. A story is to be judged by its conformity to a state of affairs. The representational view supports the proposition that a game is a simulation of or a rehearsal for life experience.

It does not take much to show that narrative does not primarily serve as a means of conveying or anticipating the facts of a situation. It is not the case that behind every encounter with narrative is a desire to be a character in the story. We do not read detective stories because we want to be detectives or solve crimes, or play *Tomb Raider* because we really want to shoot at skeletons and search through musty tombs and dungeons. A verbal narrative is not a substitute for acting out a story, any more than a conversation is a substitute for living. Narrative, conversation, discourse, dialogue belong within the realms of interpretive play in their own right. In terms of psychoanalysis, their role is more therapeutic than representative. In design the construction of narratives and counternarratives can be explained in terms of validation, exploration, question and answer, collaboration, the conversation with a design situation. If narrative has this quality, then so does the game.

Much of the impetus for the reality quest in games comes from the seduction of geometry and perspective rendering. By Turbayne's helpful account of perception as a linguistic concern, the conventions of perspectival interpretation have a strong cultural component and have to be learned.[62] Evidence comes from the fact that there are different conventions of 3-D presentation: the isometric, axonometric plan view, single point perspective, non-Euclidean projections and so on, each of which may be employed in the construction of game worlds. The human ocular apparatus seems to share characteristics with the camera, which in turn relate to the geometry of perspectival projection, but there are many differences, to do with geometry, peripheral vision, focus of attention, movement, expectation, and the whole perceptual apparatus. The reality quest assumes that the more like the photographic image, the more "real" the experience, and the more immersed we become in the game. There is little doubt that the increasing "realism" of computer games is in fact an increasing closeness to what we expect from film,[63] though admittedly with the introduction of some new conventions, such as controlled panning, zooming, overlays, and the collaging of movie clips, and interactive action. In fact the variety of conventions available in computer games highlights the linguistic nature of the visual arts. The fact that it may take a while to get used to the variable focal depth of *Myst IV,* the rendered cardboard sets and shifting camera angles of *Tomb Raider,* the rapid pans of *Quake* and *Deus Ex,* the isometric projections of *The Sims* testify to the proposition that a player is learning a new visual language, and a language of interaction, each time.[64] The player is not only learning what actions the keys on the keyboard or game pad accomplish, but how to interpret the whole experiential field of the game, which is to say, how to interact with it.

Three-dimensional games rely substantially on photographic, filmic, and painterly technique, tricks that play on conventions other than the laws of optics. For Bolter and Grusman, the dependence of one medium on the conventions of another is addressed through the idea of "re-mediation,"[65] which comes closer to understanding how media work than the idea of correspondence between image and reality. As a further example, computer games are unable to offer contiguity in the spatial experience, yet we know the rules of this aspect of the spatial game, its language. As when we watch a film, we know that we can be transported to a place in an instant through film cuts, simply walking into the cinema or positioning ourselves in front of the television, or by starting up the game to pick up from where we left off. It does not surprise us that there is no journey from here to there, no queues to get on an airplane when the action moves from Paris to New York.

Irrespective of what has motivated their development, computer games reinforce the proposition (of Heidegger and others) that spatiality is not primarily about geometrical correspondences, but about pragmatics.[66] As long as there is nothing for the game player to do, then the spatiality vanishes. Solving puzzles keeps us active within the otherwise sterile geometrical world and sustains the sense of being there. The challenges keep us repeating, which is to say interpreting, being actively engaged. This is highlighted in *Myst,* where the pictorial nature of the points of view is patently obvious. You jump from one fixed point to the next, perhaps several meters away in the prerendered geometrical field. Once the puzzles are solved, then the only recourse is to pure repetition, revisiting panoramic images of the game world, perhaps beautiful and compelling as images, but ceasing to engage us as spaces. Of course, other experiences outside the game, such as visiting and revisiting the town of our childhood, a beloved picnic spot, or our favorite museum, rarely exhaust what we can do there, and so the continuance of spatiality is assured. Space is not something to be contemplated, as if in awe and wonder (the Cartesian idea of the individual as subject positioned in objective space), but it is a matter of action. Repetition gives way to representation, but not as correspondence between an image and some real or imagined world, rather as a re-presentation and a re-interpretation.

Insofar as we see the tombs, desert landscapes, ruined temples, and railway carriages through Lara Croft's eyes, the apparent indifference of her puppet form to the unfolding visual spectacle is offset by her vicarious engagement with puzzles, challenges, and the necessary tasks of purging micro-worlds of danger. Within the constraints of the game world, these constitute actions sufficient for the player to use the language of spatiality and say they are *in* the space of the tomb, the pyramid, the locomotive, and to look back with nostalgia to places previously visited, to develop affections, and to look forward to returning. The spatiality of the game fits within a language game, invoking memory and anticipation; so too in design.

The trend in architecture is less toward the monumental, of spaces designed to inspire awe in which there is nothing to do but contemplate. Architecture on the grand scale now presents itself in terms of a stage for action, civic spaces for the enactment of demonstrations. Like their impoverished simulations in computer games, the tangible spaces of museums, railway stations, plazas, and parks are populated with opportunities for circulation, discovery, interaction, and demonstration. Their spatiality resides in this capacity for play rather than in their abstracted forms.

If design and the game have to work against the pursuit of "reality," then so too economics, or at least economic modeling. The models of Neuman, and those that derive from it, inevitably fail to account for or predict every aspect of behavior that may be called economic.[67] In this it is easy to account for the mathematical model, like the geometrical model, as fitting within a language game. Its application, which is to say its use, has to be learned, a skill developed within a discursive community. The mathematical model is less a mapping onto the reality of the world of commerce than a game, with its own rules of use, its own interpretive field.

Borrowing from the visual arts, the emerging language of computer games speaks of being there, which again shows that we need to look to the wider context of the game world to understand its spatiality. Like all linguistic activities the game fits within a communicative context.

The Sociality of the Game

Games generally require at least one player. In the case of the action and adventure computer game, the player often devotes attention to a single character, with capabilities (at least in terms of the game) supposedly in excess of the player's, much as the owner or manager of a racehorse or a prize fighter might play vicariously through controlling the selection, grooming, training, and management of their champion. In computer games the player might also control the micro-actions of their champion by selecting from a repertoire of actions, as though the player is operating a puppet. In the so-called first-person game, the combatant may be invisible (as though the view camera is located on the shoulders of the combatant). In *Deus Ex* you notice who you are when you enter a bathroom where you see yourself reflected in a mirror, or you die and your character falls into view. In the so-called third-person game, you see your character in view, as in the famous rear view of the nonchalant Lara Croft navigating her way through chambers, corridors, and crawl spaces. Games also invoke the concept of the opponent. In adventure computer games, the opponent may be expanded to a cast of characters, some of whom may also constitute members of the player's team. There are adversaries and also those who support the player's welfare and goals. Of course, there is also the possibility that these roles may change during the course of the game. You may not be sure whether a particular character is a friend or a foe, or which team they are playing for. In some games, such as *Myst,* the cast members have fixed roles and a fixed repertoire of interventions. Three-dimensional action and adventure games commonly invoke rule-based behaviors that respond in complex ways to the player's position and actions in the geometrical world. As in the case of *Quake,* there is the fascinating possibility for games to be multi-user, which is to say different players from anywhere on the Internet can assume the identity of a character and share the game play.

In the case of the rapidly developing realm of game design, there is also the computer game designer as invisible and sometimes nameless adversary, against whom game players pit their wits.[68] Amateur film critics are appraised of the greater strategic plan in moviemaking, the commercial pressures on producers, the scope for innovation, how the film under review compares with previous offerings. So, too, as testified by the evidence of online postings in discussion groups reviewing games, the reflective computer game enthusiast not only directs hostility toward the game opponents, but also the game designer(s) for making the game too difficult or easy, for bugs in the software, and for badly designed game plans, weapons, and environments. In the thick of the game, when confronted with an apparently insurmountable obstacle, the player is entitled to ask if she is playing badly, or if that part of the game is inadequately designed, or contains an error. This introduces the nature of the audience of the computer game. Filmgoing and familiarity with particular films (or any other cultural artifact) seem to be enabling and enjoyable in part due to the opportunities they provide to engage in a wide discursive, social field. The appreciation of cultural artifacts is a social phenomenon, bound to shared expectations among some group or other and to shifts in aesthetic and even political sensibilities. Computer games also seem to provide opportunities for similar participation, with magazines, fan clubs, and the more immediate medium of the Internet, chat groups, and dedicated Web pages.

As well as providing the opportunity for shared reflection, the computer game is also characterized by the possibility of saving game states. These can be collected and distributed, and they enable other players to "cheat," by jumping a level, overcoming a challenge, or replenishing their supplies of ammunition or medical packs. Cheats, graded hints, and walk-throughs describing each level of the game, provided with or without the sanction of the game producers, are free Internet goods in the game economy, as are suggestions for improvements from players to the game designers.[69] In some cases game players constitute an expectant community, aware of release dates and enjoying a sense of participation in the creation of a new game, as in the case of the staged release of rendered imagery for *Riven* prior to its full publication as a game. It is as if the player is party to the workings of a group of artisans, and able to inspect the quality of the craftsmanship pending the release from the workshop of the whole edifice. *Quake* and *Tomb Raider* also provide the opportunity for players to design environments (maps or levels) and characters (skins) that can then be made available on the Web, extending the concept of the design community to include the game player. Even isolated game play is party to the potentials of sociality. These social constituencies also populate the arena of the game. At times the game is not only a matter of finding the lost tomb, but of discovering the limits of the game designer, managing with or without the online cheats, impressing other game players with one's knowledge of the game world, anticipating the next game, inventing a better level, or contributing to the gift society of the games world, to be examined in chapter 4.

Of course, clever marketing is able to exploit the sociality of the game, and to build a consideration of fan clubs, user culture, and the expectations of communities of users into its business plans. As articulated by Kline, Dyer-Witheford, and de Peuter, the computer games industry thrives on the immediacy of feedback it can gain, its ability to tailor its products to its markets, to nurture them, and to enlist self-trained game designers from the vast pool of willing game enthusiasts.[70] Such are the opportunities provided by the high-risk, high-stakes areas of the mass media and popular culture.

Bad Taste

It is a commonplace to note that not everyone likes watching (and critiquing) the same genres of film, and there are no doubt individuals who are indifferent to the pleasures of watching movies at all. [71] In the same way, computer game players may prefer action games to flight or race car simulators, or adventure to role games. Undoubtedly there are many for whom the computer game is a matter of indifference or even repugnance. They are not prepared to invest time and money in hours of game play and do not see the computer or game console as providing a suitable environment for leisure, nor do they enjoy solving arbitrary game puzzles. The makers of low-budget films and film audiences are not necessarily averse to being among a minority of genre buffs. Budgets for computer games are now apparently on a similar scale as those for blockbuster films and so are less capable of catering to niche markets. They require very large sales to make profits. Computer games therefore cater to mass markets, pandering substantially to trigger-happy male youth culture, and are readily placed beneath the classic divide separating low from high culture. Computer games are accused of being sensationalist, overly sentimental, extremely violent, and historically and culturally naïve.[72] They are populated by exaggerated, stereotypic, comic-book characters, accommodated within architectural and geographical pastiche. Fast action seems to require exaggerated form, color, and spectacle. Perhaps the worst charge is that computer games do not stretch the medium beyond a technical agenda of faster response, greater photorealism, more rendering power, more detail, and more AI behaviors. There is little scope in computer games for the same experimentation that accompanies digital media art and its forays into new modes of interaction and novel conceptions of space. Gentler, design-oriented games such as those in the *Myst* series could be accused of being no less mawkish, with their heavily romanticized art nouveau, the expressionist and high-tech derivation of their architecture, their landscapes that draw on the languages of picturesque and sublime art and new-age naturalism, and their storylines that are derivative, quasi-epic, Oedipal tales of family affection and frailty. With rare exception, computer games do not yet indulge in the self-referentiality, or the ironic twists and turns, of contemporary artistic and narrative invention. At most, *Tomb Raider, Myst,* and *Quake* can be generously described as fitting within the genre of high-camp art, perhaps a simulated naïveté, a naïveté that accommodates the suspicion that someone in the design team at least sees the whole enterprise as a sendup, or perhaps an art form that gains its status by virtue of its capacity to attract and withstand good natured ridicule.

The concept of taste is sometimes a shorthand reference to the more complex issue of values. Irrespective of taste, the appeal of an artifact to the sensibilities of communities of users, computer games must withstand various ethical charges. Within their dollhouse existence, the states of well-being of the characters in *The Sims* game equate with the sum of their material possessions and their states of hygiene. Stallabras accuses computer games of presenting a kind of miniature capitalism, a simplistic world of points, scores, and credits, where human life is reduced to commodity and number,[73] though one could argue that non-computer games also work with this fiction. The usual complaints are that computer games risk promoting violence, using human beings for target practice, or at least may inure us to battle and war.[74] Computer games often present screen displays as elaborations on the idea of the gun sight, which increasingly bear a resemblance to the images one sees on news broadcasts of precision strikes by automated weaponry. We become inured to the horrors of killing and maiming, all but masked by the indifferent spectacle of pixels hitting their targets.

In this the consumerist enterprise that is the computer game labors under its harshest critique, as a mode of concealment. Whether tomb raider or archaeologist, Lara Croft presents as uncovering lost treasures, unlocking portals revealing successive levels of the game to an encounter with the secret of it all, the divinity (a supposed battle with the Egyptian god Horus in *Tomb Raider: The Last Revelation*), ever closer to the ultimate challenge. But in fact, under the ruse of the game, *Tomb Raider* presents a classic narrative of colonization and conquest. In the tradition of the Phantom, James Bond, and Indiana Jones stories, *Tomb Raider* participates in the invention and pillaging of the exotic other. The game designers loot imagery, mythology, architecture, and culture from countries that have historically been subjected to successive waves of conquest by Western powers. The world is turned into a stylized arena for highly technologized instrumental magic. Built artifacts (monuments, temples, and tombs) are valuable insofar as they house trophies, the magic of which resides in their capacity to act as a key to further conquest. Of course the aristocratic Lara Croft introduces an exoticized parody of the stereotypical femme fatale, designed to appear as desirable as the trophies she seeks. Under a neo-Marxist reading, the game is all the more sinister for being presented as naïve, the product of the putatively harmless fantasies of a collective nerdiness in which anyone can participate (as designers as well as players). This infantile bonhomie is one of the problems with Internet culture under the sway of capitalism, and the game producers and designers are as prone to its hegemonic grasp as are game consumers.

The game comes across as an example of technological concealment and enframing. By the constancy of her bodily comportment, Lara Croft is shown to be indifferent to whether she is in Angkor Wat, Luxor, or Venice. Whether or not she can run up a sloping surface depends on a geometry set up in the gridded world of the level editor, not on local custom, constraints of propriety, climate, or other exigencies of place. *Myst* purports to be nonviolent, but it is charged with the undercurrent of creating and destroying civilizations, the colonization of worlds. The domestic conflict, the destruction of the sons, is relatively benign in comparison to the underlying conceit of literacy, that writing books brings worlds into existence, which then become inhabited by populations of compliant savages who treat their highly educated creators as gods.

But there is a more subtle charge. Notwithstanding the possibility that players or communities of players may fall under the spell of such games and be swayed by their apparent reality to see them in other than a critical light, there is the prospect that such games inure us to the possibility that the rest of our experience is also constituted by illusion. By virtue of the obvious nature of their unreality, games inure us to the unrealities presented by global capitalism. This is the familiar charge of Baudrillard against Disneyland theme parks and similar simulated environments.[75] We are inured to the fact that the city of Los Angeles, and the country of America beyond, is an unreal simulation. Life under capitalism is fraught with the trappings of unreality: "today, reality itself is hyperrealistic."[76] Experiences that purport to show us in a highly conspicuous way what is unreality, as in the case of the spectacle of the computer game, distract us from identifying the less ostentatious unreality in our day-to-day world. So the inventions brought about by the prosaically real computer spreadsheet could be construed as unreal, raising expectations, giving credence to narratives of improvement simply by virtue of laying things out in tabular form. If a spreadsheet program bore the trappings of a computer game, we might be more correctly suspicious of what it presents. If a business report appeared from a scroll discovered by Lara Croft from within the fictional Tomb of Seth, that might indicate more accurately its spurious purchase in the realms of truth and reliability. (According to Baudrillard, it is not fiction that should cause us to laugh, but it is any claim to truth that is obscene or risible.[77]) By this reading, the danger is not that the increasing sophistication of computer games causes us to lose track of the fact that it is only play, but that we see the rest of our experience as other than play, as serious work, as outside the realms of contingency, as outside the workings of the hermeneutical circle.

Certain computer games are voyeuristic and controlling. By a variant reading, in describing the popularity of the *Big Brother* television program, from which *The Sims* has derivative appeal, Žižek draws attention to the uncanny shock of the prospect that nobody is watching us after all.[78] Our saturation in mass media and mass communications persuades us that we only exist insofar as we register in some mediated form or other in a database, on a webcam, on CCTV, or under the supposition that we might one day be on television. My sense of self-worth is predicated on my being under someone's gaze, but if it should be disclosed that there is no one looking at the monitor then my sense of self would wither. Of course I continue to exist, but the contradiction vexes my sense of being and induces anxiety. So computer game simulations operate on a complex series of disjunctions. Insofar as I identify with a *Sims* character I am under the watchful eye of the game player, and playing a putative media role. In this I am watching my own life as if observed by others from a god's-eye perspective. The prospect that no one may be interested enough to watch me, brings about a certain anxiety. This is a further realization of the problematic of the threshold condition, between the public and the private. It is a site of moral and existential dilemma, highlighted again in this case by a consideration of computer games and the mass media. The fact that I am able to watch and control *The Sims* adds further to the delusion that I am a player in someone else's game. Whereas this thought is a cause of disquiet, the prospect of the reverse, that I am not part of a game, is more worrying. This would be tantamount to the character in the film *The Truman Show* finding out in the end that his repetitive existence was in fact real, or that he was inadvertently controlling those outside the dome, or that the ratings figures were faked and no one was ever watching him.

The ostentatious simulation in computer games brings into relief the nature of design. As much as we accept the claim of the design methodologist that the process of design is constituted by successive iterations through cycles of repetition and simulation, we are inured to the fact that the design never reaches finality. The building or the manufactured artifact is still a simulation, as much as the models, drawings, and computer representations. By this critical reading, there is no end to the representational aspect of design, and to its purchase in the realms of copying, mimicry, and transgression.

Fractured Games

This criticism of computer games also works in the manner of a reversal. The real and the imaginary are presented as if a play of opposites. Global capitalism is the unreality, masked by the very real obviousness of the game's unreality. Not only does this critique advance a challenging and enticing ethical case against the computer game, an invitation to further suspicion of global capitalism, but it also advances our appreciation of play. The ethical question emerges as a matter of play, the play among conflicting images, metaphors, points of view, or formulations. Such play manifests itself in the conversations that take place within the space defined by various standpoints, which are also in play. Ethical questions are not "resolved" by appealing to a substrate of unassailable truth, rules of right conduct, but more closely match the rules of play. To play by the rules is not only to shun law breaking but to play by the rules of play. In linguistic terms this is to play according to the "rules" of the game of dialogue and negotiation. Resolution is chimerical. In the public arena, questions of ethics are repeatedly brought back into play as contexts and values change. Conservative moralists so often see this revisiting of ethical issues as a progressive liberalization, a loosening of standards, but on closer examination, insofar as there is a liberalization it constitutes a developing recognition of the complex play among images, metaphors, value systems, institutions, sociopolitical contexts, and the mass media.[79] It is a recognition of the play element in human affairs.

In this chapter, I visited several sites of play, between the protagonists of reality and play, work and play, calculation and play, an object and its simulation, the original and its repeated copying, repetition as a means or an end, representation as correspondence and representation as play, the conscious and the unconscious, the whole and the parts, object and illusion, revealing and concealing. By the account of several theorists, play operates in this "space between." For Winnicott, play is initiated in the realm of trust between mother and child: "The playground is a potential space between the mother and the baby or joining mother and baby,"[80] a precarious interplay of psychic reality and the experience of control. In Freudian mode, we could say the space between unity and individuation.[81] For Huizinga, this agonistic instinct, manifested so often as combat and competition, is "serious play, fateful and fatal play, bloody play, sacred play, but nonetheless that playing which, in an archaic society, raises the individual or the collective personality to a higher power."[82]

If some of these reversals (and the play between them) strike us as preposterous, then computer games also bring absurdity into relief and remind us of the role of nonsense in play. The computer game presents as a surreal intervention into the context of our expectations. These absurdities may arise as artifacts of technical constraint, as when the collision control of the "geometrical engine" is not able to prevent Lara Croft's leg and arm from disappearing into a solid wall if she stands too close, or if she falls headlong into a wall when she dies all that remains are her protruding legs. The absorbed player rapidly becomes inured to such anomalies and limitations as the game play takes over, though they strike the new player as strange (until she learns the language of the game).

The repetitions of which we have spoken present a certain absurdity, as the player's surrogate participates in rapid cycles of life and death. In most games it is possible to save game states, so the death of the champion does not mean the end of the game, but an opportunity to revert to an earlier saved state. The game is then not just a matter of solving puzzles or maximizing one's score, but also managing the moments of entry and exit from the game. There is a meta-game in play that enables the player to explore paths and possibilities to their fatal conclusion without jeopardizing the ultimate success of the mission. Many games have this strategic dimension that is outside the rules of the game proper: the strategic termination of an inning in a game of cricket, the prolongation of time-out for injuries in a soccer match, the use and abuse of signals to one's partner in a game of bridge. The computer game brings the meta-game to light by virtue of the game's duration, the ritual of repeated entry into the game world, and the game of manipulating computer files that record states of the game play.

If computer games participate in a meta-game of entry and exit, game designers are capable of exploiting the capacity for simulation in a self-referential game within a game. Computer games readily present simulated computers, communications devices, and screens. The precincts of Liberty Island in *Deus-Ex* are under the surveillance of synthetic cameras. You can "enter" a control room where different parts of the game world are in view from a battery of screens. It is as though the game player is controlling another game world of surveillance. At times *Tomb Raider* presents as a meta-game. In the course of *The Last Revelation,* Lara Croft encounters a giant gameboard on which she must position chess-like pieces against the countermoves of a synthetic opponent. In the process she must also guess the rules of the game. In a similar vein, the player of *Myst III* encounters an island replete with a number of elaborate oversized puzzles in various states of repair. The player has to work out what a puzzle does, repair it, and solve the puzzle at the same time. The puzzles are also of a scale that invites the player to move around its rails, ramps, levers, and counterweights to explore and repair its workings. At the end of this phase of the game we discover that the various puzzles work together to produce a larger puzzle, the solution to which rewards us with a spectacular exit from the island and another piece in the larger puzzle. This play of simulations presents the computer game at its most deliberatively surreal. In the same way that Magritte, Delvaux, or Dalí might bring the frame into relief as an issue, introduce a representation of the artist or observer into the picture, populate a painting with the tools of painting, or present a parody of painterly technique, a computer game is capable of invoking reflections on the game itself through representation, a capacity for simulation beyond the capacity of non-computer games, and perhaps beyond the full appreciation of the market to which computer games are commonly directed.

Our fascination with the meta-game may exceed our interest in the game itself. There is arguably not only more opportunity but more pleasure in contemplating an intricate maze, admiring its structure and possible significance, than in playing it. Games have the capacity to be even more enticing in their concept than in their playing, more enticing in partial than in completed form, and more exciting in prospect than in their execution. It transpires that the puzzles in *Myst III,* once repaired, are hardly puzzles at all. The game is to repair them, the restoration of games being a game in itself. For a habitual chess player, a game of chess with pieces missing will hardly warrant attention, but for the unknown game, the game for which we have lost the rules, the unfolding wooden box with a scarred playing surface and weird tokens, will excite as much curiosity as any mystery. What is mystery but a play on our expectations, a particular manifestation of the hermeneutics of play.

The corruption of games does not always present in a favorable light. Counter to Wittgenstein, Caillois asserts four ideal game types: those that play on competition, chance, simulation, and vertigo.[83] *Competitive play* is given expression in sports and becomes institutionalized in terms of economic competition[84] and competitive examinations. *Games of chance,* ostensibly found in activities that rely on the roll of the dice and gambling, find institutional expression in stock market speculation. *Games of simulation* are concerned with mimicry, theater, and the carnival, the formal expression of which is ceremonial etiquette and the wearing of uniforms. *Vertigo* concerns the thrill of speed, mountain climbing, and fairground rides, which in turn find institutional expression in various dangerous occupations, like fire fighting and sea rescue. On the one hand, there is the game activity that is at the margins of the social order (sports, lotteries, the theater, and hair-raising rides; or in the world of computer games, multi-user *Quake,* adventure games, *Tetris,* and race cars), but that leads to the acceptable and institutional forms that speak of integration into social life (economics, financial speculation, ceremony, and calculated risk taking). For Caillois, "games discipline instincts and institutionalize them."[85] On the other hand, according to Caillois, games can be corrupted. Our disposition toward competition can lead to violence, power mongering, and trickery. Chance can lead to superstition and speculations on astrology. Simulation can produce alienation and the split personality. Tests of endurance under extremes of space and time (vertigo) can give way to the thrill of chemical excess, that is, alcoholism and drugs. For some, computer gaming already bears the hallmarks of this violent, mindless, and mind-altering inauthenticity.

But if we take into account the nature of the meta-game, then we see that games can be played precisely in this space between the institutional and the deviant. Sport is not only playing with a ball or against a team but playing with the prospect of injury, both on and off the field. The world of economics involves a play between healthy competition and tricking one's customers or the competition. In the moral domain, where one draws the line is always contested. The line is in play. Each of Caillois's categories, each corrupted game, implicates the game itself. We play in the space between the safety of our imaginations, the realm of play as it is discussed by Caillois, and what we take to be the real, with its perils and consequences.[86]

The character of the game is well represented in Caillois's attempt to rescue the game from inauthenticity, which appears on a table, a five-by-four gameboard, with the column of authentic game categories on the left and their corruption on the right. We are apparently drawn by our base instincts from the left to the right, only to be persuaded by Caillois's reflections to consider the quest for the authentic game, the restored game, which presents as a unity. Caillois suggests a balance point in institutions. But the game is still in play. This is a prime example of Huizinga's characterization of the agonistics of play, the competition between opposites.

It transpires that the authentic game is more a quest than an actuality. Sports are already corrupted by the impetus for violence, lotteries are a form of superstition, schizophrenia is the basis of carnival, and extreme sports are a means of overdosing on endorphins and adrenaline: whether climbing a mountain or the Empire State Building, the setting takes second place to the intoxication. This is not to exclude a certain preference for one side or the other of the game table, nor to exclude one extreme as more socially favorable than the other, but to show that the categories are in play, and to suggest that the playing of the game (football, roulette, dressing up, car racing) is already dependent on, and derivative of, the larger arena of play.

Torturing the game taxonomy further exposes the quest for the ideal game. Games already lend themselves to the mysterious, irrespective of the "narrative content" of the game. They have uncertain outcomes, which games of chance make explicit. Games also have rules and instructions, which, to the uninitiated, appear mysterious. The skills of the player who wins more often than loses also constitute a mystery. Furthermore, like those other great metonyms, the machine and the book, the game readily serves as a metaphor for the world, the rules of which we are trying to discover. This returns us to Hesse's Glass Bead Game, the game that hippies and New Age Web enthusiasts want to believe existed. This is the quest for the perfect game, which haunts the playing of every game.[87] Like the game of unalloyed innocence, the game of games is earnestly sought but evades capture.

The search for the hermeneutical game experience with which we began also has this character of a quest. We began by thinking of play as an immersive fusion between subject and object, the text and the reader, expectation and situation, a moment when we are least self-aware, an absorbing game without objects. But clearly the game involves occasional departure from this domesticated condition. There is another opposition in play, between the world of inconspicuous involvement and that of conspicuous objects. A game is after all a game within games, a play between the inconspicuous world of absorptive play and the conspicuous world of surprise and incongruity. The play of interpretation extends to this arena, and to this tension, from Aristotle to Diogenes and back.

For Huizinga, the Stoics sought to suppress play, and the current age (or at least the late 1930s) is characterized by a utilitarianism that resists the play element.[88] Under the rubric of play, the academy invites reflection on the divine order of things and our participation through transcendence. For Plato, "man . . . has been created as a toy for God. . . . So every man and every woman should play this part and order their whole life accordingly, engaged in the best possible pastimes."[89] For the Epicurean, without Providence, the world is a game of chance. The Epicurean garden is also the leisure garden. Under the game, in spatial terms the garden borrows the character of the labyrinth,[90] the mythic game world inspired by the interconnection of all things, a hybrid concept invoking both the market and the garden, the Stoic and the Epicurean. The labyrinth also returns us to the chaos of the streets, the realm of the trickster or miscreant at the edge of the institutions. Diogenes, as much as any avatar hustling the player through the streets of a computerized adventure game, does no serious work and his rantings assume the character of the ludic, if not the ludicrous. Hermes, the god of the threshold, leads us along the wrong path with his trickery. Such is the mischief of the game.

This chapter has served to further elaborate the nature of the threshold condition, by drawing on the theory and application of the game. I did so by considering the phenomenon of repetition, which is implicated in the sense of the uncanny, the strange and unsettled in-between condition prevalent in design deliberations. I considered the concept of the level, which succumbs to a theory based on the conflictual relationships between narratives. The quest for reality is similarly fraught, in that the real as target of desire is already a product of schemas of representation, the complex play between the imaginary and the symbolic, according to Lacan.[91] A consideration of sociability, or being-with,[92] rapidly leads to the differences in reception accorded to aspects of digital media (such as computer games) in the network economy, and the agonistic play by which ethical issues are aired and actions decided. I concluded with a reiteration of the nature of fragmentation, as in the case of our intrigue with games that are partial, incomplete, and conjectural, and that present as components within larger games, which provides a fitting metaphor for the condition of the game that is the network economy. This discussion prepares us for a consideration of that other site of economic play, the exchange of gifts.

The Gift of Information

According to the received account, the Internet began in scientific research establishments and universities, for whom the maintenance of a network of contacts, collaborations, and peer esteem are the primary values.[1] Making money through the medium of the Internet is subordinate to its primary role in community building. The development of the Internet for business is comparatively recent, and it seems to bring the philosophy of the free market and self-interest into conflict with the Internet's culture of collaboration, sharing, and openness. As we have seen, there is now an interesting, and sometimes unhappy, alliance between the business and the communitarian aspects of life online, between the culture of self-interest and the culture of the gift.

The free circulation of information suggests that many people are still prepared to give away information, expertise, and advice with little or no expectation of immediate monetary return.[2] Web sites present articles, essays, programs, course material, timetables, databases, games, library catalogues, encyclopedia entries, pictures, maps, and music for free. There are also free online services for searching the Web, advising on travel routes, booking hotels, and a well-established culture of self-help, where advice seekers and counselors communicate as laypeople and professionals. Some free services are funded by advertising, and some act as promotions for services for which there will later be a charge, or, as in the case of travel agents, there is a commission hidden to the customer but ultimately paid for through the price of the ticket. In such cases, the putative generosity of the agent, mediator, or the information broker readily conforms to utilitarian understandings of the market economy.

Outside the commercial aspects of online enterprise, there is a strong culture of giving on the Net. Individuals produce and publish personal Web pages in an exchange of intimate and unsolicited disclosures. But the culture of the gift extends to areas that are otherwise the preserve of commerce, particularly among computer programmers and enthusiasts. The so-called Free Software Foundation maintains that software should be available for no cost, asserting the right to use software as fundamental along with the freedom of speech.[3] The related open-source community is a society of software developers who promote the circulation of software that is generally free, and in which computer programs can be modified and redistributed by anyone, so long as the software produced conforms to certain rules that ensure it is passed on under the same conditions. Such software is identified with the OSI (Open-Source Initiative) mark.[4] So a programmer may purchase a word processing program, and, as well as using it as a regular consumer, the programmer can modify and improve the software, then pass the improved version on to others, as long as the improved source code is also available. The open-source community claims that it promotes a highly efficient mode of organic and evolutionary software development. In the celebrated case of the Linux operating system, a single developer (Linus Torvalds) made his source code available on the Internet and invited improvements and suggestions from other programmers.[5] This encouraged the formation of a vast community of voluntary developers whose edited contributions were incorporated into successive versions of the software. The open-source community claims that this type of development is made possible by a development ethic that is anti-monopoly, is anti-establishment, and is driven by enthusiasm at the grassroots level. Some have described the OSI as a contemporary realization of the "gift economy."[6]

Open-source advocates like to contrast their approach with the style of systems development practiced within large corporations such as Microsoft. They make much of Microsoft founder Bill Gates's "Open Letter to Hobbyists" distributed in 1976, in which Gates berates the fledgling computer hobby community for distributing pirated versions of the Altair BASIC program, claiming that the consequent loss of financial return to Microsoft acts as a disincentive to systems development. The open letter goes on to suggest that no single hobbyist can develop serious software. Contrary to Gates, the open-source community has been keen to demonstrate that such development is possible, through collaboration, trust, and with virtually no management structure. The fact that the Linux operating system so produced is now one of the major operating systems in use on Web servers and elsewhere is taken as evidence that the open-source approach works.

Good software may be produced outside the commercial market, but what is the motivation, if one is needed, for individual computer programmers, service providers, and so-called virtual communitarians,[7] to promote and indulge this fellowship of the gift, of the open-source and the less conspicuous kind? There are at least four possible explanations.

First, this apparent generosity may demonstrate the true character of information. Information operates differently than do other commodities. It is possible to both give it away and yet still retain it, to be used for commercial gain. Insofar as information is understood as patterns, these can be exchanged endlessly, and in different media. We readily put a price on the labor associated with the creation of information, and the medium or hardware of storage, transmission, and decoding, but the possibility of information's endless reproduction engenders a different kind of economy, or perhaps a distorted economy. As with other commodities, oversupply diminishes prices. If information is readily available for free, then no one will pay for it. One may be more inclined to give away a computer program, a text file, or a digital image than part with hardware, a magazine, or a paper photograph, the marginal cost of production and distribution of which may be high. By this reading, Internet generosity is a cheap form of altruism.[8] The low marginal cost of the reproduction and dissemination of a computer file makes it more feasible, and even tempting, to give it away.

According to this explanation, the giving of gifts always succumbs to some form of calculation, whether consciously or not. There is a series of causes in play explicable in terms of risk, cost, and return, a kind of economic determinism. The economic benefit of the open-source approach is that it engenders the rapid development and improvement of software that is better than that produced by alternative means. For the individual there is a reasonable chance of achieving a modest return. In the closed source world there are bigger profits to be made, but at greater risk and higher cost of development.

Second, the current wave of generosity could be a sign of the much proclaimed digital revolution, which claims new ways of thinking, new configurations of self, identity, and community, or at least a revival of archaic thinking. Online altruism could be a further manifestation of McLuhan's technoromantic return to tribal society, in which commerce was dependent on kinship.[9] We are entering a digitally mediated age, where we are able to participate in an immediacy of communications formerly only enjoyed in the tribe. In the global village we are more prepared to communicate, to share, and to give than in former times, but on a global scale. A variant of this technological determinism is that we now have the medium to realize the Enlightenment dream of the free flow of information, among an active and informed citizenry. The digital gift economy is another manifestation of the new, democratic world order being ushered in by digital communications. The open-source model is evolutionary, an organic approach to software design, an ecosystem from which all participants benefit, a new and egalitarian mode of interaction determined by the socially transforming digital medium.

Third, the Internet may simply bring to consciousness something that has always been present, given new impetus by the conspicuous and socially validating products of advanced and ubiquitous technologies. According to certain anthropological studies, the economic system is parasitic on a primordial condition, a more basic form of "economics" in which the gift reigned supreme.[10] By this reading, putative generosity on the Internet is simply a contemporary manifestation of the social norm of gift exchange that predates and has survived the imperatives of modern commerce. In fact commerce could not exist were we not already predisposed toward communal sharing and gift giving. Some argue that play and the game predate work and the serious business of commerce. The exchange of gifts is a form of play, involving a to-and-fro movement, the nonserious business of chance, and a flirtation with risk. Gift exchange is the primordial root of contemporary economics. Economics is subservient to the gift.

Fourth, the gift may present a profound disturbance to the economic order, a point that resonates with the claims of the Internet to radical social alteration. The OSI is subversive and perhaps unsustainable. It plays a role, sets a model of an alternative, and provides a provocation. So, through the Internet, and other media of late modernity, the commercial transaction, or the exchange, encounters its opposite, which is the gift. An analysis of the radical aspects of the gift can be taken further. The social defects inherent in the commercial transaction have been well aired, but giving is also a fraught enterprise, on the Net as elsewhere.[11] It can be a means of exploitation, coercion, graft, and deception, with unpleasant outcomes not so far removed from those of theft. As well as play, the symptoms of the gift are perilously close to those of terror, crime, and the worst of mercantile excess. An analysis of the tortured relationships engendered by the gift may be instructive of the network economy and contribute to a further understanding of the connections between commerce and design. From this point of view, the gift brings to light the role of transgression in social relations, on the Internet and elsewhere.

I have just identified four explanations of the gift: (1) a raft of positions that cluster around utilitarianism, or economic determinism, advocacy of free-market economics, the subservience of all social relations to economic (and util-itarian) considerations; (2) the romantic utopianism of much of the popular literature on the digital age; (3) the argument from anthropology of the primacy (or primordiality) of the gift; and (4) the transgressive position that seeks to unsettle any certainty about commerce or the gift. In order to set up a matrix for further discussion of the gift, I will consider three of the gift's main charac-teristics. These also structure my discussion of the network economy in general.

Three Characteristics of the Gift

Cultural theorists and philosophers have subjected the gift to substantial scrutiny, the terminology and definition of which was established through the seminal essay by the anthropologist Marcel Mauss.[12] For Mauss, the principles underlying the exchange of gifts predate and underlie the modern commerce of Adam Smith and juridical understandings of contracts.

Surprise

According to Mauss, the gift has its seeds in concepts of the festival and in extra-ordinary events. As neighboring tribes negotiate the fine line between conflict and alliance, isolation and trade, they move to excesses either of spectacular gen-erosity or insane destruction.[13] For my purposes here I will characterize this as-pect of the gift in terms of *surprise,* though it is not a term Mauss uses. The surprise aspect of the gift is promoted by Jacques Derrida in his commentary on Mauss. For Derrida, the gift must be unforeseeable, or "appear chancy."[14] Derrida makes much of the meaning of the word "surprise" as "overtake" (best preserved in the French: *sur* as "over" and *prise* as "to take"), the giving of gifts be-ing a way of taking hold of the receiver, as if giving an obligation.[15] For Mauss, in tribal societies the gift seems to be the norm and the expected, though its timing is not necessarily so. But for Mauss, the very idea that the gift should be so prominent a feature of tribal societies is a cause for surprise, expressed through a question: "What rule of legality and self interest . . . compels the gift that has been received to be obligatorily reciprocated?"[16] So in the context of the free market, the idea and perpetration of the gift comes as a source of surprise if not any particular gift itself.

Excess

Mauss also draws attention to the role of *excess* in the purveying of gifts. Gifts are often useless trinkets, in archaic societies as in our own. They represent a surplus, something not really needed. The festive occasion of their giving is also characterized by exuberance, demonstration, squandering, and other trappings of excess.

Difference

The giving of gifts also promotes unequal relations between members of the tribe. Whereas modern commerce seeks to render everyone equal as long as they have the capacity to pay, and modern conceptions of equity and justice are predicated on the need for balance, evenhandedness, and fair play,[17] tribal gift exchange involves unequal exchange. The gift reinforces differences in rank and status independent of talent or earnings, or modern concepts of justice. We can recast the value-laden concept of inequality in terms of *difference.* The gift amplifies difference, in status, class, wealth, age, rank, ability, access, freedom and education.

So I will adopt these three characteristics of the gift to help structure further discussion of the apparent altruism of Net culture: surprise, excess, and difference, which are not so far from contemporary understandings of the gift. Other concepts I may care to invoke in explanation of the gift cluster around surprise, excess, and difference: concepts of a giver and receiver, exchange, circulation, contract, social norms, kinship, domesticity, altruism, celebration, special occasion, timeliness, and delay. The identification of surprise, excess, and difference also enables the consideration of phenomena and events that at first glance seem to have little to do with the gift, but can easily be coaxed into its orbit, such as design and creation, as well as crime, terror, exploitation, and injustice.

How is the gift revealed in contemporary culture? When we think of the contemporary gift, we readily think of surprise. Gifts are frequently unexpected, or at least the object given may be unknown until it arrives. It is considered good form to evince surprise, even if one expects the gift. The gift also equates with some notion of excess. It is often in the spirit of the gift that it is something the receiver does not really need. We are entitled to wonder if the gift cost the giver anything, or if it derived from the giver's surplus. The gift is also implicated in difference. Small children and the needy may receive gifts from their elders or benefactors without the expectation that they must return in equal measure. There is commonly an imbalance in the benefits that accrue to the giver and the receiver of the gift, exaggerating difference.

Many narratives can be invoked to show evidence of this tripartite character of the gift. Writers of children's stories know how to exploit the dramatic potential of the gift in these terms. Harry Potter receives the gift of a broomstick, which is unexpectedly dropped by owls onto the breakfast table, "knocking his bacon to the floor."[18] It is a witch's broomstick with specifications in excess of the norm, a souped-up "Nimbus 2000," and he is enjoined not to let the other pupils of the school know of this favoritism or they will all want one.[19] The gift upsets some expectation of balance and fair play, highlighting Harry's difference from the other pupils. The elements of surprise, excess, and difference also resonate in nobler narratives of redemption. Luther's "break through"[20] is that salvation really does come as a gift (grace) from God, that God's favor is born of excess (grace abounding),[21] and that the moral account is unevenly balanced. In narratives less sublime, the emerging stories of Internet economics suggest we should be surprised that informational goods are sometimes given for nothing. It is a remarkable feature of the emerging medium of digital communications. The medium is already laden with an excess of information,[22] bandwidth, computing power, software, capacity to copy and transmit, even time[23]—the raw materials of hacker production.[24] Some have remarked that on the Internet we will always receive far more than we can possibly give away.[25] The question arises as to how fair it is that some give and others receive without giving in equal measure. The Internet raises questions of equality of access. The poor are further socially disadvantaged by being unable to participate in the network society. The Internet and Internet culture are permeated with the trappings of difference and inequality, within which the putative gift economy seems to trade. Digital media obscure certain differences but amplify others.

As a further example, I can cite Derrida's exploration of the theme of the gift in *Given Time: 1. Counterfeit Money*, which contains Charles Baudelaire's short story of an apparently simple exchange between two gentlemen and a street beggar. Having donated money to a beggar, one gentleman remarks to other: "next to the pleasure of feeling surprise, there is none greater than to cause a surprise."[26] Part of this surprise was that the gift offered was apparently in excess of what one would expect, and it was complicit in various asymmetries: one gentleman gave more than the other, and the beggar was potentially even more the loser because the coin offered was counterfeit, which could get the beggar into trouble if he attempted to pass it on. The gift served to amplify a series of differences, not the least of which was the beggar's inferior social standing compared to that of the gentlemen, and issues of the true and the counterfeit, the just and the unjust action. For Derrida, the gift is characteristically fraught in this way, presenting various irreconcilable differences, and as such it also provides a model for understanding communication, language, and commerce in general.

I will examine this tripartite character of the gift (surprise, excess, and difference) in the philosophy of free-market utilitarianism, the gift in romance, its role in an intellectual schema that seeks for a primordial condition prior to free-market exchange, and the Derridean construction, which purveys the gift as a mode of transgression. This strategy will help position design and the network economy within the culture of the gift. Insofar as I can identify these features in the network economy, they provide evidence of the gift in germinal or residual form.

The Utility of the Gift: Classical Economics and Risk

Smith's philosophy of the free market does not address the gift overtly.[27] The philosophy of the free market ostensibly eschews the characteristics of surprise, excess, and difference. The free market obviates the element of surprise. Though it gives rein to the "invisible hand" of free competition, through the principle of self-interest, it relies on the availability of information, so that good and certain choices can be made.[28] As an emerging science, political economy was concerned with establishing the means by which predictions could be made. The economic world is ideally a predictable world. For Smith, a free market involves laborers trading the surplus of their production above their own needs with the surplus of others,[29] but this requires prudence: "every prodigal appears to be a publick enemy, and every frugal man a publick benefactor."[30] Though profit is the accumulation of surplus, in most other respects the philosophy of the free market eschews excess. We have to be prepared to save, and not squander what we produce.[31] A free market also means equality of opportunity (the suppression of difference), a fair price for labor and goods, ensured by competition. In keeping with Smith's philosophy, predictability, frugality, and equality are stoic virtues, particularly when translated into trust in Providence,[32] Prudence,[33] and Order.[34] Of course these are ideals, and though Smith does not present them dialectically, they are clearly at war with their opposites. Against certainty, Smith draws attention to uncertainty, speculation, risk, and chance, and how merchants and carriers insure against the calamity of shipwreck.[35] Against prudence, consumption can have the appearance of prodigality. Against equality, everyone is clearly not equal in the marketplace, in Smith's time due to slavery,[36] and in the free market prices get out of balance, even if temporarily.[37]

The three terms (surprise, excess, and difference) here find some kind of unity on the issue of knowledge. For markets to be fair and "perfect," with no party suffering unduly, there has to be knowledge. For the twentieth-century economist Friedrich Hayek, building on Smith's analysis, economic systems are driven by certain foresights and anticipations. We make plans as individuals and as groupings of individuals. So in a perfect market situation, where there is complete knowledge, the suppliers of building materials produce quantities of bricks and pipes in the expectation that the quantities will be consumed by people who want houses. In turn, potential home buyers save money in anticipation that they will be able to make a purchase one day, and that there will be a supply of the necessary materials.[38] Some kind of equilibrium is reached within this network of expectations. One hopes that supply and demand match up: "under certain conditions, the knowledge and intentions of the different members of society are supposed to come more and more into agreement or . . . the expectations of the people and particularly of the entrepreneurs will become more and more correct."[39] Of course, there is no perfect knowledge. Suppliers and consumers do not know each other's plans and anticipations in their entirety. There are surpluses or deficiencies in supply. There can be insufficient or excess demand. In a healthy market, these discrepancies eventually dissipate (prices fall if there is oversupply, etc) and the system tends toward an equilibrium. Our three terms of surprise, excess and difference are translated into anticipation, marginal errors in the system, and equilibrium. We are surprised by a mismatch in expectations. Excesses in supply or demand are transient market errors, on the way to the obviation of difference and a state of equilibrium.[40]

Under a system of perfect knowledge there should be no surprises, the free and ubiquitous flow of information being one of the means by which digital communications is said to promote the free market. According to Gates, the currency market already comes close to Smith's ideal, thanks to "nearly complete, instantaneous information," contributing to "friction-free capitalism."[41] In the free market, surprise is understandably accompanied by suspicion, a sense that information has been suppressed, or is being restricted. Countless Web sites attempt to sustain this suspicion by exposing inside information on the policies of major corporations, such as Microsoft. Surprise also comes in the form of a disruption to the economic system, such as changes in interest rates, sudden withdrawal of labor, sudden limitation in supply, the vagaries of the stock market, disaster, loss of confidence, a sudden find or decline in raw materials.[42] Risk takes on a particular complexion in the period of "late modernity." For the social economist Ulrich Beck, risk is now often insidious and invisible, presaging epidemics, toxic pollution, the leakage of nuclear waste, the bitter fruits of overproduction.[43] Enemies can be invisible, and stateless, revealing themselves sporadically, and operating under the cloak of existing economic, technological, and social systems. Surprise can arrive from within or without. Risks can now also present as cataclysmic, affecting all of humankind and life on the planet. Risks are also unevenly distributed, as in the case where floods affect those less able to afford to live on safer ground. Risk is also treated scientifically, through measurement, empirical records, and calculation, though it is also accompanied by mistrust in those methods. With an intensifying suspicion of experts, people are becoming increasingly responsible for their own assessment of risk and rely increasingly on compensation and litigation as a means of ameliorating its costs. Risk can be revealed gradually and without drama, as the accretion of latent threats, as in the subtle buildup of an epidemic, but risk is certainly epitomized by surprise.[44] Disaster comes as a shock to the system, a breach in the fabric of our certainties and expectations.

Computer systems also bring to mind the element of surprise through concepts of risk. We have become dependent on large, dispersed information systems. We are familiar with the complaint of the desk clerk or telephone call operator for whom the computer system has "just gone down," bringing all transactions to a halt, and with the effects of losing an entire hard disk of data due to a technical failure. Information in digital form is easy to replicate, back up, disperse, in order to minimize the risk of corruption and loss, but redundancy also entails risk, through the proliferation of versions, security measures, and the extra burden of managing the multiplication of data. As the assurances and reliability of data increase, so do the consequences of loss and corruption become more catastrophic when they occur. The consequences of rampant computer viruses, security breaches, and cracking[45] are well known.[46] Communication systems, and no less the widely accessible Internet, are also implicated in the perpetration of subversion, terror, and surprise, as in the plotting and coordination of the surprise attack, the poisoned gift, the Trojan horse.

Risk is clearly a feature in the financing of computer systems' development and exploitation, particularly through venture capital.[47] A business plan is formulated to encourage trust by investors in an adventurous and possibly risky proposal. The investors may be led by an entrepreneur, who participates closely in the startup firm, monitoring its progress. The risks are high but so are the potential returns, and the venture capital will be withdrawn if the project seems not to be succeeding. What is success? Success is not necessarily or immediately based on profits earned by the company set up to develop the project, but in its ability to maintain the momentum and profile of the project to the extent that the company can go onto the public market, that is, it can raise shares with an investment bank that are then put on the stock market.[48] Income from the creation of shares will be raised on the expectation that the company will soon become viable (return profits) or it may be bought out by a bigger company. Judgments about timing are crucial. The enterprise relies on the manipulation and management of risk and expectation, as much as on the project itself.

The venture capitalist is often regarded as far removed from the passions of those proposing and developing the project, interested only in a quick return on investment, and through an investment of other people's money. As a dealer in the medium of time, the venture capitalist may withdraw from the project or sell out at any time, both managing and perpetrating the element of surprise. Under the title of "angel," the provider of the gift of capital deals in beneficence, guardianship, and the ephemeral. Internet innovation and its funding are closely allied. The sociologist Manuel Castells argues that the Internet and related electronic networks provide the necessary conditions for the financing of high-risk e-business and computer systems development projects.[49] Electronic networks have encouraged the interdependence of financial markets across the globe, which in turn facilitates the rapid deployment of large quantities of capital for high-risk, high-return projects.

Surprise is partly countered by *excess*. Venture capitalists finance more projects than they expect will succeed, to counteract risk. Shrewd investors organize portfolios of shares that include both safe and risky investments. Economic systems have a resilience to certain kinds of shock, through the storage and management of savings, reserves, insurances, and underwriting.[50] Borrowing, the issuing of promissory notes and the "exchange" of debt, is possible due to the excess of funds in some part of the system. A surplus of cash, money, capital, value, or promise does not necessarily equate with a surplus of information, but the structural redundancy built into digital communications provides a parallel function. The Internet, for example, offers a certain resistance to the shock of outside interference. The network contains redundancies, so that information is redirected through different parts of the system or through different media in the event of disruption or congestion. Information is backed up or cached on proxy servers, and duplicates of files can be kept on different servers, ranging from major data storage sites to the hard disks and removable media of desktop computers and handheld devices. Though money and information are dissimilar in many respects, there is an inertia in both economic systems and the Internet that acts as a buffer to surprise and attack, an inertia made possible by the capacity of money and information to be held in reserve, a means of making use of excess.

The Internet also supports and purveys gossip and news, raising the profile of its own products, and further promoting a sense of excitement and inflated expectation, as well as some skepticism. This intricate series of links contributes to the volatility of the dot-com phenomenon, which has seen periods of extreme inflation and deflation of stock values, and many businesses folding.[51] The performance of dot-coms has also been one of excess, with talk of overvaluation, irrational exuberance, and the bursting of the dot-com bubble.[52]

On the matter of difference, the model of the free market calls on metaphors of balance. Prices, interest rates, and economic indicators can fluctuate around a mean as in the behavior of a steel spring, which oscillates around a stable position at which it can rest. In some economic models oscillations occur about a series of points that are never reached, known as "strange attractors."[53] Complex systems are those where the values of parameters (such as stock values against time) fall into regions of smooth and stable behaviors, interspersed with wild and apparently random fluctuations. As mathematician Benoit Mandelbrot and others have shown, even simple formulas or algorithms can generate complex behaviors. In calculative terms, surprise reveals itself as a sudden discontinuity in a trend, a brittle edge, a shear fracture, also addressed in "catastrophe theory."[54] Excess is accounted for in terms of reserves and momentum. Difference, or balance, is a matter of movement around or toward some stable condition, a trend, mean, asymptote, or strange attractor.

In isolation these factors do not demonstrate automatically that the world of commerce is permeated by the gift. But they are suggestive of certain similarities and differences between both the gift and commerce. In the context of risk, there is the language of stewardship: that the earth's resources are a gift that should not be taken for granted and that need to be looked after. On the other hand catastrophe comes as a "gift" that is unwelcome, unwanted, and in effect poisoned. The business loan sometimes has the appearance of a gift. It is born of excess, and is returned, but with interest, and under contractual obligation. The to-and-fro of the gift and countergift has the appearance of stable and random oscillations. I will return to these concepts subsequently.

If this is how free-market economics deals with the elements of surprise, excess, and difference, the constituents of the gift, then how does it deal with the gift proper, the gift identified as such? Free-market economics sees no need to provide special account of the gift. The free market is not opposed to the gift, but subsumes it. There is a benefit in giving services and goods to a communal pool.[55] The giver takes risks, calculable or otherwise.

The gift is often accounted for in terms of altruism. The utilitarian account of the gift finds extreme expression in the political scientist Robert Axelrod's description of the so-called prisoner's dilemma.[56] Two prisoners who collaborated on a crime are under interrogation in independent cells. If only one prisoner provides incriminating evidence against the other, then he will be freed and the other will receive the harshest sentence possible. If each provides incriminating evidence against the other, then they will both suffer a medium penalty. If neither informs on the other, then they will both suffer a light penalty. The stakes are different in each combination, but neither prisoner has sufficient information about what the other prisoner may do, and each would seek to gain the lightest sentence. This highly artificial example provides a microcosm of the general dilemma of altruism from a utilitarian perspective, as an exercise in maximizing one's self-interest. There is insufficient information, one must calculate risks, compounded by the fact that there may be a vast number of agents involved.

In the context of our exploration, the confession has the character of a gift, to the police, or to an accomplice. The confession and the gift entail risk, a matter of surprise, a shocking disclosure. The confession is also born of excess. The impulse to disclose all may not be vital for criminal prosecution or even exoneration. It is sometimes telling more than people want to hear, or want to be heard, analogous to the redundant disclosures of the personal Web page, the flamboyant bio line or profile of the MUD citizen. The confession is intent on establishing and exaggerating difference, between innocence and complicity, truth and falsity, providing an opportunity for the accomplices to mark out their differences from each other.

Of course, the risk to the giver (of a confession, information, consideration for the welfare of others, or tangible objects) is diminished if the gift is from the giver's reserves, from an excess that will not be missed. Objects or funds are also diminished as gifts if they are not the giver's to give, but borrowed on the strength of a promise, as in the case of venture capital for a project.

From a utilitarian perspective, for rational beings the books can be balanced. The difference between the conditions of the giver and the receiver can be bridged, even for open-source computer systems development. For Castells, businesses make profits from open-source development by designing commercial application programs that are built on top of the open-source programs, by selling services, by packaging and customizing, or by selling hardware that works well on open-source technology. In other words profits are not channeled through the sale of open-source products but through the proprietary closed-source products that support or feed off them. The giving of gifts is in order to reap the same or better not only in terms of monetary reward but in terms of feelings of satisfaction, pleasure, or social approval. The system of balances is complex, and the payoff is a sense that one's reputation is being enhanced.[57] This view is well expressed in an account of the apparent altruism of the OSI. According to Torvalds: "Open-source hackers aren't the high tech counterparts of Mother Teresa. They do get their names associated with their contributions in the form of the 'credit list' or 'history file' that is attached to each project. The most prolific contributors attract the attention of employers who troll [sic] the code, hoping to spot, and hire, top programmers. Hackers are also motivated, in large part, by the esteem they can gain in the eyes of their peers by making solid contributions. It's a significant motivating factor. Everybody wants to impress their peers, improve their reputation, elevate their social status. Open-source development gives programmers the chance."[58] It also does this in a highly public and accessible way. The Internet is a medium well suited to the circulation of reputations.[59]

Such utilitarian justifications do not explain how it is that some individuals are disposed to this style of social facilitation and others move to its converse: the closed-source model. It could be that the utilitarian argument is simply a post facto justification for the way certain people feel disposed to act in any case. The appeal by benefactors to utilitarian arguments can also be read as an expression of humility: "I am not only being generous or public spirited; I am also in this for what I can get out of it." In the business world, to be seen as giving is also to be construed as naïve and lacking in acumen or guile, a charge avoided by demonstrating that the apparently altruistic act is in fact calculated and self-serving. This humility is perhaps offered as a kind of gift, a gift of denial that one is giving.

Toward the end of this chapter, I will examine what happens to elements of the free market, such as selling, competition, borrowings, and shock, when they are taken as dealing in the gift, that is, when commerce is examined more directly through the metaphor of the gift.

The Romance of the Gift

Utilitarianism objectifies the concept of "feeling good" about one's altruistic acts, such as giving gifts, as an emotional state. The payoff for altruistic behavior is not only the ability to survive better, or improved chances of reciprocation in kind in the future, but also personal happiness. For the utilitarian Jeremy Bentham, the principle of utility means that we should approve of actions that augment "the happiness of the party whose interest is in question."[60] The giving of gifts can engender good feelings, and this is an individual matter, society being just the sum of individuals and the social benefit being a sum of the benefits to individuals. The greatest happiness for the greatest number of people becomes the chief moral guide. Though opposed to utilitarianism in other respects, Romanticism shares this Enlightenment preoccupation with the individual and with feeling. This Romantic subjectivism elevates feeling, emotion, and sentiment.

Surprise, or the pretense of surprise, provides an opportunity for the outpouring of emotion. Ruskin's ecstatic description of St. Mark's in Venice reads as an attempt to capture and relive a moment of awe, wonder, and surprise, as the tourist progresses from the vulgar and narrow alleyways of the city to the grandeur of the piazza and the "sculptured spray" of the church's roof line. For Ruskin's Romantic naturalism, "vital sensibility" rejoices in "its own excessive life, that puts gesture into clouds, and joy into waves, and voices into rocks."[61] It is not the pure Platonic forms, but ornament (which can never "be overcharged if it be good"[62]) that provides the arena for the exercise of imagination and design. The Romantic sensibility trades in the "imperfection and variety of things professing to be symmetrical."[63] As in ornament,[64] so in life, the Romantic impulse is characterized by a celebration of the unexpected, of excess, asymmetry, and a generosity of spirit that does not require the books to be balanced. For Ruskin the archetype of self-sacrifice resides in the soldier, who must face the shock of danger. He lives a reckless life, an excess of pleasure or adventure, and is prepared for the ultimate inequality, of being slain on behalf of others.[65] And so the gift finds a ready home in the Romantic age: as a spontaneous and exuberant expression of generosity, inevitably linked to emotion and self-sacrifice. It is this sentimentalization of the gift that we have inherited—and that finds expression on the Internet, as it does in print media—of online greeting cards, the dispatching of floral tributes, effusive correspondence, and other opportunities for personalized outpourings of familial sentiment.

Romanticism also lays claim to the role of the creator, who is disposed to self-sacrifice for the sake of art. Creativity takes on the trappings of the gift. It fosters the element of surprise. Of course, the calculative (utilitarian) tradition is also capable of presenting creativity as such. For the AI apologist, Margaret Boden, "a creative idea must not only be new, but surprising,"[66] in her case accounted for in the language of mappings, search, rules, randomness, prediction, and determinism. For the Romantics, on the other hand, surprise defies calculation and arises from some flash of inspiration or genius. This surprise either wells up from within, the innate genius of the artist, or is planted from without, a "holy gift to men"[67] from the daughters of Zeus, the Muses. As pointed out by Jacques Godbout writing on the primacy of the gift,[68] generosity often extends to attributing the gift to another source, as in such dubious benefactors as Father Christmas, the tooth fairy, or the gift of the secret Valentine's Day admirer. For the Romantic sensibility the gift of the Muse scarcely conceals the false modesty of creative prowess.

The creative person demonstrates prowess in *excess* of basic skills. Creativity is a supplement, and the benefits of its exercise provide in excess of economic return. Godbout makes clear the supplemental character of the artist's worth: "An artist is hired for a concert and we must pay to attend. The bond between artist and spectator is, it would seem, entirely quantified. But neither one is satisfied. Both want more than an objectified relationship. The artist wants to be applauded, the spectator wants to applaud; both want to establish a tie that is nonquantifiable, disinterested, that cannot be absorbed by the market."[69] As a further defender of the gift, Lewis Hyde asserts that "a work of art can survive without the market, but where there is no gift there is no art."[70] In the case of a gift, there is no expectation that creativity is given and rewarded in equal measure. Its reward is other than reciprocal. Designers commonly complain of an imbalance in this regard, that clients will more willingly pay a building surveyor or accountant for a routine service in measurement or calculation than they will pay an architect for producing a sketch design. Would-be commercial Web site designers seem equally prone to the expectation that their services will be offered as a gift, perhaps pending approval prior to a full commission. Creative output seems to be caught up with expectations of approval, and design presents as merely a forerunner to a calculative exercise. Like the conditions of the gift, designing appears open-ended, in duration, in its interpretation and its valuation. The point at which a client or patron may be obliged to pay the account is uncertain—the point at which the work and the claimed remuneration are in balance. That design celebrates its qualities in surprise, excess, and difference assists designers and clients alike in regarding the production and presentation of a design as a gift, outside the normal realms of obligation and contract.

Torvalds, the inventor of Linux, states (and overstates) the case for why a computer program (as design) is not just "intellectual property" but comparable to art: "It's not property to be sold like chattel, it's the act of creation, it's the greatest thing any human can ever do. It's Art, with a capital A. It's the Mona Lisa, but it's also the end result of a long night of programming, and it's an end result that you as a programmer are damned *proud* of. It's something so precious that selling it isn't even possible: It's indelibly a part of who you are."[71]

These sentiments also take us perilously close to the myth of the designer as misunderstood hero, prone to working without adequate appreciation or reward, suffering the indifference of aesthetic ignorance from patrons, clients, and users, the criticism of the tasteless public, the constraints of bureaucracy and soulless economics. Of course, the calculative tradition has sought to bring design into the orbit of the measurable and the remunerable, though against the resistance of the Romantic impulse that prefers creativity and design to be reckoned otherwise.

Design has long held a trade in shock and surprise, in keeping with the tenets of the gift. The Internet no less must bear the burden of maintaining its newness. As I have examined elsewhere, the burden of utopia placed on the digital realm continues the Romantic legacy, in technological form.[72] At the moment the pundits of digital media seem to exhibit an inexhaustible capacity to present the medium as a source of surprise. Facts, statistics, and projections are proffered as if to take our breath away. Design and innovation on the Internet in this context bear a further burden, that of living up to expectations, perpetuating surprise and excess, and fulfilling the expectation of the Internet as gift economy.

The society of the gift also resonates with McLuhan's account of social transformation brought about by electronic communications, and is classically utopian. There is a better future, implicating concepts of wholeness and unity, but this future is also a return to when things were better. The current age is marked by some form of fragmentation, a transitional state between a past and a future unity. From the phenomenological point of view, to be examined next, the Romantic craving for a unitary state, utopia, betrays a more basic human propensity to always project forward. The romance with utopia, in which the promotion of innovation in digital media trades, is but a diminished or limited manifestation of our capacity for projecting expectations.

The Primordiality of the Gift: The Future

For Castells, Internet entrepreneurs "sell the future because they believe they can make it."[73] To appeal to the future in this way suggests a condition of being driven, of an agent caught up in a field of expectations. By various accounts, anticipation is a basic human condition and a hallmark of the creative impetus. The gift is characterized by surprise, genuine or acted, and the gift is caught up in expectation, eagerness, or dread. In this the gift gives potent expression to the condition common to us all. We are ever redolent with expectation for our world, constantly projecting forward; in the language of Heidegger, we are thrown into a fore-project.[74] In any situation we bring with us a fore-conception, a predisposition, or an anticipation. When we come to interpret a situation, or a text, we already have a pre-understanding, perhaps recognized as a prejudice.[75] In the case of the gift, we expect one thing and receive another. We expect a purely contractual exchange but then someone throws in a free gift. It is against this field of anticipation that events strike us as surprising.

Surprise gains its impetus by way of presenting a contrast within a field of expectations. Utopian dreams, hopes, narratives of technological and social progress, and the optimism that supports the financing of computer systems development are derived from this predisposition. The artifacts and systems of information technology present as gifts to ameliorate the problems of our current condition: conflict, poverty, environmental degradation, inefficiency, uneven access, oppression. For the digital utopian, the Internet is the technological equivalent of the gift of salvation or redemption, and the gift is not yet with us but is to come. Its residence is the future. But for Heidegger, our primordial condition is already of care and expectation, the concept of the future follows, as a particular form of explanation of our involvement in the world of technology.

In this light, digital technology is characterized by the "not yet," a term developed at length (with no reference to digital media) by Ernst Bloch in his treatise on utopia and the future, *The Principle of Hope*.[76] Is the world a better place due to digital communications? Does the Internet presage a free market? Will the dot-com return a profit? Is consumerism being supplanted by the society of the gift? Well, not yet, say the pundits, but it will be.[77] The concept of the future assumes an important role in the face of the increasing inadequacies of digital technology compared to the promises made of it. The future serves as a repository for the unfulfilled ambitions of digital technology. For Bloch and the phenomenological tradition, the "not yet" is a suitable name, a placeholder, for the condition of being unsettled in the face of hopes and desires. Our primordial condition is of care and expectation, the concept of the future follows, as a particular form of explanation of our involvement in the world of technology.[78]

The concept of "the future," purveyed so enthusiastically in the popular media, does not do full justice to the "not yet." The future is the way the "not yet" is revealed when we wish to exercise our interest in control, in the face of the unrealized promises of technology. In calculative terms, "future" names the part of the time vector extending from the present, and which is contiguous with the past. It lends geometrical legitimacy to the play of extrapolation, prediction, goal setting, and method. Time constitutes the axis on the graph showing progression to bigger, smaller, faster, further, closer. If we can predict how digital technology is shaping up, then we can control how we position ourselves in relationship to it, instrumentally and rationally. By this reading, time is a derived phenomenon, not some fundamental, as is so often assumed. In contrast to time, the phenomenologist would not so much assert the fundamental nature of *care* and *anticipation* as assert their primordiality. *Care* comes before in an ontological sense, which is not to presume time, but rather a basic dependence, later on in our reasoning interpreted as something coming before something else in time. Phenomenological concepts of surprise develop within this framework.

If time and the future are dependent on something more primordial, then similar claims have been made of the basis of modern-day commerce. Independent of the Internet gift economy, some claim that commerce builds on the more primordial condition of the gift. The economic system is parasitic on a primordial condition, a more basic form of "economics" in which the gift reigns supreme: helpfully named "stone age economics" in the title of a book by Sahlins.[79] By this reading the supposed generosity on the Internet is simply a manifestation of the social norm of gift exchange that predates and has survived the imperatives of modern commerce. In fact commerce could not exist were we not already predisposed toward the giving of gifts, toward communal sharing.

By this reading the conditions for surprise are socially decided, licensed, encouraged, and validated. We allow ourselves to be shocked and amazed by certain events in certain contexts, and by the ordinary or unusual gift. The capacity of people to give of information on the Internet is surprising if we are in a context where we are looking for surprise, for new claims of social transformation that can be attributed to digital communications. Equally, surprise is accommodated by the expectation of its converse: where we expect no social transformation, but it presents itself to us nonetheless. Surprise seems to be born of extremes, heightened anticipation or extreme complacency, the stock in trade of the journalistic populism of the Internet, in any case abetted and sustained by a social condition.

Surprise and the Thing

Openness to surprise also implies an openness to possibilities, a freedom, a letting things be as they are, rather than requiring them to conform to some schema, system of classification, or measurable property, such as market value or price. One of the complaints against commodification is that the things we encounter in the everyday world of commerce fail to instill a sense of wonder or surprise.[80] The spoiled child epitomizes the submissive consumer, the infantile seeker of instant gratification soon bored with the demanded and expected gift. The transient fetish for objects of consumption is one manifestation of Marx's identification of mechanization, where we and our products feature as so many incidental and expendable machine components, or of Heidegger's complaint about the reduction of all things to objects under the regime of a technological mode of being.

For Heidegger, the items of mass production as consumer objects have lost (or never had) the capacity to *gather,* to be the center of focal practices, to operate within a historical continuum, or a web of interconnected circumstances and events. The jug, as family heirloom, as precious thing around which the family gathers for sustenance and communion, is displaced by the mass-produced object of mere convenience or fashion.[81] The jug as commodity can be replaced by any other. Any container will do: ceramic, glass, steel, or plastic. The jug as commodity is within a class of objects with particular properties and functions: capacity, weight, cost. By way of contrast, for Heidegger, the jug as *thing* invites consideration of its own particular characteristics, its own uses and attendant practices. The authentic thing is objectively neither a collection of properties nor something over which one throws subjective feelings, as the romantic might sentimentalize objects by projecting on to them meanings, values, and a right attitude. Nor is the thing an object of contemplation, in the manner enjoyed by the sentimental poet concocting a sense of the sublime or wonderment, removed from the thing: the city dweller in naïve veneration of the rustic heirloom, or in awe of nature as spectacle. The thing is first and foremost authentically itself, to which we can attend, and which reveals new and surprising aspects of itself and its context in situations of use.

By this phenomenological reading, the thing (as opposed to the object, or item of consumption) is marked by this capacity to disclose, to reveal, not in the sense in which it might yield properties of weight, color, capacity, and price to scientific or commercial scrutiny, but in the sense in which it discloses the character of its context, which in turn informs us of the thing. So the bridge as thing discloses something about the strength of the river, the nature of the banks, and the needs and aspirations of the communities on either side of the river that it connects.[82] Without the bridge these factors would not necessarily be brought to light. Of course the bridge also changes things: the current of the river, the stability of the banks, and the interaction between the communities. To disclose is both to reveal what is already there and to create a new condition. For the thing appreciated as such, neither is predetermined.

Against this background understanding of the thing, as connected and disclosive of context, we should have no difficulty understanding Mauss's description of the nature of the gift in archaic society.[83] As opposed to the denigrated object of consumption in contemporary society, the archaic gift seems to participate fully in the character of the thing as described by Heidegger. For Mauss the archaic gift is implicated in what he terms a "total service" between two tribes or factions, an alliance implicating ritual, marriage, inheritance, legal ties, and rank.[84] Cooperation between tribes involves all of these issues. The gift is never a mere commodity, with exchange value, but it is a thing, or even a person, ensuring a kind of connection between parties. So the archaic gift participates in the thingly character as outlined by Heidegger. It participates in a larger series of interconnections and practices. According to Mauss, in archaic societies the gift is also described in magical or idealistic (Platonic) terms of having "soul." So for Maori culture, "a tie occurring through things, is one between souls, because the thing itself possesses a soul, is of the soul. . . . to make a gift of something to someone is to make a present of some part of oneself."[85] Archaic society apparently expresses the thingly character of the gift in terms of its agency: "Invested with life, often possessing individuality, it seeks to return to . . . its 'place of origin' or to produce, on behalf of the clan and the native soil from which it sprang, an equivalent to replace it."[86] The gift, as for the thing, has the capacity to reveal itself other than through generalized categories. In this it participates in a kind of surprise.

In contemporary terms, where giving is marked so much by the pretense of choice, finding the right gift rather than following a venerable rite or sacramental convention, we might ask what the gift reveals about the giver and the receiver. The gift provides the opportunity for surprise, in terms of unusual, appropriate, or inappropriate choice, but also in its timing, how it will be received, and whether or not it will be reciprocated. According to Godbout, the gift operates within the realm of freedom: "the more convinced I am that the other is not 'really' obliged to reciprocate, the more the fact that he does so has value for me, because it means that he is acting out of concern for the relationship, to foster the ties between us, that he is doing it for . . . me."[87] Among other things, the gift is disclosive of a series of social relationships. Software modification under the open-source regime seems even to have this character. Each contribution is disclosive of the community in which it is purveyed. Open-source narratives are bent on persuading us that open-source is about community and not commodity.

Surprise and Repetition

The communal aspects of giving suggest that the gift is not just a one-off event, but part of a pattern, a repetitive movement. Surprise reveals itself in terms of a breach in a sequence, as when a sequence yields a number as a discontinuity in the established pattern (e.g., 1, 3, 5, 7, 48). The cycle of giving and receiving suggests a repetitive movement, the alternation of gift and countergift. By a Freudian reading, as in the case of the game, the medium of repetition, or the thing in the repetition, is of less relevance than the repetition itself. Objects have psychological associations and trigger recollections and traumas certainly, but the repetition itself can also be the source of disquiet. Even a cotton reel with a piece of string attached can be implicated in a reenactment of something as "universal" as the loss of a child's union with her mother.[88] The object disappears from view, then is brought back, only to be thrown away again, a cathartic repetition, implicating deep-seated family relationships. With the cycle of the gift, the giver loses the object only to have it returned, albeit in a different form. On the one hand, this narrative diminishes the thing, turning it into a mere object of exchange, a surrogate character in a psychic drama. On the other hand, the thing gains its significance by virtue of its role in a larger practice, which in turn implicates mother, father, union, symbolism, and language.[89]

In many respects, Freud's psychologistic construction of the world of objects is at variance with Heidegger's phenomenology of things. But here there is some agreement, in that for Freud the thing is never just a mere thing (object, commodity), but is implicated in a larger picture of practices, and in a history and a continuity.[90] In the case of the child with the favorite toy or blanket it is no easy matter to effect a substitution. Not all blankets, cotton reels, and teddy bears are the same. By this reading, the cycle of giving and receiving gifts participates in the compulsion to repeat. Godbout describes this, with no reference to Freud, in terms of "the strange law of alternation."[91] When two people play a game, they take each move in their turn. In combative games each delivers a blow in succession. In the case of battle between warring tribes there is the strike and the counterstrike, the act of aggression followed by the act of revenge. So with the gift, the repetition is amplified by the to-and-fro movement of the gift and countergift, giving and receiving.

In the case of general benefaction, as in public-spirited Internet exchange, the contribution to a common pool, the cycle of gift and countergift, is sometimes hidden. Contributing in a generous way to a common pool does not seem to participate so fully in the cycle of repetition. But perhaps the repetition of the gift is also manifested in other ways: in the regularity of subscriptions, the calls for donations, the seasonal requests from charitable organizations, the ritualistic call for alms from the street dweller, and the various repetitions engendered by the ritualistic use of the Internet: connecting and disconnecting, immersion and retreat, opening and closing files, applications and connections, and the relentless deleting of "spam" email. But perhaps, too, the cycle of the gift and the countergift is after all evident in the operations of the open-source movement. There is the cycle of procurement, development, and passing on. The software loses its origins but exists as a proliferation of copies and improvements. The developer offers the source code as gift, which is then "returned" with something added.

But Freud also implicates the gift in his intriguing account of rites of passage. The young child (exemplified in the behavior of girls) seeks to win the approval of the father or father substitute through the offering of gifts.[92] The immature, narcissistic stage of development is characterized by self-absorption, holding back, not being prepared to give, not passing through the infantile phase of self-gratifying anal eroticism. For the girl, it is also a state of anger at the mother.[93] The child must progress to a state whereby she comes to terms with her estranged condition. She undergoes a rite of passage. Freud's complex and varied accounts of the human psyche connect the gift, the rite of passage, repetition, money, and gold. The contents of the bowels represent the child's first gift: "by producing them he can express his active [104] compliance with his environment and, by withholding them, his disobedience."[94] Later in life the body issuance of waste becomes associated (by the girl) with the gift of a baby.[95] The gift of feces can also be transferred to the giving or retention of money.[96] The miserly, acquisitive, and exploitative individual is immature and self-absorbed, that is, he or she has not passed through the narcissistic phase.

Freud's account serves several purposes here. It provides further support for the proposition that the compulsion to exchange gifts, to transact, to repeat, to engage in the cycle of taking turns, has its basis in the body, Freud's account of the way the small child deals with excrement, and with basic sexual drives. Freud serves the cause against idealism of various kinds: the Enlightenment concept of freedom, free-market economics, the greatest good for the greatest number, and the elevation of honor, duty, and noble ideals. Contrary to Enlightenment and Romantic idealism, for Freud human motivations are explicable in terms of sexuality, the body, and the pathology of family relationships: narcissism and the Oedipal condition. Freud is also instructive on the matter of suspicion. His exhortation to be suspicious of the surface phenomena of human behavior and look to the unconscious has been likened to the neo-Marxist critic bent on uncovering various modes of domination beneath the surface of bourgeois manners, the securities, promises and hopes of the capitalist system, themes taken up in various ways by thinkers such as Marcuse, and Deleuze and Guattari.[97]

Continuing our sideways look at Internet culture, we can also observe Freud's account surfacing in popular narratives about the OSI. The OSI purveys the concept of a society of computer systems developers that is giving, able to share, and in a sense mature and sociable. By way of contrast, the world of closed-source development is made up of individuals who are comparatively self-serving and therefore presumably narcissistic. The theme of maturity and psychic development recurs throughout the populist account of computer hacker culture. For example, open-source pioneer Torvalds berates his own obsession with solving technical problems, his enjoyment of solitary work on the computer over social relationships, and his lack of dress sense—in short his "nerdiness": "only a certain kind of person is able to sit and stare at a screen and just think things through. Only a dweeby, geeky person like me."[98] This social reserve also comes down to a lack of business sense, that is, a greater interest in resolving a technical problem than in working out whether one is being appropriately remunerated. The idea of the computer nerd buys into the romance of craft, the artisan or artist dependent on the business acumen and sponsorship of the patron, the altruistic artist dedicated to his work.[99] But the nerd is also defined in terms of sexual inadequacy. He or she is too distracted to engage in dating and courtship, has limited sexual experience, and is awkward and childlike in seeking and relating to potential intimate partners: "the only time I brought girls home was when they wanted to be tutored. . . . and it was never my idea."[100]

At least this is the self-narrative so constructed. Schooled in the art of Freudian suspicion[101] we are perhaps familiar with the oblique (and negative) reference: talking about money when we mean sex, and sex when we mean money; apparently downplaying our strengths and elevating our weaknesses in order to present the reverse; pleading poor when we really mean to announce our riches, and celebrating abundance when in penury. We describe ourselves as contrary to what people actually think of us, wanting to avoid the stereotype, our unconscious apparently employing every ruse at its disposal to keep our actual condition hidden. So the profiteer wants to appear benevolent. The public-minded wants to appear self-serving. The self-deprecation of the nerd has now become a "defense" against the charge of altruism, a narrative implicating sexual development: I may appear generous, but I am actually a victim of repression; I may appear enterprising, but I am sexually awkward and have not yet grown up. In the cases cited here, the complex play of narratives by which we attempt to reposition ourselves in the estimation of our critics and peers encourages reference to sexual experience. Instead of owning up to either the profit motive or altruism, we talk in more covert terms of success or otherwise in sexual relationships. Were the hidden motive to defend a position of sexual prowess, then we might well resort to money to make the point.

These tortured, Freudian readings of Internet altruism speak of surprise if nothing else, particularly in the denial of stable categories. For free-market economics, the enemy of surprise, everything should be in its place. The Romantic resists categorization and all similar machine-like and reductive schemas, while introducing (or reviving) Romantic categories: nobility, duty, sacrifice. The phenomenologist seeks to invert the basic categories: free-market economics is not the substrate of sociality, but rather it is preceded by the conditions that the free marketeer thinks follow it. The gift is not a particular manifestation of free-market commerce, but commerce is built on the gift. The gift is in turn prone to repetition, the body, family relationships, and sexuality. Any challenge to categories and their status is a candidate for surprise—a kind of gift.

The Potlatch and Conspicuous Excess

The propensity toward excess further supports the primordiality of the gift. It is in the anthropological account of the gift that the concept of excess finds its most startling expression. Mauss draws attention to the phenomenon of the potlatch,[102] that archaic custom whereby different groups, villages, or communities would attempt to outdo one another in generosity, often to the point of squandering their own resources, and impoverishing their own community. For Godbout, "often a bit of squandering goes along with the gift, a bit of excess, of folly, a superfluity that keeps the object's utility or exchange value at arm's length."[103] The remarkable feature of the potlatch is that it is a form of giving and self-sacrifice that might be carried through to near self-destruction, where the community's own "slaves are put to death, precious oils burnt, copper objects cast into the sea, and even the houses of princes set on fire."[104] The "rival" community is expected to reciprocate at some stage, and with interest, that is, a further excess of self-destruction. Failure to reciprocate indicates defeat, suggests loss of status, and in archaic societies requires ritualized restitution. So, contrary to war or competitive games where the aim is to vanquish the enemy by superiority in combat, the potlatch seeks to establish superiority by a contest of giving and self-sacrifice. Mauss indicates the remnant of this kind of practice in beer-drinking and food-consuming competitions, where "one is committed to gulping down large quantities of food, in order to 'do honor,' in a somewhat grotesque way, to one's host."[105] By this account, the gift is explicable not only in terms of altruism and generosity, fellow feeling, public spirit, and wanting to see the lot of the other improved by one's generosity, but in terms of competition.[106] The giving is to be excessive and bring one to the verge of one's own demise, which in turn indicates one's strength: If I can withstand all this giving, then I am indeed stronger than you. The contest may even bring down the opposition. One gives in excess in order for the opponent to reach the limit of his or her giving, and to be incapacitated or shamed. In modern society we may suppose that this aspect of the gift appears as a highly ritualized, bounded form of self-destructive giving, accompanied by posturing, genuine or false modesty, subtle appeal to humble means, the ruses of symbol, substitution, and oblique reference we have already identified in the context of Freudian negation.

Georges Bataille, the twentieth-century neo-Marxist essayist and surrealist further promotes the potlatch as providing the primary aspect of the gift.[107] The potlatch (and the gift) is a form of exchange without bargaining. Classical utilitarian economics regards barter as the precursor to economic exchange. It also assumes a deficiency of resources.[108] Following Mauss, for Bataille excess and the gift are the harbingers of economics. Community life naturally generates surplus, more of its own produce than it can consume (excess food, clothing, livestock), which needs to be dissipated. An excess of produce beyond one's immediate needs indicates prowess, status and prestige. In agonistic society (where there is conflict between neighboring communities), the most spectacular means of demonstrating this prestige is not simply to give away the excess but to waste it. So, in societies in which the potlatch assumed importance, this profligacy involved burning one's own possessions, murdering one's own slaves, in a public display. This occurs with the purpose of "humiliating, defying and obligating a rival." The receiver must "respond later with a more valuable gift, in other words, to return with interest."[109] For Bataille, the gift has its origins in this idea of destruction and loss. That someone receives something of benefit through this process is incidental and constitutes a later embellishment to the notion of the gift. The ostentation of the potlatch is the preserve of the aristocracy, who truly have the means to squander. For the middle classes, living and producing under the shadow of the aristocracy, this destruction of goods is carried out in private. It is translated into what we know as consumption. Consumer society is perpetuating the potlatch in its own diminished and machinic way. The bourgeoisie spends "for itself."[110] Whereas the exceedingly wealthy aristocratic class sacrificed its own slaves, the bourgeoisie class (the capitalist "bosses") sacrifices the laboring classes: "The end of the workers' activity is to produce in order to live, but the bosses' activity is to produce in order to condemn the working producers to a hideous degradation."[111] So, for Bataille, the origins of the gift take on an ignominious cast, they reside with the potlatch and lead to conspicuous consumption, capitalist domination, and the oppression of labor.

So conspicuous consumption is explicable as a diminished form of ritual profligacy by which one participates in a contest of the squandering of wealth—in popular terms, in keeping up with the Joneses. From a position different from Bataille's, the twentieth-century economist John Kenneth Galbraith also observes that we feel wealth must be displayed, hence the advertising of one's wealth through "obtrusively expensive goods,"[112] an unsatisfied craving for the latest model car, fashionable clothing, accessories, and entertainment, "for the entire modern range of sensuous, edifying and lethal desires."[113] This sentiment is also given a Marxist orientation by Debord, for whom capitalism has reduced everything to a commodity for show, and the show is everything: "It is not just that the relationship to commodities is now plain to see—commodities are now all that there is to see."[114] We are a society of the spectacle. This finds linguistic expression with Baudrillard, for whom it is not goods that are being exchanged so much as signs,[115] that is, visible indications. Bataille adds pessimistically that these symbols communicate in terms of excretion, death, anal eroticism, and sadism.[116] The reference is also to de Sade's grotesque story of gluttony and sexual excess, resulting in mutilation and death for just about all concerned.[117]

The excesses of the impulse to consume are no more evident than in the perpetration of pornography on the Internet. Certain scholars argue that "for some individuals, excessive Internet usage is a real addiction and of genuine concern,"[118] particularly insofar as the Internet is "anonymous, disinhibiting, easily accessible, convenient, affordable, and escape-friendly."[119] Addiction is the obvious characterization of the tendency toward excess. The fetish constitutes a further manifestation of excess. Marx drew attention to the "fetishism of commodities,"[120] whereby mass production detaches the things produced from the social relations of labor and ordinary usage, to stand as something transcendent. Desmet provides further insight into the Web page as fetish object.[121] As an exercise in substitution, and therefore of metaphor, the fetish makes its appearance on Web sites in a manner similar to the positioning of personal objects around a sacred shrine. After all, personal Web pages often make a fetish of images of pets, possessions, details about the owner's life, and her favorite things. The sacred fetish is a substitute for the inaccessible that directs attention elsewhere to some putatively transcendent condition. The fetish object is burdened with significations in excess of its ordinary use. By a Freudian reading, the fetish can also serve as a substitute for the object of sexual attention, and as such also represents a fixation.[122] The fetish soon gets caught up in talk of repetition, obsession, and addiction. Addiction in turn is characterized as a self-destructive impulse, not far removed from the potlatch.

Earth, Excess, and the Community of Strangers

The network economy is commonly characterized as detached from location, geography, and sources of supply. For Castells, we are tending toward "a horizon of networked, ahistorical space of flows, aiming at imposing its logic over scattered, segmented places, increasingly unrelated to each other, less and less able to share cultural codes."[123] One location can be substituted for another. Insofar as it participates in locality, the network economy is "at home" in the non-places of airport concourses, call centers, shopping malls, and the "generic city."[124] But the economic legacy is not so aloof from its grounding.

By way of contrast, the putative origins of the economic legacy indicate a greater bonding with place. According to the economist Thorstein Veblen, the profligacy of conspicuous consumption draws on the bounty of the earth as a model. The potlatch is a surprising phenomenon in an economic world, but in some respects is simply following nature's model, or at least the model of the earth, a model of excess and oversupply. The earth "gives up" so much, at the cost of its degradation.

On the one hand, the earth stands for substance and origin, a condition with which human endeavors must make contact for validation.[125] Here the earth is the progenitor of economy, a grounding in the essential rather than the excessive. As expounded by Vitruvius, the Stoic, buildings and towns establish their affinity with the earth, through their origins in the stake, the pole, the primary gnomon, the scribing of the circle, and the establishment of the cardinal directions by the shadow from the rising and setting sun.[126] By this geometrical means the town, the city, and the dwelling trace their origins to the earth and the earth's relationship with the cosmos.[127] Among the variants of this myth is nineteenth-century architect Gottfried Semper's account of the mound of earth as the primary origin of the dwelling, the mound being above the earth, but also of the earth.[128] So the earth stands in for the fundamental, the original, the essence, the parsimonious, the economical, but on the other hand the earth also provides a model for bounty and excess. The identification of the earth with motherhood, fecundity, prodigality, and wealth is also an ancient legacy. Hesiod referred to the "broad-breasted Earth," mating with Chronos to bring forth Zeus.[129] For Carlyle, the Romantic: "The land is *Mother* of us all; nourishes, shelters, gladdens, lovingly enriches us all; in how many ways, from our first wakening to our last sleep on her blessed mother-bosom, does she, as with blessed mother-arms, enfold us all!"[130]

The provision of the earth also features in various accounts of economics.[131] The earth is one of the primary sources of wealth, through the mining of gold and other precious materials. For Smith, land is in the company of labor and capital as one of the primary constituents of the economic system, with rent from land as a stable and abiding source of wealth. Following from Smith, the canon of political economy presents us with Thomas Malthus's pessimistic warnings against overpopulation, acknowledging that the earth does not yield up infinite resources. Subsistence is the base measure of production, with agricultural production at best increasing arithmetically with improved farming methods (and population increasing geometrically). But nature presents an "infinite variety of forms and operations"[132] that tax the intellect and "improve the mind," if not the body.

In archaic society, the earth was also the source of "the given." For Godbout, in archaic society, in "a world populated only by autonomous powers that cannot be subjugated, . . . nothing is produced, everything must be given."[133] Birds are available for consumption only if the forest has been persuaded to make a gift of them. Women do not produce children, but "are their provisional custodians and must be convinced to give them away, in other words to put them into general circulation."[134] The earth, and then nature, is the original source of the given, the primary gift.[135] For Bataille: "The sun gives without ever receiving . . . they saw it ripen the harvests and they associated its splendour with the act of someone who gives without receiving."[136]

In philosophy, Heidegger posits earth against world; the former is resistant and unyielding, the latter is constituted by science, nature, human history, or all of culture.[137] For Heidegger, the relationship between earth and world is agonistic, in the manner of a conflictual game. It is as earth thrusts through world that Being reveals itself.[138] Apart from its intellectual basis in a philosophy of the primordial, commentators have identified Heidegger's reference to the earth with the somewhat diminished concepts of the Fatherland, the Germanic and neo-Romantic folk legacy celebrating blood and soil, a further struggle that reminds them of the agonist game.[139] Clearly the land is commonly associated with intense national allegiance, undergoing reconfiguration in the global economy.

How does information technology relate to the land as source of the given? In the network economy, the land is commonly identified with constraint, something to be overcome. Land implies boundaries, the specifics of location, the constraints of space, nationality, and distance, the allocation of uses, and the articulation of resources. If the earth is the rock solid given, then communications technologies represent release from the earth—a movement to new possibilities and new worlds. Participation in the network economy provides the hallmark, the quintessential sign, of advanced industries, participation in which provides a measure of progress, economic adaptability, and distance from dependence on the raw earth. Primary industries extract materials from the land, secondary industries add value to the earth's produce through manufacture, tertiary industries provide services that further cushion our dependence on location. Sometimes we add knowledge-based industries as a fourth category, businesses that specialize in data processing or the development and use of information technology.[140] Famously, Internet economics attempts to break with spatial and geographical constraints. Much store is placed on the Internet as a means of breaking with the boundaries that support extremes of nationalism. Contrary to being bound to the earth, e-commerce seeks to position itself in terms of crossing spatial boundaries, overcoming distance, creating new virtual spaces, reducing space to the head of a pin.[141] This rarefied discourse readily transports e-commerce into the technoromantic realms of the digital ideal, the "not yet," the transcendent, ignoring the grounding of political economy in social and material contingency. The validating narratives of e-commerce tend to abrogate or deny the earth, and they attempt to get away from the contingencies of real estate, rent, land value, and the specifics of location.[142]

In the mythos of the global Internet, unconstrained by the earth and spatial boundaries, there is now one community. In the global community, gifts are no longer needed to propitiate relationships between rival communities. The stranger is already within the fold. In fact, we are constituted as a "community" of strangers.[143] The Internet gives scope to the category of giving Godbout defines as the gift to strangers. In archaic community, there are no strangers save those outside the group, with whom interaction is guarded and polarized, driven either by war or peace, the battle or gift. In urbanized, industrialized, and now globalized communities, informed by the mass media and advanced communications, there is the possibility of interactions within whole "communities" of strangers. Once the earth, land, and space are transcended, there are no boundaries. Large numbers of people who have never met can share very similar values and sense that they are part of a larger community under the cloak of anonymity.

In this context, self-help groups develop, a modern phenomenon recently abetted by the supposed dissolution of spatial constraints, the globalization of community, and now the Internet.[144] In self-help groups such as Alcoholics Anonymous (AA), individuals can leave the sphere of the family, friends, and neighbors and disclose their condition to strangers with similar problems. Such groups rely on there being a large pool of people, as in cities, from whom to draw sufficient numbers of like minds and to preserve a sense of anonymity.[145] They rely on being able to uproot from the constraints of location. Such groups are typically nonprofit, relying on the contribution of care and expertise from among their members, operating a kind of gift economy. Advice, comfort, support, personal disclosures, and confessions are given without obligation to repay. Arguably, such developments are now abetted by the Internet, and the dissociation from the land and place that is characteristic of late modernity.

Leisurely Self-Destruction

The degradation of the earth and the depletion of natural resources read as symptoms of overconsumption. By a certain classical reading, there are two models of production. One pertains to tending the earth, the other to the hunt— the ancient distinction between agricultural and nomadic life. Writing soon after Marx, Veblen constructs an account of the origins of the class system in these terms.[146] He sets up the mythic origins of the social and economic order in terms of the male-dominated role of the primitive hunter. Hunting in groups carried dangers and required absence from the clan, but it was not particularly time-consuming and the spoils of the hunt would keep the clan in food for a substantial period. On the other hand, the role of preparing food, tending the family, and working the land required constancy. These tasks were labor-intensive and largely the preserve of females. The hunter traversed the land in search of prey, while domesticity and agriculture engendered settlement and stability. As the demands of hunting became less onerous and more domesticated, the ethos of the hunt became more leisured. Hunting even becomes a pastime for the privileged classes rather than a necessity. Veblen associates the remnant of the hunting ethos with the upper classes, those who, rather than actually producing, enjoy a life of managing and living off those who do. This connection is obvious in the association of hunting as sport with the aristocracy.

In contemporary terms, the sociology of labor is characterized by two poles. The managerial class constitutes the leisured hunters. The laborers are the hardworking homebodies who do the work. They are also those who cultivate the earth.

Whereas the land is associated with nurture and toil, the hunting class is aligned with conspicuous leisure. Veblen's myth is far-fetched, but what credibility it has is gleaned from the associations it engenders with earth, bounty, and excess, albeit in an inverted manner. The hunt is associated with an excess of time, whereas tending the earth is associated with sober hard work. The suggestion is that the hunters rape the earth, exploiting its bounty giving nothing in return, whereas the cultivators tend the earth, plowing back from what they have reaped. Exaggerating the distinction, the suggestion is that the hunt pertains to capitalism, whereas those on the land participate more fully in the culture of the gift. The origins of capitalism reside with the predatory instinct; the origins of the gift reside with the earth. From Bataille's point of view, both the hunters (capitalists) and the cultivators (society of the gift) draw on the profligacy of the potlatch. The gift is already fraught and contains within it the seeds of capitalism, through the degradation of the potlatch to its bourgeois form as conspicuous consumption.

For Veblen, one of the effective ways of demonstrating membership of the leisured class is to show that one has time to spare, that one is not caught up in the necessities of survival or making a living. This does not necessarily engender sloth, but a frantic occupation with activities that are patently time-consuming and ultimately unproductive. Veblen gives examples of affectations of grammar and manners that could only be acquired by many hours of labor, or rather by the abundance of time left over from necessary labor: the use of difficult words, mastery of foreign languages, dressing for dinner, skill at cards, embroidery, dabbling in arts and crafts, and other nineteenth-century parlor activities. There is a strong vicarious component to conspicuous leisure. The gentlemen and ladies of the leisured class maintain a retinue of servants and service providers whose labor is to sustain the industry of conspicuous consumption, which also becomes a sign for those who aspire to the same leisured status. Whether or not one has the means to live as such, conspicuous consumption is largely an aspiration, a way of identifying with the good life, dealing in its signs.

These associations seem quaint in the network economy, where video gaming becomes the benchmark for contemporary leisure skills, relying on instantaneity and adaptability rather than the measured exercise of time-honored skills. But mastering computer games is time consuming if nothing else. For Veblen's theory to be applicable, it is only necessary that we aspire to the conspicuous leisure practices of the hunting class. As with other hobbies, computer gaming shows the trappings of vicarious participation in leisure skills, and of the complex of pastimes from which it derives: cards, chess, reading, sports, and overt participation in the hunt; through the vicarious exercise of martial arts, target practice, archery, sports car racing; and of course the gentlemanly pursuit of war games and armed combat. For Veblen, juvenile delinquency is not so far from the barbarism that constitutes the origins of the leisured class: "The traits that distinguish the swaggering delinquent and the punctilious gentleman of leisure from the common crowd are, in some measure, marks of an arrested spiritual development."[147] By this reading, the supposed delinquency of computer video games, including their extremes of violence—for example, the tribal plunder of *Doom* and *Quake*—are also forays into the officer's mess of the upper class, or at least participation in its sign system.

The ambition toward leisured consumption turns to conspicuous signs of self-destruction, the death instinct,[148] and is not always associated with refinement and good manners. David Fincher's controversial film *Fight Club* depicts the persistence of the group hunting ethos in terms of secretive male clubs bent on self-destruction through displays of bloody raw-fisted combat, recalling the excess of the potlatch.[149] The clubs are fraternities of anonymous strangers—in fact, self-help group dropouts. The male fight is portrayed as a foil against the feminine,[150] the domestic sphere, the trap of compliant labor consigned to meeting the incessant demands of domesticity and self-improvement. The tables are turned though. The film associates domesticity with conspicuous consumption against the raw, earthy violence of the men's club. The self-help group also comes under criticism as belonging within the domestic sphere. The elements are similar to those propounded by Veblen (earth, hunt, domesticity, consumption), though the roles are reversed in part and confounded. In Bataille's terms, this is a story about the battle between two versions of the potlatch. There is the form that claims authenticity in terms of primal, agonistic, and bloody self-destruction, and the aberrant form of the bourgeois potlatch with its investment in conspicuous consumption.

For Veblen, domesticity, emerging from toil on the land, is also the site of creativity. Within professional endeavor, the designers, creatives, and engineers are the remnant of the productive labor force who tends the hearth. Veblen's hope was that some day the engineers, rather than the laboring classes, would rise up against the managerial class and reassert the role of creative production. Of course, for the neo-Marxist critic, this is just a feud within bourgeois culture.

Veblen's narrative therefore focuses on concepts of excess and on the earth. Leisure pertains to an excess of time above the necessities of subsistence and the labor to achieve it. Consumerism and conspicuous consumption are symptoms of this excess. For other critics, this consumption is elaborated as the malevolent purveyance of signs with no substance.

Veblen's account of the archaic origins of the class system predates the structuralist school of anthropology that bases its theories on the workings of signs and language. It is on the subject of difference that the structuralist anthropological account of the gift articulates its stand against free-market economics.[151]

Veblen's narrative presents a series of dichotomies pertaining to class, but ignores the *system* of oppositions and differences that pervade cultural phenomena. From Mauss's account of the gift derive Lévi-Strauss's theories of culture and language. Lévi-Strauss acknowledges his debt to Mauss in articulating the central role of exchange in archaic communities, particularly the exchange of women as marriage partners between communities.[152] The exchange of women brings to mind its opposite, which for Levi-Strauss is incest, marrying one's own kind. The need for genetic diversity engenders a sense that one should not stay with the same but participate in the realm of the different, take the risk of venturing into the world of a collective that is not one's own. The gift, whether a marriage partner or an item of jewelry, is already a sign of difference, a symbolic encounter with the other. The theory of language and culture known as "structuralism," to which Lévi-Strauss subscribes, is pervaded by concepts of difference. The structuralist project also informs Bataille's, Debord's, and Baudrillard's tortured metaphors of difference, and the linguistics of spectacle, symbol, and sign. I will return to the matter of difference under the theme of transgression.

Internet Society and the Gift

In examining the gift society, we should note that giving on the Internet offers some major differences to the ancient legacy of giving. The Internet gift society is a highly globalized and technologized entity, a product of late modernity. To ignore as much is to fall into the trap of the technoromantics, to see the Internet as providing a nostalgic return to an idealized tribal or craft-based condition.

Castells provides a helpful account of the social structure of the Internet in support of the presence of the substrate of the society of the gift. For Castells, it is the techno-elites that have formed the basis of Internet culture.[153] As we have seen, the development of the Internet was driven by a meritocracy rooted in universities and scientific research establishments, for whom the maintenance of a network of contacts, collaborations, and peer esteem are the primary values, above pecuniary interest. This scholarly community is supplemented by those university workers and graduates who constitute the hacker community: dedicated, technically skilled, and creative communities of programmers who sustain and enhance their productivity and sociability through the Internet. Participation in open-source development captures the ethos of this culture. "Virtual communitarians" are the diverse hobbyists and users of the Internet who thrive on life online and who promote its benefits, as exemplified by the

users of the WELL in the 1980s, online descendants of the 1960s counterculture movements as celebrated in Rheingold's book *Virtual Communities*.[154] Then
there are the entrepreneurs who trade on the promise of the technology to gain
financial backing and bring innovations to the marketplace. For Castells, these
four cultures (the techno-elites, the hackers, the virtual communitarians, and
the entrepreneurs) interacted to conceive and determine the character of the Internet as we see it today. Presumably this is in contrast to comparable ubiquitous technologies conceived and promoted through business motives, such as
the development of other forms of telecommunications, the railroads, the spread
of the automobile, or the development of pharmaceuticals or biotechnology.
Castells's account of the culture of the Internet diminishes the pecuniary motive in favor of a giving one. Even Internet entrepreneurs seem driven by noncommercial motives. They are "creators rather than businessmen, closer to the
artist's culture than to the traditional corporate culture."[155]

Castells does not explore this issue, but it seems to me that Internet culture
(so presented) gives conspicuous expression to what is evident in so many other
areas of work. The idea of "the professional" has always been an attempt to
demonstrate that a discipline is above its self-serving business interests. Education, health care, law, architecture, and engineering come to mind as areas of
work in which a sense of responsibility toward some cause outside self-interest,
and dedication beyond what is remunerable, are enshrined in codes of conduct,
and the disciplines' exemplars, histories, and canonic texts. Such an appeal is no
less evident in the tradition of trades, guilds, and unions. It is corporatization,
the profit motive, and self-interest that have the character of a late arrival.

Sociologists, particularly from the political left, might think an apologia on
behalf of Internet economics is necessary on three counts. First, the disciplines
implicated in the Internet's development have not traditionally been those that
formalize and restrict entry on the basis of an ethical code, as do the learned professions. Professional organization, rigorous entry criteria, and codes of conduct
are not as powerful among the sciences that were served by the embryonic
Internet as it is among more clearly defined professional communities. More
particularly, entry to the disciplines of software engineering, computer programming, and digital design are less regulated than other fields. Appeals to the
altruism of its founders, the valorization of open-source and gift economics, are
as much about a series of disciplines seeking professional identity as is the discovery of new forms of sociality and production, or the revival of the sociality of
the gift. Second, the conspicuous promise of lucrative reward and the rapid

growth in e-business have amplified the commercial aspects of the Internet. There is some justification in reviving the Internet's history and origins in a grassroots meritocracy, as a way of distancing it from vulgar commerce. Third, commerce is such an important part of contemporary society, including the Internet, and the causal narrative of self-interest is so potent, that any means of rehabilitating commerce is to be welcomed by those who would hold to the grassroots and egalitarian ethos of the Internet. It is not just that the Internet will be restored to its rightful condition, but economics might be rehabilitated.

The philosophy of the gift society is expounded by and developed from Mauss's attempts to subvert the hold of free-market economics, utilitarianism, economic rationalism, and economic determinism. The philosophy of the gift provides a potent antidote to Smith's assertion of self-interest as the primary motivation of human transactions and exchange. If exchange is founded on the culturally rich interactions of the gift, then self-interest is simply its modern manifestation, a feature of certain limited economic models and practices. The gift brings to mind the character of modern economics by way of contrast. For Godbout, "the gift slips through the cracks everywhere, spills over, finds its way, adds something to what the utilitarian relationship tries to reduce to its simplest expression, a monetary expression."[156] The primordiality of the gift points to a substrate of complex and conflictual social interactions, without resorting to Ruskinesque concepts of honor, duty, or sacrifice.[157] As Derrida says of Mauss's case for the gift, it is motivated by "an ethics and politics that tend to valorize the generosity of the giving-being."[158]

The Transgressional Gift

But as suggested by Bataille, the gift, particularly in its manifestation as potlatch, bears the seeds of class struggle and oppression. The gift already transgresses.

Contrary to the gift, in the economic transaction money is exchanged for goods or labor. The transaction may involve a promise to pay or a promise to deliver, invoking concepts of credit and guarantee. The economic transaction also participates in a contract between two parties, the buyer and the seller. If either party is unhappy with the transaction, or it does not take place as agreed, then the buyer or the seller might go to the competition, which may provide better value for money, or a better offer. In support of the free market, there is also recourse to the paraphernalia of the law. Under the free-market economy, there may also be state intervention to ensure that the market remains free, that is, that monopolies do not develop that diminish competition or restrict freedoms (as exemplified in the antitrust case against Microsoft). There are various safety nets, such as state-funded welfare, for those who cannot gain enough for their labor and those who cannot pay. Taxation is levied for those goods and services that cannot be provided by the free market and to pay for the services provided by the state. Of course, governments seek to control economies, by legislating how much money banks may lend, by adjusting their own spending, and by adjusting the rate at which interest is charged on lendings from government reserves.[159] By way of contrast, the gift society operates outside the public scrutiny of the larger economic system as laid out by economic theorists such as Smith, Ricardo, Marx, Marshall, Keynes,[160] and Friedman.[161] A dealing in the gift lacks the "disinterestedness" of the economic transaction.[162]

Though there may be much to learn from the archaic gift society, it unfortunately offers a poor model for the late modern world. In the contemporary gift society, there may be obligation but there is no security. Dependence on gifts entails risk. We are familiar with the supposed generosity of the feudal nobility and its remnant to provide for servants and laborers, with no recourse if enough is not given. Today there are still those who rely on the handout to make a living, the need in some quarters to rely on gratuities, or tips, for services, and the lot of clerics in some religious establishments to rely on voluntary contributions for support. Gifts are offered in lieu of wages and retirement benefits. There is also the situation in which an employer may be generous with discretionary gifts and bonuses, while unforthcoming with adequate wages and work conditions, or the tenant or debtor who would give gifts and participate in the game of gratitude, but fails to pay the debt or pay it on time. There is also the bribe, the gift as an accompaniment or inducement to an economic transaction, a variant of the gift that is not particularly welcomed, but that places the receiver under an obligation, or absolves the giver from the penalty of some misdemeanor or other. Such gift practices fit uncomfortably with the modern economic order, not least in the difficulties they present in settling disputes and their operation outside the tax system.

As a leading example of gift culture at work in the modern world, the open-source ethos may be limited to certain spheres of operation. According to Torvalds, the development of the Linux operating system depended on the "benevolence" of his "dictatorship." There were apparently hundreds of thousands of volunteer software developers working on improvements to the operating system. Torvalds would not delegate but wait for people to come forward with changes, which he would approve or reject. Apparently the motivation for people contributing to the enterprise was that they enjoyed what they were doing, they were committed to the open-source philosophy, and the developers would gain recognition, which would make them more marketable to employers. For Torvalds, the system worked on trust, which the volunteer developers were prepared to invest in him. He led by example, in his technical skill, his dedication, and the trust that he was not creaming off profits from the free labors of others. The gift of such labors seems to work well in the hobby context of hacker culture, but Torvalds admits difficulty in translating the philosophy to the corporate world. Why should a volunteer developer contribute to a corporate enterprise and see no financial return? How does a corporate executive develop the same kind of moral trustworthiness and engender the same respect for technical expertise?

For Romantic critics of free-market economics, and for Marx, it is in the malformed contracts for wages and labor that we look for exploitation, domination, and oppression, and those who seek control over profits: those who own the capital or control the labor. But we can also look to the gift itself for what is corrupt and exploitative. As we have intimated from Bataille, the gift is already fraught with aberrance and unfair dealing, well understood in the destructive practices of the potlatch. It promotes difference and relies on maintaining an imbalance between giver and recipient. There are many types of gift exchange, not all of which speak of beneficence: the unrequited gift, the unwelcome gift, the poisoned gift, the withdrawn gift, and the gift as a transgression of good and appropriate contracts.

For Derrida, the latter is summed up by the gift of the counterfeit coin in the short story by Baudelaire. This marginal transaction brings to light the problems and contradictions inherent in the idea of the gift. As explained at the start of this chapter, the story concerns two gentleman friends who leave a tobacconist's. One has been shortchanged by being passed a coin that he sees is obviously counterfeit. The gentleman chooses not to return to the shop or report the passing of the coin to the police. But the two men soon encounter a beggar in the street, and both offer him money. The gift from the gentleman with the counterfeit coin seems particularly generous. The friend is clearly impressed until it is pointed out that it is the fake coin that was passed on. So begins a series of speculations about the value or otherwise of the giver's putative altruism. As is common in Derrida's writing, the example given is one that we might regard as unusual and marginal to normal exchange, but it becomes a new transgressive prototype on the basis of which to conduct a discussion of the gift.

At the outset we can observe that the passage of counterfeit money suggests a chain of transactions, each of which is problematic. The coin can be traced through a series of transactions, each of which might be fraught with similar tales and doubts. Should the coin be passed on, returned, or reported to the police? The beggar might indeed be arrested for unwittingly passing the coin on to someone else.

Derrida presents the dilemma of the counterfeit coin as the problem not only of the gift, or even of commerce, but of simulation in general. We could relate the problem of the gift of the counterfeit coin to the problems encountered in relation to text and image files in digital communications, in Internet economics. The medium invites so much copying and duplicating that we may well be suspicious of the authenticity of the objects presented through it, or of their status as gifts. As for the counterfeit coin, giving on the Internet can be a cheap form of altruism, trading in mimicry, ruse, and subterfuge.[163]

The gift is ostensibly given and received without obligation. The thing exchanged, its value, the timing, and a sense that it will be returned are uncertain. As we have seen, the gift can be characterized by surprise. If these characteristics were fixed, then we would be in the realm of obligation and contract. But in spite of this indeterminacy, one gift does lead to another. There is, after all, something expected about the gift. It is predictable, intentional, in archaic society as well as in our own. The giver offers a box of chocolates. Some moments, days, weeks, or months later the receiver returns a meal, or a bottle of wine, and the cycle of reciprocal giving continues if the relationship is to remain in the same condition, or the cycle is perhaps terminated.

For Derrida, this dual characteristic of the gift—that it is both unexpected and expected, accidental and causal, conditional and unconditional—constitutes a paradox. The gift is at precisely this juncture between surprise and certainty: The gift (and the event) "are decisive and they must therefore tear the fabric, interrupt the continuum of a narrative that nevertheless they call for, they must perturb the order of causalities: in an instant."[164] In everyday language the idea of the gift relies on narratives of reciprocation, expectation, anticipation, returning like for like, appropriateness, social norms and practices, appeasement, ties within the family and across communal boundaries. The surprise of the gift translates into a paradox. Not only is the gift a transgression against the modern transaction, its contracts, and its obligations, the gift is also a transgression against common sense, against a coherent understanding.

What of excess as transgression? For Bataille, the gift is born of excess, the potlatch, and is already transgressive. Derrida also provides an account of excess in his critique of those who appeal to the reality of essentials (such as free-market "fundamentalists").[165] For free-market economics, the gift is an excess. It is not essential to economic transactions. It is also subsumed within economic models. The important thing in the market is economic exchange. That people might wish to give things away for nothing belongs within the realm of individual motives, and is outside the study of economics, which is only concerned with its economic "effects." For Marshall, the economist does not seek to study individuals by their "mental and spiritual characteristics,"[166] but in terms of what people are prepared to pay. So we cannot fathom how a person values drinking coffee compared with getting home early. But when a person is unable to decide between spending his loose change on a cup of coffee or a bus fare, then we may assume they are valued equally on that particular occasion.[167] For free-market economics (and utilitarianism), altruism is equally private and can be dealt with only in terms of outward manifestations of utility. Economics lays claim to the essential scrutability of monetary value and the monetary transaction, and it consigns altruism, and the gift, to the secret realms of private motivation and the inner life.

As made vivid in Derrida's account, philosophy has long traded in the polarity between the essential and the inessential, or essence and accidence. There are essential characteristics of an object without which it would not be what it is. The accidental properties are incidental, are supplemental, and represent an excess. So we might say that the essence of the economic exchange is what people end up paying, whereas motives are accidental (supplemental) to an understanding of the economic system, or we might assert that self-interest is the essence of the economic system, whereas altruism is inessential.[168] Such discussion participates in the metaphysics of excess, that there is an essential core, an authentic origin, against the inessential.

Arguably, in opposing itself to the economic order, the case for primordiality participates in this metaphysics, in its assertion that the culture of giving and receiving gifts comes before commerce and more accurately reflects the character of the human condition. For the phenomenologist, economic exchange is supplemental. It represents an excess. The aim of such an argument is to decrease the importance of that to which we normally ascribe essence, and to privilege the inessential or excessive.[169]

So the arguments for the primordiality of the gift suggest a reversal. If the cultural practices of the gift are the norm, then altruism is no mystery. In fact, we do not need a word such as "altruism" to bring to account our preparedness to give, the development of the Internet, or the workings of open-source software development. We are already giving beings. In Heidegger's terms, we are already "being-with," or in sociological terms we are social beings.[170] From this perspective, the interesting question is: How is it that we are able to convert certain social interactions into this rarefied understanding known as "self-interest" or "utility?" By the logic of this inquiry, the gift is not incidental but essential. It is the rarefied construction of the economic transaction that is superfluous to an understanding of the human condition. The economic transaction is a limited form of the gift, which denies the whole complex of human relations and the character of the thing.

But Derrida further makes the case that both economics and the gift are subject to something more basic. Following his strategy of deconstruction (in the case of writing and speech), we could identify this fundament as the "proto-gift," and its characteristic of circulation.[171] We have already made reference to the primacy of repetition and circulation. Derrida draws attention to their working: "circular exchange, circulation of goods, products, monetary signs or merchandise, amortization of expenditures, revenues, substitution of use values and exchange values. This motif of circulation can lead one to think that the law of economy is the—circular—return to the point of departure, to the origin, also to the home."[172] The gift, as well as economics, participates in this game of return, though it also tries to break the circle. So both economics and the gift are indebted to circulation, as a founding characteristic. By implication, everything comes back to repetition.

But Derrida goes even further than these attempts to establish a foundation to sociability, when he asserts that there is no essence or foundation in any case. Neither the gift nor the monetary transaction warrant the designation of being essential. Another way of putting it is to say that the essential is already full of problems, contradictions, and paradoxes. If the gift forms the basis of the transaction, then it does so as an impossibility. The gift is, in fact, an impossibility. If you expect a gift or feel it is your due, then it does not function as a gift; rather we are in the realms of obligation and contract. The gift is also "annulled each time there is restitution or countergift."[173] So receiving something back, as in the seasonal exchange of gifts, is not really giving at all, but exchanging.[174] We still talk about the gift, but it is a paradoxical giving. Less obviously, Derrida also asserts that to receive the gift also negates the gift: "As soon as the other accepts, as soon as he or she takes, there is no more gift. . . . There is no more gift as soon as the other *receives*—and even if she refuses the gift that she has perceived or recognized as gift. As soon as she keeps for the gift the signification of gift, she loses it, there is no more *gift*."[175] Once the gift is received, it is the receiver's property, and it ceases to function as gift, even if the receiver chooses to hold on to the object received as significant by virtue of being a gift (e.g., from one's grandmother). The gift kept as a trophy is even less the gift as the moment has passed. If the giver acknowledges that she has given or is about to give a gift then it is already reciprocated by "symbolic recognition." The accompanying self-congratulation of the giver symbolically gives back to the giver the value of what he has given, or is about to give. So if the gift is to feature as a primordial entity, then it does so as "an impossibility." For Derrida, this is no denigration of the gift, or insult to the scholarship surrounding it. Rather the gift typifies the paradox of all transactions, or all foundations, and, a familiar theme of Derrida's, of language and textuality: "language is as well a phenomenon of gift-countergift, of giving-taking—and of exchange."[176]

What of difference and its amplification in the gift? Derrida problematizes a series of differences, keeping them in play as differences, presenting them as irreconcilable: the commercial transaction and the gift, the authentic and the counterfeit, the gift and the countergift. He also shows that each is already imbued with its opposite. Each is already implicated in the agonistic play of differences for its existence.

Derrida also introduces time into a consideration of the reciprocation of the gift and countergift. The imbalance engendered by the gift implicates time. The reciprocation of the gift can be at some time distant from the giving. For Godbout, "Time is at the heart of the gift and reciprocity, while the elimination of time is at the core of a mercantile relationship."[177] The cyclical movement of the gift and countergift, or of the spiral of extravagance that is the potlatch, suggest a momentum created by a state of imbalance. It is not that the books have to be balanced, but that each time a gift is reciprocated then the imbalance has to be reinstated by one or other of the parties. As with any competition, the objective is not to form some state of equivalence with the opponent but rather assert a difference, an inequality. The practices of the potlatch make this obvious in the case of the archaic gift society. Whether the imbalance is to a superior or inferior position is also only a secondary consideration.

As well as promoting difference, what is offered in the gift is time, the possibility of delay before the gift is reciprocated. The promises purveyed by Internet culture, of free, open, and egalitarian access to all information and to one another, is a gift that exploits time in this way. The gift of utopia is on hold, exploiting the license granted to the gift for indefinite delay. Digital utopia grants time (as gift) to stave off complaint about the current, inadequate state of digital technology.

The Event

The gift also takes place at a moment in time. In Baudelaire's story "Counterfeit Money," the gentleman wished to create an event in the life of the beggar, a moment of significance. Giving often has this character. Everything leads to the moment at which the gift is revealed, with little thought for its persistence as gift beyond that event. Of course, the event has soon passed. What little presence the gift has is only for an instant.

In this respect the gift constitutes the archetypal event, a moment in time. What is an event? An event may be one of a series. There is the historical event, the political event, the event as reported in the news, a festive occasion, an event in a play, a move in a game, a language event, a computer event, a great moment in economics, the stock market crash, a perturbation in the linear flow, making one's first million, going bankrupt, winning the lottery, or receiving a spectacular payout. An economic transaction can appear as an event. Whereas for Heidegger we are driven by a sense of expectation, for Derrida the chief characteristic of any event is that it takes us by surprise.[178] It creeps up behind us. We really do not know what is coming next. Surprise, discontinuity, and rupture are the basic characteristics of the event. As for the gift, the event is also animated by contradiction and paradox. This contrasts with the moment within a teleology, the original or final moment, the moment within a causal chain, or in the grand sweep of history. For Tschumi, the architectural design theorist, the event is as the surrealists saw it, the incongruous moment, a sewing machine and an umbrella on a dissecting table.[179] The event as such contrasts with great moments in the development of political economy, communist revolutions, the growth of the Internet, urban developments, and architectural accomplishments. The event is that which has not yet been incorporated into the grand narrative, or it is the event unpicked from its teleology and re-presented as a disconnected moment.[180] The event is most typified by transgression: breaking and entering, an eruption of violence, the suicide attack, all in the spirit of the bloody self-destruction of the potlatch.

The paradox of the gift is also the paradox of the event. What happens to events when we describe them as gifts? What happens to the regular transaction seen as a subspecies of gift, or as a transgressive gift, the gift as a metaphor for the transaction?

Transaction as Gift

We have considered the gift as a transgression against the transaction. The gift is also transgressed against. It can be appropriated and violated by commerce. The gift can be offered as a ruse to conceal a commercial transaction. It can appear as an abuse of the good faith engendered by the gift. An examination of the transaction in contemporary economic practices makes gestures toward the gift society, or at least it participates in the "aura," or ruse, of the gift. How does the e-commerce transaction appear under the metaphor of the gift?

Retail companies are anxious to tap into an impression that they and consumers are participating in the culture of the gift. As an obvious case, it is in a company's interest to be seen to be supporting charitable causes, even if doing so with the profits earned from the investment of its clients and the sale of goods in the market. More significantly, the enthusiasm within corporate retail at providing a service beyond the mere provision of the goods on sale suggests a propensity on the part of the seller to convey an aura of generosity toward the customer.[181] Such generosity extends to free samples, special offers, price reductions, and opportunities to try something out before buying it. In any transaction a certain amount has to be given away. As designers, artists, and tradespeople know, it is often necessary to offer the proposal, the sketch, the competitive tender as gift. Purchasing an online train ticket offers a buyer free timetables and planning services. For other goods, free catalogues exist. Not only is this information needed in order to make an appropriate purchase, or to make comparisons with the opposition, but it is an excuse for fostering a sense of participation in the beneficence of the retailer. The vendor gives the appearance of generosity, of an openness, which perhaps engenders trust.

In terms of their interaction with consumers, the gift ethos also provides the impression of a diminished obligation on the part of the buyer. There is a freedom to purchase or not to purchase, freedom to choose from a range of goods, and even a freedom to withdraw from the purchase, change one's mind, and return the goods. As for the gift, goods do not have to be received or reciprocated. There are also schemes to promote customer loyalty, as if the consumer is participating in a community based on a particular product line, supplier, or service. Not only is the consumer encouraged to purchase regularly from the same supermarket, or online store, but she is granted a membership or loyalty card, which entitles her to certain benefits, some of which are overtly presented as gifts. Presumably this sense of participation in a gift regime, whether appropriated or not, compensates for the inconvenience to the customer of maintaining records of, and redeeming, such benefits, not to mention the added cost of administering the scheme, which is passed on to the consumer. Of course, such ruses serve to maintain the repetitive aspects of consumption. The ambition of the retailer is to encourage repeated return and a regular commitment to shopping at that source. Within this regular regime the retailer is interested in providing an opportunity for surprise. Seasonal sales and special offers may wear thin, but retailers are constantly looking for opportunities to play with the rhythm that further promotes the sense of the gift.

The gift also speaks of the event, the special occasion. The retail experience is never just a matter of selecting goods, parting with money, and accepting delivery. It is clear that retail philosophy seeks to make an event out of shopping.[182] Part of the gift aspect of the retailer is to provide an entertainment, a festive event, for free. So there is the pastime of window shopping,[183] the opportunity to promenade down the high street, the opportunity for the chance encounter with friends and familiar faces, pastimes with which the paraphernalia of online shopping must compete. Goods are often packaged to defer or prolong the sense of surprise and occasion. Much is made of the micropractices of receiving goods. We say thank you, and some people even evince extremes of gratitude for what they have just paid for. We expect the gift of purchased goods to be accompanied by eye contact and a smile, even from the checkout teller. Even vending machines are capable of providing a sense of occasion, inducing a mechanical operation to return a prize. Home delivery amplifies the trappings of the gift, as the gift is conveyed to one's doorstep. Apart from these modes of delivery going wrong, there are alternatives that diminish the occasion of the purchase as gift. Having someone else do our shopping, stocking the refrigerator, secreting a new shirt on a hanger in the wardrobe, or invisibly installing a brand new hi-fi may carry its own benefits and the trappings of the leisured classes, but each denies us the sense of occasion associated with the gift. So, too, one suspects that the gift occasion is diminished by having to stand in line at the rear entrance of a furniture store to take possession of goods, to make a purchase and then wait a week for it to arrive in the shop, or to conduct purchases through the usual business-to-business procedures involving purchasing departments, catalogues, anonymous purchase orders, requisitions, and invoices. Presumably smart retail policy treats the transfer of goods in the spirit of the gift, even for business-to-business transactions, where gifts, free samples, visits by sales representatives, invitations to trade fairs, and product launches compensate for the sterility of the transaction as event. Online retail attempts to substitute other means for maintaining the gift character of the consumer event, including dynamic graphics, and interactives that give consumers the impression they are customizing products to their own requirements, that allow product selection and combination, and that present information, links, activities and games as free gifts.

A further means by which retail shows its commitment to the ethos of the gift is in the diminution of the occasion of the transfer of payment. Whereas much can be made of the receipt of goods, the transfer of cash is diminished. In retail, the need to negotiate price is long abandoned, except in certain well-defined cases (bazaars and auctions). Clearly it is less important to carry cash in the electronic economy, and funds can be accessed immediately. The use of direct debit and credit cards diminishes the occasion of money transfer further. Such facilities render the transfer of money invisible and incidental. With credit it is possible to defer the balancing of the books, for those within the credit system. Uncoupling the receipt of goods and services from the transfer of cash is a long-established practice in the case of professional services beholden to the gift ethos, where an invoice might be dispatched at the end of the month for services rendered by the dentist, accountant, or architect. The use of regular subscription services provides a further example of this uncoupling of service from payment, where roadside car repair, heating maintenance, and the insurance payout comes as if a gift from some benevolent carer.

Retail can also participate in the gift ethos by facilitating giving to others. The obvious case is by tapping into and even inventing seasonal and festive occasions. Shops and online retail provide gift tokens and wedding list services. For some products it makes good sense to encourage the formation of communities of consumers, as in the case of specialized computer software: computer-aided design systems, for example. User groups form around such software with individuals providing support for each other and feedback for the developers. Such software is not always a one-off purchase. Consumers might purchase an annual license, which entitles them to upgrades and special assistance with problems. Utilitarian arguments can be drawn in support of the approach, but the value of the social aspects of consumption is undeniable. This sociality also implicates the gift. Members of the user community give freely of their expertise and labor in the interest of the group. The publication of reviews from purchasers by online booksellers, however suspect, also taps into this aspect of the gift society. Sometimes there is "behavioral feedback" through monitoring of purchases and navigational activity in online retail sites. Castells sees this "co-operation" among customers and providers as the key to innovation in computer systems and e-commerce: "customers are producers, as they provide critical information by their behavior, and their demands, helping e-companies con-stantly to modify their products and services."[184] Sometimes consumers dem-onstrate a power to transform commodities and render them in some way "authentically" their own, as in the case of fan clubs able to appropriate and transform soaps and popular programs presented in the mass media to their own ends.[185]

Retailers, traders, and advertisers are undoubtedly skilled at exploiting any means to improve sales. By the construction presented here, they do so by tap-ping into the many aspects of the gift society, and this not only because people like to think they are getting things cheaply. There is the suggestion of surprise, in the unexpected experience, the special offer, the unexpected and incongruous element of an advertising strategy. There is the suggestion of excess, in creating an impression of limitless product ranges, freedom, choice, and the advertised wealth, health, and happiness in excess of the norm to be conferred by the prod-uct. There is the suggestion of amplified difference, in the bargain, as if the seller is offering us a product that is better than our money can buy, and customer ser-vices, the cost of which is entirely in the consumer's favor. It is possible to see the consumer as being duped in this enterprise, but it may also be the case that consumers want it to be so. They would rather see themselves as participants in a culture of the gift than calculating players in the instrumental utility of the free market. The free market as gift society is clearly fraught with paradox, which, according to Derrida, is within the nature of the gift. It is not simply that the gift is offered in opposition to the free market and self-interest but that the appeal to the gift already invokes concepts of the market in its explanation, at least as presented in the primordial account, by Mauss and others.

The potlatch reminds us of conspicuous consumption, certainly, but also the agonistic, competitive aspect of buying and selling. Not only is there competi-tion between sellers, but between sellers and customers. The process of hag-gling, bargaining, and various forms of auction are obvious examples, and they exploit the game quality of commerce. But the extent to which retailers can trade on the gift is also a game. To what extent is the consumer taken in by the aura of the gift: corporate courtesy, extended services, sales, prizes, loyalty schemes, and user groups? In the case of auctions and haggling, there is competition, but there is also a meta-game in play. If consumers think they are not getting a good deal, or that the game is rigged, then they will not want to play. The game becomes a matter of just how far the game can be taken. The rapid evolution of diverse advertising and marketing strategies attest to this, as do the restless changes in online retail strategies.

Retail and commerce can adopt the overtly transgressional aspects of the gift, as in the gift as bribe. The free sample, special offer, two-for-the-price-of-one, can be construed as the offer of gifts intended to instill an obligation, a debt, to buy, a sense of loyalty to the seller. This works to the extent that buying and selling build on the gift ethos. Sellers can resort to any number of means to invoke an obligation to buy, or to trap buyers into a commitment. There are many examples of such strategies in software and hardware sales. Buyers get caught in a spiral of upgrades, which initially are presented as a privilege. Buyers are exhorted to upgrade to a better operating system, which in turn requires more hardware memory to operate optimally. In spite of promises that the application programs will run on the new operating system, there are the inevitable bugs, requiring patches and upgrades. One has to be a committed hobbyist, a hacker of sorts, to fully participate in the benefits of computer culture and its gifts of more and better, and to be prepared to partake in a cycle of upgrades, patches, and online problem solving. The analogy has been drawn to using a car, as if one has to read car magazines, join car clubs, or become a mechanic to keep on the road. Much of the electronic gift culture seems designed to draw one in not only as a participant, but as a pundit, an unwilling member of a family rather than just a user. Not everyone is interested in, or capable of, full membership. Digital culture provides exaggerated demarcation between being in or out of the consumer family.

The gift is worthy of suspicion in other ways. What of the poisonous gift? The obvious case is the computer virus that comes through the Internet, the Trojan horse as emissary of destruction. In turn there is anti-virus software, co-implicated in a kind of arms race, for all we know marketed by the perpetrators of the poisoned gifts themselves, engendering suspicion of a form of commerce not distant from a protection racket.[186] There is also the unwanted gift of email (spam) clogging up the world's mail servers and frustrating the management of personal and business correspondence. We are also aware of the role of communications technologies, including the Internet in the promotion of various forms of terror: the organization of a living missile dispatched from the blue of the Manhattan sky, an incendiary carpet dropped over the Tora Bora mountains.

What of the counterfeit coin? This is the gift that is not what it purports to be. It is in fact worth substantially less than its face value, or it will get us into trouble if cashed in. The obvious example is a gift of "cracked" software by a friend or illegal dealer. The gift ethos brings to mind the black market in software, which seems to hold sway in the domestic sphere at least, where it may so far go undetected. In some cases the major burden of paying for software seems to reside in institutions and companies who are readily audited. While they could never openly sanction the trade in pirated software, it may be that software developers and publishers have at least some interest in the clandestine and illegal distribution of their software, through the preparation of an informed and committed clientele, who may later have an influence in business and institutional purchases.[187]

But then, in keeping with the tenets of conspicuous consumption and its bourgeois inheritance in the potlatch, so little of what is presented in the marketplace is what it seems to be. Advertising renders products counterfeit. The product is other than what the brand name and its promise purport it to be. Sometimes we buy the brand without paying heed to the product, and in some markets it is possible to buy watches and clothing that bear the favored brand and the appearance, but not the originality, nor often the functionality and performance. As in the trade of counterfeit coins, consumer culture trades in promises—empty signs, many of which can never be cashed in.

Then there is the gift that never arrives, or arrives late. There is the promise of the next release. Or instead of the product as contracted, we receive a trifling gift, or a further promise. In fact, many consumers don't want superior software with more features in the future. They just want the current offering to fulfill its contract, to work properly. Then there is the promise as the basis of the financial system, payment in stock options rather than cash or capital, or the Internet entrepreneur's raising of funds by selling the future. For Derrida, such promises characterize language in general. There is no actual delivery, just the purveying of a series of interlinked signs (or signifiers). Nothing is signified by a promise apart from another promise, in endless regress.

Insofar as commercial strategies and consumer culture exploit the gift, they may also have to bear its burden. Overindulgence, the bribe, poison, the counterfeit, and the delayed arrival are not alien to the gift but characterize it, because they characterize language.

The gift is already transgressive in that it crosses boundaries. One tribal community passes something of its own to another community. The gift keeps alive the idea that something that is yours was once mine, or perhaps is still mine. It is sometimes easier to ascribe a gift to its previous owner than it is to recall from where something was purchased. In terms of language, the gift provides a tangible instance of metaphor,[188] ascribing the thing a name that belongs to something else, putting something into the "wrong" category: a house is a machine; the chief is an eagle; the computer is a brain. In the case of the gift, this is translated to the transferal of category membership: my pound note is yours; my bottle of wine is his to keep; this jewelry that she bought with her own money is her friend's. Like metaphor, the gift has the capacity to provoke by virtue of its transgression, and it does so with full recourse to its paradoxical and ambiguous character. The metaphor of the gift can also illuminate, through an examination of the commercial transaction *as* gift.

We can think of the unusual gift and its capacity to provoke disturbance, suspicion, and new practices and understandings, revealing a complex of relations through its intrusion. According to one commentator, the gift society of the Internet contributes to a new and subversive kind of democracy, but it is one that includes "aspects of trickery, pleasure, fluidity and self-gratification,"[189] and the acquisition of small freedoms from corporate structures through subterfuge. As gift, we may suppose that the Internet, and its content, constitutes an intrusion as it conducts its e-business, revealing and concealing aspects of the network economy and of the homely securities into which it intrudes.

The persistence of the gift stands out as an anomaly in the network economy. I defined the gift in terms of its investment in *surprise, excess,* and *difference.* To the extent that we can identify these phenomena in the network economy, they provide evidence of the gift, at least in rudimentary or remnant form. The contribution of each was discussed under four headings, four explanations, provided by scholars to account for the gift. The *utilitarian* explanation seeks to position the gift within usual economic considerations. People give that they might get something back, or contribute on the basis that the greatest good is being promulgated. The *romantic* position appeals to motivations that are placed above commerce, such as altruism, the preserve of the artist and creator. The *phenomenological* position develops from the primordiality of the gift, that is, the evidence from anthropology that commerce is already imbued with the characteristics of the gift. In a lengthy excursion, I considered the contrast often promulgated between commodities and (authentic) things, the role of repetition in surprise, the peculiar practice of the potlatch as a manifestation of the propensity toward excess, the relationship engendered by the gift and its affinities with the ground (the culture of agriculture versus the hunter), and the nature of the impulse toward "self-destruction" within consumer culture. I related all of these to the gift in the network economy. My conclusion is that, whatever the primordial status of the gift, it represents a disturbed category of social interaction, fraught with contradiction. The gift belongs within a culture of *transgression*. This brought to light the disjunctive character of "the event" and provoked a consideration of how the transgressive character of the gift is present in economic transactions. Theories of the gift provide a valuable entry point to understanding the unusual aspects of the network economy, but this position is eclipsed by the importance of the threshold, and other metaphors of boundary and transgression, to be addressed in chapter 5.

Whether or not we agree with the primacy of gift culture, the chapter has served as a means of structuring and canvassing many of the major issues that confront the network economy: risk, open-source and free software, software piracy, prediction, investment, conspicuous consumption, commodity fetish, addiction, online pornography, globalization, leisure, professionalism, competition, and marketing strategies. I have attempted to align these issues with the design thinking with which this book began. Edgy design does not take much for granted and seeks out the marginal, the odd juxtaposition, the hybrid condition, and the strange metaphor. This sets the stage for my final foray into the network economy, the position of the gift in narratives of the threshold.

5

Liminal Computing

Economic activity hits limits. According to the economist Alfred Marshall, a businessperson will increase her capital investment until reaching an "outer limit, or margin, of profitableness."[1] This is a point beyond which further investment will hardly produce any profit, and she may even lose money. This is a limiting moment in the growth of a business at which profit turns to loss. Growth is limited in any case. For Malthus, "Population is necessarily limited by the means of subsistence."[2] Population growth has its ceiling. No one yet knows the limits to growth of the network economy, or the limits of the Internet. In fact, the story put out by the enthusiasts is of "limitlessness potential," freedom to move across boundaries without constraint. For some the Internet is a medium without limit.

A limit is simply a line defining a region, and it is related to the word "limen," or threshold.[3] The line marking the limit of one territory and the beginning of the next constitutes a threshold. The threshold is a helpful concept that allows for the possibility of passing over limits. Limits can be exceeded, which constitutes a move across a threshold from one condition to another. The visitor moves across the threshold from outside to inside. The threshold is marked architecturally by a doorway or step. It signifies a discontinuity in surface, environmental quality, security level, or comfort. Similarly, a Web portal provides a threshold, gateway, or door to information, resources, other Web sites, sometimes mediated by security systems, log-ins, firewalls, cryptography, and access protocols.

The threshold also describes a step in a process. If the temperature of water is raised slowly, it will reach a value where a very small increase will be accompanied by a threshold transition from a liquid to a gaseous state. Signal processing also invokes the concept of the threshold. For example, an increase in the intensity of a sound reaches a level (threshold) at which another state sets in, perhaps distortion, or a pain threshold in the listener. Electronic networks can be organized in such a way that the nodes of a network transmit signals when the intensity of the inputs from adjacent nodes reaches a certain threshold level. The propagation of signals in a neural network seems to depend on these threshold characteristics, from which the phenomenon of memory derives.[4]

The Latin for "threshold" is *limen,* a word stem that appears in variation in several important words.[5] The *subliminal* pertains to thought that is below the threshold of consciousness.[6] To *sublimate* is to push into unconsciousness. It also has a meaning derived from alchemy, apparently still used in chemistry, in which a solid substance turns into a vapor without melting, or a vapor condenses into a solid without passing through the liquid phase. It is also a purification process. According to some commentators, this is the derivation of the strange word *sublime.*[7] We think of the sublime as an elevated condition above the line, and yet its formation suggests a condition beneath (sub) the line. According to this reading, the sublime is a condition that undercuts, or exceeds, the threshold (between solid, liquid, and gas). Through an interesting inversion the sublime is therefore above the threshold. To the category of the sublime is attributed not only the uplifting and the pure but the inexpressible. For Lyotard, the sublime motivates the avant-garde painter in enabling us to see "only by making it impossible to see," or to "please only by causing pain."[8] In this the sublime is a transgression, a boundary crossing, the indeterminate condition reached at the limit. Digital networks can be described in these terms, as occasions that defy representation, or that in themselves attempt to give expression to the unrepresentable. It is not that the digital network raises us to a higher level of aspiration, but it arguably presents "the fact that the unpresentable exists."[9]

In digital circuitry a threshold is marked as a sudden step from one state to the next. In binary logic a signal is either on or off, or some intermediate condition derived from an accumulation of on-off states, according to the binary number system. The design of computer systems has to contend with and resist the abrupt nature of binary thresholding. The material world of doorways, steps, ledges, fences, and lines in the sand affords complex edge conditions, and ambiguous, rich, hybrid, and creative possibilities, without effort. In the binary world, it seems these complexities have to be deliberately manufactured.

In this light the gift presents as an archetype of the material threshold phenomenon, entailing complex human relationships. On the other hand, economic exchange appears as a harsher process, with greater affinity to binary functionality. To overstate the distinction, it seems as though each pertains to the threshold, but the threshold is either a complex transition (in the case of the gift), or tending to an abrupt demarcation (in the case of economic exchange).

The Gift and the Threshold

I concluded the last chapter by considering how the gift is implicated in transgression. Transgression is a matter of crossing boundaries, being where you are not supposed to be, occupying the wrong space. The gift is implicated in the boundary condition in several ways.

A community of friends and kin enjoys the free exchange of gifts. According to Aristotle, the household is an "association of persons, established according to nature for the satisfaction of daily needs."[10] In this community, goods, sustenance, and nurture are freely shared. The exchange of presents gives formal expression to this domestic communalism. In a family one takes for granted that gifts will be exchanged on festive or special occasions. The giving and receiving of gifts is the norm. This is not to say that gift giving is unconstrained or indiscriminate, or that all is harmonious within the aura of the gift. The gift may even be at the center of friction among family members. But the business of the gift is rightly conducted in the household. One way to mark the boundary of the household is to map this circuit of intimate gift exchange. With the family at the center of our conception of community, the gift marks our participation in any inner circle, favored group, community, polis, or nation. For Aristotle, we begin with family membership and proceed to citizenship in the city-state. By extension, participation in the exchange of gifts marks us as a community. Some commentators remark that this is the role of the gift in digital communities. We give time, service, and resources, and follow the appropriate conventions, to gain acceptance as a member of the digital family.[11]

The gift also serves to mark relationships across communities. As such it can appear as an ostentatious gesture, as when the representative of one nation brings a gift to the leader of another, or a business associate from one country brings presents to the household of his host in another. Here the gift may be presented from a respectful distance. It is not that the giver and receiver are now of the same ken, but the exchange is a gesture, a symbolic act, a sign, a simulation of what happens between intimates in the family. Such is the condition for so-called newbies in digital communities. Someone who wishes to gain entry to a circle of online friends, or garner information from a specialized support group, will take into account the appropriate exchange of information as a means of gaining access. Gift giving serves to demonstrate friendships and affinities between communities, while at the same time possibly highlighting their differences. Here the gift is at the meeting of boundaries. As well as the site of inter-community giving, the boundary is also the site of its malevolent obverse—siege, war, infiltration, and theft.[12] As suggested by Godbout and Hyde, were we not exchanging gifts, or trading, we would be exchanging gunfire and missiles.[13] Those malevolent toward digital communities resort to a similar arsenal: barraging someone or a group with unwanted messages, "flaming" with incendiary insults, propagating viruses, digital espionage, and "hacking."

Gifts between nations and families may also facilitate transition from one community to another, as when courting couples move into each other's spheres of intimacy. The gift eases the transition from the outside to the inside. Boundaries are reconfigured, or rather the gift is a way of gaining access to the inner circle. In each case the gift is implicated in the concept of the inside and the outside, whether it is an indication of the solidarity of the group, a means of one group dealing civilly with another, or a way of securing passage into the group.

So the gift brings to mind the boundary condition. In keeping with our philosophical legacy, we can think of the ancient Greek city, its fortification, and its sometimes hostile relations with neighboring cities. Several personalities inhabit the boundary condition, whose roles embody the institutionalized boundary. The bearer-of-gifts is the ambassador at the gate, waiting to cross the threshold. The enemy may also be there—the infiltrator, warrior, invading force, terrorist, the enemy laying siege, seeking entry, and conquest. Both the ambassador and the enemy momentarily occupy the boundary condition in crossing it, and their presence is transient and cataclysmic, presenting as an unusual event, or a breach. At the boundary there are also the asylum seekers, the refugees, the emigrants, the exiles—those seeking a safe haven either inside or outside the city. The condition of such people readily presents as the condition of the hero, the crosser of thresholds, the novitiate undergoing a rite of passage.[14] This is the subject of the heroic narrative, the first person in the computer game. In the Odysseus story the hero undergoes several transitions, a descent to the underworld, the return home, the passage from one island to the next, beset with perils, threats, temptations, rocky coastlines, and shipwreck.[15] The odyssey takes the hero across a steady succession of perilous thresholds.

But there are those who make their living from the edge condition. These include the border guard, the patrol, the protector, the concierge, the doorman, and the keeper of order. This person is the gatekeeper whose role it is to include or exclude, to ensure safe passage or to deny it. It is also the role of Janus, the two-headed god in Roman mythology, the god of gates and doors, looking in two directions, looking forward and looking back.[16] It is also the ferryman, Charon, who could be bribed with a coin to secure safe passage of the dead across the river Styx to Hades.[17] In folktales, the gatekeeper is commonly characterized as an ogre, a dragon, or a monster. For theorist of narrative form Joseph Campbell, the transition involves an entry to and emergence from the womb-state, a passage from the mortal to the suprahuman realm, as if through the belly of a whale: "That is why the approaches and entrances to temples are flanked and defended by colossal gargoyles: dragons, lions, devil-slayers with drawn swords, resentful dwarfs, winged bulls. These are the threshold guardians to ward away all incapable of encountering the higher silences within."[18] The gargoyles are the teeth of the whale. The boundary is also the condition of hybridity, of exaggerated difference, of the reassembly of parts. The monstrous Minotaur, Cyclops, Medusa, and Cerberus are antagonists in episodes of trial. Their conquest also marks the transition to the next region, a further stage in the journey.

Technologies feature in some people's narratives as monstrous. We recall Ruskin's account of the monstrous steam engine, the image of which arguably impedes his progress as a journeyman, or perhaps his progression across the threshold of acceptance. Negative accounts of the computer are frequently delivered as stories of impediment by the inscrutable thinking machine, resisting our commands, getting upset, breaking down through our own fault, and able to return vengeance. The computer is readily described as an enabler, but to the extent that it impedes progress it is commonly characterized as monstrous.

The power to include or exclude is also monstrous, and even mindless. The gatekeeper just carries out the orders proclaimed from the center. As at the customs desk, the student registry, or the door of the nightclub, the rules of civility are applied with a broad brush. For literary theorist Lewis Hyde, there is the law of the altar and that of the gate. Just as the hearth is at the center of the home, the altar is at the center of the city: "A person is treated differently depending on where he or she is. At the edge the law is harsher; at the altar there is more compassion."[19] Once you have entered then you are free to enjoy the benefits of admission, but not until there is a clear determination that you belong on the inside. The boundary offers resistance to entry. Digital networks provide a ready example of mindless adherence to the rule, and as such are positioned at the edge, devoid of compassion, and barring entry. There is no point in arguing with an ATM cash point, ticket machine, electronic gate, or security log-in.

Unlike the impersonal threshold condition of digital networks, the role of the gatekeeper implicates the gift in some measure. A bribe might be offered to appease the gatekeeper, and infiltration may be accomplished through the faux-gift, as in the case of the Trojan horse. The person on the edge is also implicated in commerce. In distinction to the gift or the act of violence, the commercial transaction is the third way of conducting affairs between those inside and those outside the community. Commerce enables interaction and the necessary passage of goods, without needing to appeal to family ties and the various obligations of the gift. It is a disinterested means of interaction, and thus of negotiating across the boundary. For Hyde, the most blatant extreme of commerce, which most marks the boundary, is usury, where money is loaned at interest to yield more money. So the moneylenders and usurers constitute another category of threshold inhabitant. Aristotle despised usury for its violation of the order of the household. Wealth should be earned through the honorable and necessary practice of household management, rather than making gain out of money itself: "the birth of money from money,"[20] which is altogether "unnatural." For Hyde: "Gift increases inside the circle, capital gains interest at the boundary."[21] So commerce is another way of marking the boundary. This is where money takes over from the gift and reinforces institutionalized boundaries. Of course the whole financial sector, amplified through the instantaneity of digital networks, is founded on usury: money is lent at interest; charges are levied for exchanging assets of varying degrees of liquidity; there are bankers, brokers, and agents. Funds course through networks, accreting profits independent of the labors and goods at the points of production and consumption.[22] These aspects of the network economy are at the edge of the familial confines of the city.

Liminal Dwellers

But there are those whose mode of being is precisely the threshold condition, yet who fall through the gaps set up by the state and its institutions. We can identify at least three characters who occupy the liminal condition, the thresholds and gateways of the city, though their influence extends beyond: the beggar, the trickster, and the cynic. I introduced the beggar in chapter 4, in Derrida's use of the story of counterfeit money by Baudelaire.[23]

The beggar's participation in the gift society marks him as an outsider to the group. The beggar at the gate can never participate fully in the community within. The beggar has nothing to give and at most is in receipt of the handout. The handout is not a means to inclusion, but is a further sign of exclusion. The beggar, unable to look after himself, is offered charity to keep him at bay, to stop him from being a nuisance or otherwise disturbing the sphere of the citizen. The beggar is readily discussed in the singular. The beggar is not really a participant. If he has the wit and the interest, then he is positioned as an observer outside the system. The beggar is also victim. Our narratives about the beggar show him as helpless, not in control, subject to disease or addiction. We assume the beggar is not at the boundary by choice. In *The Odyssey,* Homer describes the beggar as "a lounger at men's doors, rubbing his back against the posts, seeking for scraps."[24] In contemporary terms, we think of the homeless. Of course, the beggar category can be given too romantic a cast. In contemporary urban sociology, homelessness is a complex problem, involving individuals in a variety of life circumstances, each with their own condition and social situation. At the very least, they are in the company of those with very limited access to what commerce and the state have to offer, including global communications. Of course, in a pique of appropriation, we may think of the Internet as the province of vagrancy. There are chat room lurkers, and individuals cruising personals pages and erotic Web sites. But the metaphor is limited. The truly dispossessed are those excluded from this technological cornucopia. One needs to be part of the system, have the appropriate level of educational and training, and have a credit card and a home in order to connect to the network economy.

In contemporary usage, there is another word for the nonparticipating individual. This is the cynic. As we have seen, Diogenes the Cynic resided on the street as the homeless fanatic, ranting against the corruption of the city. He was reliant on the citizens' generosity in order to subsist. In contemporary terms, we readily ascribe to the corporate critic the term *cynic.* This is the non-believer, the skeptic of technological progress, the rejecter of the ideal and of utopia. The cynic may be skeptical of the gift, and may offer a gift or a complement as a joke, with feigned sincerity, or even offer a dangerous or demeaning gift. The cynic may be on the outside, the one passed over for promotion as not participating in the corporate ethos, being unhelpfully critical. The cynic is the one on the edge, looking in. Though not necessarily in penury, the cynic sometimes shares the demeanor of the aggrieved beggar.

As the first enthusiast of Net culture (before it existed), Diogenes famously declared himself "a citizen of the world."[25] When the citizens of Sinope sentenced him to exile, he said he would sentence them to stay at home.[26] For Diogenes, global citizenship had a negative connotation. It meant he was a non-participant in any particular locale. He was not cosmopolitan, nor the well-traveled person of letters interested in foreign cultures, but rather someone who saw himself as outside the citizenship of any Greek city. The claim to universal citizenship was a way of declaring that he was against the citizen.

In an alternative but not unconnected usage, we readily ascribe cynicism to those who are successful in the corporate world, able to turn the appearance of beneficence to personal gain.[27] There is the suggestion of caring for clients, customers, employees, and the social good, but the motive is personal gain. In this usage, the cynic is a deceiver.

The third occupant of the threshold condition is the trickster.[28] The corporate achiever may also be a confidence trickster, a con artist, who dupes employees into working under oppressive conditions or the consumer into purchasing inferior goods.[29] The similarity between the cynic and the trickster resides in their attitude of externality to the system, in manipulating it as if from outside. This is also the demeanor of the clandestine merchant, or scalper, who operates in the streets, looking for buyers, but ready to retreat from the police, who knows the limits of the law, and is above it, so long as she is not caught. The trickster/cynic amalgam is also in the company of the unscrupulous entrepreneur, the ambitious corporate leader who manipulates circumstances and bends the law to his own ends. The trickster is also the middleman, who does not produce but lives off those who do. As a character in digital narrative, the trickster appears as the successful dot-com opportunist, the one who promotes an idea on the strength of promise and has every intention of selling the enterprise to someone else before it proves unworkable.

But the trickster also has a benign and pleasant aspect. The trickster is of the street, among those who offer the gift of performance, music, trinkets, or good luck, the carnival magicians, fire-eaters, jugglers, comedians, jesters, crowd pleasers, and others who operate opportunistically, through surprise and caprice. Each can turn a trick, be it the trick of amassing a fortune by keeping one step ahead, or the trick of surviving by keeping the crowds amused. In the era of media saturation, the trickster assumes the cast of celebrity, adding the manipulation of the mass media to her arsenal. On the Internet, which affords instant celebrity, Web sites that are controversial but cool and amusing thrive on the trickster ethos.

To the extent that commerce is outside the boundary of the community, the preserve of the gift, it can already be construed as a cynical and tricky enterprise. Taking the gift as primary, commerce offers a simulation of community exchange, a reduction of the complex of human relations to commodity value, demand, and self-interest. As we have seen, the commercial world is capable of explicitly trading on the aura of the gift, pretending to be what it is not. The con artist further pushes the rules of commerce, promising more than can be delivered. For Hyde, this involves "creating belief."[30] Advertising strategies sometimes epitomize the trickster (and cynical) attitude, offering commodities as if gifts, claiming participation in the sphere of the domestic. Consumer culture requires that this be the case. As I will demonstrate subsequently, as a dealing in tricks, the origins of commerce fall into the company of thefts and lies.

It takes little persuasion to see how the network economy is caught in a cynical and tricky game. E-commerce brings certain features of the world of commerce into sharp relief. There is the incursion of commercial activity, which supposedly corrupts the gift culture of those scientists and academics with whom it had its origins. There are the practices of companies that seek to monopolize markets through limiting the capabilities of browser software and controlling applications development by dominating the supply of operating systems. There are the overt confidence tricksters who try to trap vulnerable consumers into a sale, manifested in the practices of spamming and pyramid selling.[31]

Commerce involves exchange at the boundary between the inside and the outside. Globalization due to electronic communications is simply an extension of the sphere of that trade. It seems it is possible for the wares of the small trader to be purveyed internationally simply by being accessible from a Web server. In this respect, Internet economics adds little to the notion of the boundary between the inside and the outside. There is no wholesale dissolution, blurring, or dissolving of boundaries. Boundaries still exist, though they may be reconfigured. I will examine the boundary in more detail. The boundary is where things appear into and retreat from view. It is the site of the agonistic game of revealing and concealing.

To resort to character types as inhabiting the threshold region is to appeal to archetypes, which is already a problematic strategy. The point of the next section is to show that the trickster is a type that already contradicts the idea of the archetype. Readers who have no trouble with the ironic use of archetypes may care to skip this section.

Types and Boundaries

Throughout this book, I have used certain metaphors to provoke thought about aspects of the network economy and design: the home, the machine, the game, the gift, and the threshold. There is a marginal aspect to these terms. Whereas economists readily talk of capital, land, and labor, or in contemporary terms of free markets, community, trade, globalization, fiscal policy, and integration, the terms I used are at the edge of the discourse, though arguably more central to design discourse. In its own right, the introduction of such metaphors can serve as a provocation. I have used the word *metaphor* here. For some theorists these metaphors are types, or classes, of things. We are familiar with the marketplace as a type in architectural discourse. The marketplace has certain definable characteristics, and a spatial arrangement (the classical stoa and open space) that can be deemed to fall within the type. Insofar as we are beholden to types, they are reputedly undergoing reconfiguration in the digital era. The school, the museum, the hospital, the home, the market, and the shop are seen afresh in the light of digital media. They are no longer simply buildings, if they ever were, but networks and systems. The location, form, scale, and composition of buildings has always been in flux, but especially now as we think about how they accommodate digital technologies, the emerging practices of digital technology usage, and the changing functionality of global networks.

Economics is less concerned with spatial typologies than is design, but is no less committed to classification schemas. There are clearly different types of commercial organizations and institutions (banks, limited liability companies, small businesses, e-retailers) and different types of commercial transactions, as might appear on a ledger, such as credit, debit, direct payment, on account, or pay on delivery. The design of e-commerce systems sometimes calls on the concept of the type, at the most prosaic level revealed in terms of "templates." So the designer can select from a range of predesigned forms, database formats, and Web site layouts, and modify these to fit the particular context. There are also types of e-commerce systems and Web sites: business-to-business, business-to-consumer, travel itinerary, online auction, exclusive, open-ended, and so on. The gift can also be treated in typological terms. There are types of gifts: the festive, the unexpected, the anonymous, gifts among friends, gifts from strangers, the gift of passage, the poisonous gift, the Internet gift, and so on. The gift per se can also be treated as a type, with characteristics that are repeated in each instance: there is a giver, a receiver, a thing, a time delay, a thank you, a reciprocation. But as is evident from the discussion in chapter 4, the gift gains its potency in social discourse not by defining a class of things but by presenting a provocation against something that already assumes much greater authority in modern discourse, namely, the commercial transaction. As presented by Mauss and others, the gift is an irritant to the accepted convention of what constitutes exchange. In turn, the gift is interesting insofar as we explore its edges, where it fragments community rather than builds it, and where it is implicated in profligacy and theft rather than beneficence. So it can be with any consideration of type. Typological study is undoubtedly useful, but the intellectual interest resides in the exploration of its boundaries: the zone of hybridity and transgression.

In this case, is not the pursuit of type misleading? Why not talk instead about metaphors, images, or provocations? Perhaps there is no necessity for the Platonic concept of the type, the appeal to an ideal, something that does not actually seem to exist in the material practice of day-to-day work and life. It was Marx who complained that the idealists talk about "fruit" rather than "apples" and "pears,"[32] that is, generalizations rather than specifics. The appeal to type is simply one discursive strategy among many. In argument as well as in design, there is value in starting from the center, then moving to the edge condition. This is to start with a confidence in the type, then examine how the type breaks down at the edges, or how the integrity of the category is challenged by the edge condition. The center may after all be transformed in the journey, or rediscovered. The journey to the edge may even show the center to be similarly infected with hybridity and transgression. The center may take on the character of the threshold.

So our study can begin with the idea of the type, or the first type, as a means to examining the boundary. The word *archetype* suggests a first instance, which defines the ones that follow, or that exemplifies the type. So the agora of ancient Athens (or Cnossos, Delphi, or any other disputed origin) is the archetype of all marketplaces. The concept of the archetype gains discursive impetus not from architecture but from psychology, from Carl Jung,[33] and we have already made appeal to the archetype in referring to the beggar, the cynic, and the trickster. For Jung, the archetype is an appeal to universals, "a common psychic substrate of a suprapersonal nature which is present in every one of us."[34] Archetypes are the content of the "collective unconscious," that substrate of hidden memories, primordial conditions, and repressed anxieties, not privately owned, but born by all of humankind and revealed in its stories. Jung's named archetypes typically include "concrete personalities," such as the mother, the wise man, and the trickster. For Jung, their presence recurs throughout narrative, legend, folk tales, and dreams, with extension, elaboration, and variation. Archetypal status may be attached to nonfictional, historical characters, exaggerating their traits in order to render them larger than life, universal, and exemplary. By the Jungian reading, there is no truly new archetype. Every new encounter is but a manifestation of an established archetype.

An archetype serves to establish connections between character traits. In the case of the psychological relationship between a child and its mother, "all those influences which the literature describes as being exerted on the children do not come from the mother herself, but rather from the archetype projected upon her, which gives her a mythological background and invests her with authority and numinosity."[35] It is not so much that any particular mother does her best to make her child feel love, security, guilt, or gratitude, but any specific relationship bears the burden imposed by the archetype of the all-beneficent mother. Jung is also keen to indicate the primordial character of the archetypes: "archetypes are not whimsical inventions but autonomous elements of the unconscious psyche which were there before any invention was thought of."[36] Jung famously also constructed theories of psychological types, particularly the introvert and the extrovert,[37] with other categories derived from these. Though less interested in his appeals to mythic origins, the corporate world has made much of the psychological type,[38] as a means of explaining company roles against structure (the manager, the loafer, the cynic, the industrious hack), and of personality. In the world of commerce it is thought imperative to know with whom you are dealing.[39]

Though Jung has contributed to the development of theories of personality types, it is perhaps more useful to think of an archetype as a character in a narrative rather than a category to which any individual may be assigned. So the story of any individual can be woven into a narrative, and onto this role is assigned a particular archetype. So the popular imagination portrays the Dali Lama as the wise wan (Socrates), Marylyn Monroe as the seductress (a Siren, Pandora, Calypso), Elizabeth I as the great mother (Maia, Athena), and Frances Drake as the adventurer (Jason, Odysseus), depending on context and narrative purpose. In fact, it is much easier to think of fictional rather than historical characters as exemplifying an archetype, since much depends on the way the life is recounted. The movie celebrity can be portrayed as seductress or victim, as universal mother figure or naïve child. Furthermore, appeals can be made to different actual or mythic characters as exemplifying the archetype. It is also the case that each of the types can be of either good or evil intent. The great mother can be instantiated as the good witch of the East or the wicked stepmother. The wise man and the trickster can be either demonic or benign. In psychological terms, we are caught up in self-narratives, in which we and the characters in our lives assume such roles. Archetypes are revealed in our dreaming and narratives of self-construction.

Narrative self-construction along typological lines is evident in amateur and personal Web site design, or in the bios of chat room participants. Most of the "technological subcultures" identified by Bell,[40] Turkle,[41] and others fall under the trickster archetype: MUDders (online role game players), cyberpunks, and hackers. For Bell, the latter often fulfill the role of "folk devils,"[42] who appropriate technology in unorthodox ways, and whose activity is on the edge of criminality, if it is not illicit.

Jung also elaborates on archetypes of process. So there is the archetype of rebirth, or transformation, implicating the passage from one state or condition to another, often marked by transformation rites. So the archetype implicates the passage across boundaries. This is the structure of the myth seen in archetypal terms. For Campbell: "A hero ventures forth from the world of common day into a region of supernatural wonder: fabulous forces are there encountered and a decisive victory is won: the hero comes back from this mysterious adventure with the power to bestow boons on his fellow man."[43] As we saw in chapter 3, for Freud, the archetypal process of transformation is given expression in the Oedipal myth, the working out of the relationship between the son and his mother, where the son inadvertently marries his mother and then blinds himself out of remorse for breaching the taboo of incest, and for killing his father. Freud gave expression to the archetypes of mother (Jocasta), father (Laius), and the son (Oedipus). According to Jung, Freud only discovered a limited formulation of the archetype, which Jung claimed to extend to other types and further narratives of transformation.

For Jung, archetypes are given expression in only diminished form in modern culture. Thinking of the distortions created by figures prominent in politics and the mass media, particularly the European fascists of the 1930s and 1940s and their idealization, there is a moral imperative to return to archetypes in their authentic form. A strict Jungian reading provides little support for the identification of a cybercultural typology. Jung's is a highly developed form of Platonism, a return to authenticity and indeed an appeal to the restoration of a lost unity.

There are problems with archetypes. The school of psychology known as the *archetypal school* follows from Jung, and, according to Jungian scholars, is averse to pinning down the term *archetype*. According to Adams, "there are no *archetypes* as such . . . there are only phenomena, or images, that may be *archetypal*."[44] For archetypal psychology any phenomenon is a candidate for consideration as an archetype, though not all carry the same weight, or have comparable structure. In fact, any noun or name can be turned into an archetype simply by capitalizing or italicizing it, though not with equal authority. For example, the great mother carries resonances and a primal significance not yet enjoyed by the entrepreneur, the nerd, the MUDder, and the hacker. Authority is everything in the identification of an archetype. According to Russo's commentary on Jung: "Literary artists instinctively mold their narratives around characters, situations, and dramatic sequences that carry a high 'payload' of emotional and spiritual impact."[45] According to Adams, an archetype is "a 'flexible matrix' that will allow different cultures to place their distinctive or local stamp on a universal figure."[46] In recent times we have the cyborg, given the status of a primordial category, and drawing on the authority of NASA research in the 1950s.[47] The category is all the more intriguing by virtue of the mystery of its instantiation. It is a type that includes everyone and no one.

If we think of the archetype as metaphor, as expounded in chapter 3, then the archetype offers an invitation to consider similarities and differences, to consider what any archetype reveals and conceals. To recall your favorite schoolteacher as a wise man reveals something about mentoring, intellectual and emotional co-dependence, and perhaps conceals the teacher's own propensity toward naïveté, a sense of fun, and ignorance.[48] What does the trickster reveal? Not only is the trickster an archetype and a metaphor, but archetypes and metaphors are themselves tricky. Jung devotes many pages to the elaboration of the trickster as an archetype. The trickster is at the edge of the type, and his chief mischief is on the idea of the type itself. The trickster is the type that crosses boundaries, or that denies categories. In fact, following an argument I presented elsewhere,[49] from a Freudian perspective it can be argued that there are only three "archetypes": that which unites, that which individuates, and that which confuses. The great mother stands for the unity: "the love that means home-coming, shelter, and the long silence from which everything begins and in which everything ends."[50] Then there is the father, who, according to Freud, Jung, and Lacan, individuates; that is, he lays down the law. For Jung, "it is always the father-figure from whom the decisive convictions, prohibitions, and wise counsels emanate."[51] The impetus to categorize belongs with the law of the father. The tension between the mother and the father in this psychic alchemy constitutes the basis of the Oedipal condition. The agent of confusion is variously attributed. For Lacan, there is the notion of rupture, the destruction of either unity or individuation, the recognition that each inheres in the other and that the unity (the real) is already characterized by rift and division.[52] Insofar as we need archetypes, the trickster personifies this factor, the agent who subverts categories.[53] This subversion is evident as we think of any category and its inadequacies, no less so than in attempts to ascribe computer users or cyberculture participants to a typology. People assume different roles in different situations. The authoritarian "father figure" at work can be playful at the domestic dinner table, and a MUDder at the computer. That people shift between categories does not automatically imply trickiness, but the preservation of categories is tricky at the edges.

The Trickster Conceals: Proto-Encryption

Confusion at the boundary is well described in terms of concealment. The threshold provides the opportunity to retreat into shadow, or to disappear inside. At the threshold, it is an easy matter to say you are either in or out depending on what is most convenient. Lying is a mode of concealment, exemplified by attributing a thing to the wrong category, saying you are inside when you are in fact on the outside, presenting a watch as a Cartier when in fact it is a fake, promising delivery within five working days whereas in fact it always takes more than ten, saying a new operating system will support the old software when in fact it requires upgrades. So the adventurer (Odysseus) in disguise as a beggar constitutes a lie: one archetype masquerading as another. A lie is also a theft. We anticipate one thing and receive another, or nothing at all. Thieves lie in order to cover their tracks, and lying is closely related to theft as a mode of concealment. The lie and theft are in opposition to the promise and the gift, which bear the character of a disclosure. A gift is a laying bare, a celebration of vulnerability, a symbol of openness within a community, an invitation, an open door,[54] evidenced by so many online disclosures and the vulnerabilities they entail.[55] Thieving provides the converse. Things are not given but taken, the transaction is not willing but by force, the result is not openness but suspicion, and the result is the closed door, the password, and the firewall. In fact we are well able to cope with such categories as the giver and the thief. The intrigue or distress of trickery lies in never being sure as to which category an event belongs. There are those who give with one hand and take with the other. In the threshold condition, the door is never so much open or closed as ajar, or in flux. With online life, one is never entirely sure of the reliability or trustworthiness of the service, site, agent, or individual at the other end of the line. The portal is neither entirely encrypted nor open-source, but permeable.

Accounts of the "first lie" are revealing of this condition of concealment and ambivalence. The beggar, the trickster, and the cynic merge in several related stories, notably, in the legends of Odysseus, Hermes, and Prometheus. Homer's story of *The Odyssey* tells of the mortal Odysseus[56] who embarks on the long journey home after fighting in the Trojan wars. Presuming him dead, his wife is being pursued by several unscrupulous "suitors," who seek a stake in his household. After many adventures, Odysseus arrives home disguised as a beggar, which constitutes a deception. He observes the household and even wins the respect of the suitors before revealing his identity in an archery contest. He eventually slays the suitors. Odysseus is in many respects the hero figure, but he is also described as wily and in possession of cunning.[57] Whereas the hero typically wins against opposition by courage and strength, Odysseus does so by "clever manoeuvring."[58] He does not battle directly with the Cyclops, but hides, sees most of his companions killed while he waits, blinds the Cyclops while sleeping to gain an unfair advantage, then escapes by suspending himself beneath a sheep.[59] At one stage, he is abetted by the intervention of Athena, goddess of cunning intelligence (Metis).[60] That he (and Athena) chose the disguise of a beggar is appropriate to the boundary condition. He appeared in his hometown as "an old, wretched beggar, stooping over a stick and with dismal rags about his body. He sat down on the ashwood threshold inside the doorway, leaning against the cypress pillar which a master carpenter long ago had smoothed deftly and trued to the line."[61] The habitual location of the beggar, the threshold, was the perfect place from which to observe, to scheme, and to be noticed if need be. It is also a relatively easy disguise. Anyone can more easily disguise themselves as a beggar than a king.

It happens that Odysseus's grandfather was the god Hermes.[62] Classical glossaries describe Hermes as the god of translators and interpreters. He was a messenger to the other gods and is associated with wealth, good fortune, commerce, and fertility. He brought the souls of the dead to the underworld, and he escorts Odysseus there on a visit. He is also associated with thievery and assumes the role of the one who told the first lie. In "The Homeric Hymn to Hermes,"[63] he is described as "a wily boy, flattering and cunning, a robber and a cattle thief, a bringer of dreams, awake all night, waiting by the gates of the city."[64] In his youth Hermes stole his brother Apollo's cattle. Hermes coaxed the cattle to walk backward to give a false impression from their footprints, and he wore sandals of his own devising that concealed the theft. He then lied about the theft, but he ultimately earned his brother's affections by presenting him with a gift, a musical instrument, a lyre of his own making. Hermes is often depicted as a youthful messenger with wings on his sandals and carrying a rod with entwined snakes. In preparing a meal from some of the cattle, Hermes is attributed with inventing fire, or at least using fire sticks, as a trick.[65] A similar story tells of Prometheus, who attempted to trick the god Zeus by concealing the good portions of meat from a slaughtered ox. Prometheus also stole divine fire and gave it to humankind.[66] Both Hyde and Russo construct a composite picture from these three characters: Odysseus, Hermes, and Prometheus. The trickery of Hermes includes disguise and the ability to become invisible, which are forms of concealment. He is responsible for clever and useful inventions (e.g., fire sticks, the lyre, sandals). Russo describes this composite Hermes character as the patron of "mobility and exchange between zones—as patron deity of transactions and interchange he is the god of travelers, crossroads, traders, and interpreters."[67]

By now the affinity of Hermes with the threshold should be apparent. Statues of Hermes would occupy the threshold in ancient households: "as god of special and liminal spaces his statue stood in public places and at entryways to private homes, presumably for his protective powers in general and protection against thieves in particular."[68] Jung further amplifies the threshold status of Hermes (Mercurius), who "consists of all conceivable opposites."[69] Jung describes Hermes as "a duality," whose "innumerable inner contradictions can dramatically fly apart into an equal number of disparate and apparently independent figures."[70] For Jung, Hermes can assume the converse of a benevolent deity: "He is the devil, a redeeming psychopomp, an evasive trickster, and God's reflection in physical nature."[71] In an extensive analysis, Hyde elaborates the role of the trickster: "He is the spirit of the doorway leading out, and of the crossroad at the edge of town (the one where a little market springs up). He is the spirit of the road at dusk, the one that runs from one town to another and belongs to neither."[72] As the middleman, the trickster is close to commerce, as well as a confuser of distinctions.

In short, trickster is a boundary crosser. Every group has its edge, its sense of in and out, and trickster is always there, at the gates of the city and the gates of life, making sure there is commerce. He also attends the internal boundaries by which groups articulate their social life. We constantly distinguish—right and wrong, sacred and profane, clean and dirty, male and female, young and old, living and dead—and in every case trickster will cross the line and confuse the distinction. Trickster is the creative idiot, therefore, the wise fool, the gray-haired baby, the cross-dresser, the speaker of sacred profanities. . . . Trickster is the mythic embodiment of ambiguity and ambivalence, doubleness and duplicity, contradiction and paradox.[73]

For Hyde, boundary creation and boundary crossing are related, and "the best way to describe trickster is to say simply that the boundary is where he will be found—sometimes drawing the line, sometimes crossing it, sometimes erasing or moving it, but always there, the god of the threshold in all its forms."[74]

So the narratives developed around the trickster involve cunning, deception, disguise, creativity, concealment, revelation, transformation, interpretation, breach, and theft. The trickster is the concealer, and the deceiver, skilled at setting and evading traps, the legitimate inhabitant of the threshold condition. According to our characterization of the creative process, the trickster is also the designer, the artist, the risk taker, and the adventurous entrepreneur.

If nothing else, this foray into ancient mythology serves to demonstrate the persistence of the long-standing legacy of trickiness. If we think of a "postmodern condition" as upsetting convention, then it is a condition in which we recognize what was already in place, though concealed through a selective reading of the tradition, generally in favor of a particular reading of Plato. The resurrection of the trickster is on a par with Nietzsche's elevation of the Promethean tradition, the so-called gay science,[75] and Heidegger's elevation of the pre-Socratics. Lest we think that cyberculture and the network economy throw all modernist ideas of rationality and order on their heads, this is a task begun at the dawn of storytelling. The trickster myth is now revived in digital narratives.[76] For Haraway, the trickster is the human-machine hybrid known as the cyborg, who crosses category boundaries and irritates the capitalist machine.[77]

The symbolic potential of Hermes (or Mercury) in corporate branding has not escaped the world of global telecommunications, though obviously in his role as messenger without his cunning or boundary ambivalence. The trickster's character comes through nonetheless, and, as I will examine subsequently, the threshold condition is everywhere in global communications.

The Cynic Reveals: Open Source, Open Mind

What is a cynical posture toward the network economy? In everyday usage, the cynical attitude is negative, critical, and resigned, without commitment to detailed analysis, diagnosis, or remedy. The cynic may even assume a position within the very systems she criticizes and benefit from them. That is, the cynic may use computers while being critical of them, profit from e-business while decrying its shortcomings, lament the exploitation of cheap labor while setting up an offshore call center. But, understood historically, the cynic represents an even more interesting program. The network cynic seeks to expose the pretense of commercial hyperbole, and to advance alternative, provocative constructions of what the network is all about. She will probably advance her critique from a moral position, though without recourse to rules, standards, and ideals. The network cynic may attempt to set intellectual traps and do so with an economy of means.

If the trickster has his ground in concealment, the lie, and theft, then the cynic starts with the pretense of exposure. The cynic does not feature among Jung's archetypes, though certain of his aspects appear as the wise man: "a magician, doctor, priest, teacher, professor, grandfather, or any other person possessing authority."[78] On the other hand, the wise man is supposed to appear "in a situation where insight, understanding, good advice, determination, planning, etc., are needed but cannot be mustered on one's own resources."[79] The wise man may do this by providing unexpected responses, asking questions, or provoking reflection by other means. Socrates, as described by Plato, typifies the wise man, whereas Diogenes counsels, or rather provokes, by causing offense. Diogenes went around as a beggar, and so was in a position subservient to the citizen. As a master of ironic self-deprecation, he once asked for a statue to be made of him. When interrogated on his reason for asking, and aware of the unlikelihood, he replied: "I am practising disappointment."[80] Self-deprecation is endemic as a means of indicating its converse, from the confession of nerdiness by the accomplished computer programmer to the self-proclaimed Luddism of the competent computer user.[81] Such assertions lose their cynical edge when employed to excess.

If the trickster has his being in concealment, disguise, thieving, and lying, then the cynic presents a kind of obverse, not in beneficence but exposure through critique, and not through extended argument but by provocation of words and actions. The trickster and the cynic are provocateurs, but the cynic takes the high moral ground and does his work by exposing the pretense, hypocrisy, and moral turpitude of others. Diogenes would walk the streets in broad daylight with a lighted lantern supposedly looking for an honest man. His teaching is commonly associated with illumination. When Alexander the Great came to Diogenes and asked if there was anything he wanted, Diogenes replied dryly, "Stand a little less between me and the sun."[82] Arguably the Cynical aspect of illumination has been overtaken by the concept of *enlightenment,* as a progression to higher levels of attainment, which pervades the heroic rhetoric of the network society. For the network cynic, the idealistic rhetoric occludes the source of that illumination. More tellingly, it produces shadows. The enlightened disposition contains dark recesses, all too evident as we reflect on the nefarious aspects of Net culture.

The main source of information on the Cynics is the second-century historian Diogenes Laërtius, who introduces Diogenes of Sinope (the Cynic) as implicated in counterfeiting.[83] The father of Diogenes the Cynic was a money-changer, or banker, and was forced to leave his native city under the accusation that he had "adulterated the coinage." The charge extended to the son, Diogenes, who therefore began his philosophical career at odds with the law and as an exile. There are two interpretations of the story about the coinage. The obvious meaning is that Diogenes and his father were forgers. The second meaning is that they destroyed the face of coins to diminish or conceal their value, an act of anarchic protest. It is supposed that Diogenes was in fact critical of the institutions of commerce, and that it was the coinage in circulation that was already "falsely struck," giving a sense of false value. The moral point of his demonstration was that the coinage needed to "be defaced and put out of circulation."[84] Promissory notes now replace coinage as currency,[85] which circulate through digital networks. The network cynic recognizes that the value represented on ledgers and bank statements is contingent on the maintenance of the financial system and the social practices of exchange.

The Cynic is ostensibly against rule, order, and institution, bent on exposing the weakness of established social structures. Diogenes' mission was to provoke against convention, and his daily life was to be the prime example, over dialectic or allegory, that is, over words.[86] In this Diogenes has been counted as "one of the great forerunners of anarchism."[87] The twentieth-century anarchist Kropotkin refers approvingly to the *Republic of Zeno,* written when Zeno was under the influence of Cynicism.[88] For some, the independence of the Cynic aligns with the pioneering spirit, its self-sufficiency and contempt for law and authority,[89] and hence the putative anarchy of the Internet, and the countercultures of cyberpunk and cypherpunk.[90]

Cynicism is also a philosophy that is parasitic on authority. A world populated entirely by Cynics is untenable. Against whom would they rail? As for anarchism, it is a case of demanding the impossible.[91] Diogenes' demonstrations gained their impact from the context of his protest. As for any aphoristic teaching, the burden of understanding fell on the recipient of his barbed attacks. The network society is assailed with a volley of (cynical) assertions that require extensive contextualizing to provoke understanding: information wants to be free, the network economy is friction-free, think different,[92] computer design needs to be user-centered, the cyborg is our ontology,[93] the Net is an anarchy.[94] The cynic's proclamation presages the radical design manifestos of the early twentieth century.[95] For the Futurist Marinetti, "No work without an aggressive character can be a masterpiece" and "what we want is to break down the mysterious doors of the Impossible."[96] The impossibility of the cynic's exhortations is reflected in the Web space given over to trade in absurd aphorisms: hit any user to continue; our software never has bugs, just random features; in cyberspace no one knows you are a dog, and so forth.

The cynic is supposedly without shame or modesty, demonstrating an attitude that is against concealment. Cynics practiced a way of life that was shameless, as are dogs, who apparently don't mind how they appear in public. The dog is not beneath modesty but superior to it. Dogs also exercise a kind of revealing, by sniffing out quarry, and can distinguish between friends and enemies. Diogenes enjoyed the hunt, and he is recorded as taking people on regular hunting trips.[97] His behavior was aligned with that of a threatening dog: "He was a dog whom all admired, yet few dared go hunting with him."[98] Dogs are good guards, as are the Cynics of their philosophy. They drive enemies of their philosophy away by barking after them.[99] Diogenes apparently said he was a dog because he fawned on people who give him anything, he would bark at those who give him nothing, and he would bite the rogues.[100] The anonymity afforded by the network society enables the cybernaut to roam the streets of cyberspace without shame, and to lurk, flame, and bark with impunity, though the cynic is the one who is prepared to declare her identity.

A dog-like affinity is expressed in the word *cynic,* which can be traced to the ancient Greek term *kunikos,* meaning "dog." The dog is also a prominent theme in trickster stories.[101] The indigenous folklore of North America makes much of the role of the coyote, as wandering inhabitant of the threshold condition, both foolish and wise, deceiving and exposing. The coyote also taught the first hunters how to make traps to catch prey,[102] an attribute also of Diogenes in winning arguments. The network economy is rife with traps, identified as scams, viruses, adware, spyware, and spam, and it offers tips on safe surfing.[103] The traps of the Net cynic are of a different order, however, akin to Baudrillard's intellectual trap of the simulacrum: the circular paradox that the computer simulation blinds us to the reality of the rest of existence, which is the actual simulation.[104] The trap is the paradox, or the circular argument.

Apart from the hunt, Diogenes demonstrated an affinity with animals in other ways. He took his example from the subsistence tactics of animals and is said to have been inspired in his philosophy of simple living by observing a scampering mouse. He insisted on the self-sufficiency of the individual,[105] stripping back necessities to reveal the animal within. The Cynic is equated with asceticism, denying personal comfort, by training the body. Diogenes would roll in hot sand in summer and snow in winter.[106] Dudley identifies the legacy of the Cynics within the asceticism and wisdom of various traditions.[107] Dominicans were sometimes known as "Domini canes," "the Cynics of the Lord,"[108] and the Franciscans lived by wandering the world and begging. Diogenes' teacher was Antisthenes, a student of Socrates. It is said that Antisthenes "learnt the art of enduring, and of being indifferent to external circumstances."[109] Asceticism resonates with the Neoplatonic body-loathing that finds expression in those aspects of cyberculture that speak disparagingly of the body as meat, as transient, disposable, and eventually to be replaced by pure mind as information,[110] though the cynic rejects the idealism in such assertions.

Diogenes was a rival of Plato, who said of Diogenes that he was Socrates gone mad.[111] For Diogenes, "most men were within a finger's breadth of being mad."[112] From a Freudian perspective, the human psyche is driven by a struggle with the Oedipal condition and with incest. To Diogenes is attributed (probably by his enemies) advocacy of the violation of various taboos, such as incest, stealing from temples, eating any kind of meat, and eating human flesh.[113] He was certainly against marriage and the exclusive union of one man to one woman.[114] In supporting incest, the Cynic therefore diminishes the significance of family relationships, and hence, unwittingly, the archetypes: the great mother, the wise man. According to Jung, Diogenes in fact ridiculed the incest tragedy of Oedipus,[115] with a "denial of the substantiality of the generic concept."[116] As anti-idealist, the Cynic is opposed to universals: "The accent is laid upon the individual thing."[117] In his account of classical philosophy, Jung shows that the Cynics were thus in the company of those opposed to Plato's *ideas*. According to Diogenes Laërtius, Diogenes the Cynic railed against much of the idealism of Plato: "That mathematicians kept their eyes fixed on the sun and moon, and overlooked what was under their feet."[118] In contradistinction to the supposed illumination of Plato's exemplary discursive methods, Diogenes criticized Plato's dialogues as obscuring the truth, as presenting disguise.[119] Here the Cynic has more in common with the contemporary scholar concerned with the social practices that develop around the Internet, and who positions various net ideologies as storytelling, or narrative constructions.

The Cynic is clearly against idealism and embraces the materiality of the human condition. Diogenes' protest against religious regulation about what you may and may not eat was founded on materialism. According to Diogenes Laërtius: "In reality everything was a combination of all things. For that in bread there was meat, and in vegetables there was bread, and so there were some particles of all other bodies in everything, communicating by invisible passages and evaporating."[120] In this there are resonances with the Stoic assertion of the interconnectedness of all things, and with Epicurean materialism,[121] which we have already related to aspects of Net culture.

As for the trickster, Diogenes is readily associated with the threshold. He endorsed the condition of being on the verge of some important life event but not proceeding, as in the case of someone reneging on a decision to marry, take a voyage, or rear children.[122] Such recalcitrance at the edge of an important decision strikes us as weakness, but also as a resistance to the norm, a determination to follow an alternative path, a characterization of the creative designer, the e-entrepreneur, or the Net critic. Jung supports the view of Cynics as on the edge. In his account of classical philosophy and the archetype, he describes Diogenes' teacher, Antisthenes, as "of the periphery."[123] Diogenes had a disciple known as Crates who was also called the "door opener." Crates embodied the idea of the Cynic as watchdog, working in the interests of humanity.[124] Crates, renowned for his jesting and laughter, was apparently welcome in any home. His reproofs would be offered in a kindly manner, unlike those of Diogenes, of whom it was said he chose to bite his friends for their own salvation.[125] The Cynic was the watchdog at the doorway.

So the Cynic is entitled to a place on the threshold, as liminal inhabitant, inquisitor of hypocrisy, immodest joker without a smile, dealer in particulars, doubter, wise fool against the state. Both aspects, concealing and revealing, reside within the composite trickster/cynic, exposing the nature of design, and the language by which they are articulated.

The Trickiness of Communication

Electronic communications mediate across thresholds. We might wonder at the reliability of communications networks for getting across what we have to say. But language is already tricky. Referring to the "weakness of language"[126] Plato notes that it is already a mediation. For example, if we are to comprehend what a circle is, then we must resort to an image, to the principle of reason, and to the ideal of a circle. This is in addition to the devices of language: the use of names and definitions. Language on its own can be deceptive. Elsewhere Plato attributes language to Hermes, specifically in relation to speech: "the name 'Hermes' seems to have something to do with speech: he is an interpreter (hermeneus), a messenger, a thief and a deceiver in words, a wheeler-dealer— and all these activities involve the power of speech."[127] Then he describes Pan, the double-natured son of Hermes, who is half-man and half-goat: "You know speech signifies all things (to Pan) and keeps them circulating and always going about, and that it has two forms—true and false? . . . the true part is smooth and divine and dwells among the gods above, while the false part dwells below among the human masses, and is rough and goatish."[128] Contrary to the Epicureans and the Cynics, for Plato there is always some transcendent truth to which words attempt to refer and are but a pale representation, and in the realm of words there is every opportunity for persuasion by devious argument, trickiness, and deception. Language as spoken is thereby defined as already falling short of the ideal. It is already predicated on the lie and duplicity.

Of course there is the modern tradition of language study that attempts to subject language to the rigors of "reason and right opinion,"[129] culminating in the methods of logical positivism in the twentieth century, by which ordinary language is translated into formal propositions, which are precise, and can be subjected to verification and proof,[130] and digital processing. The trap that logical positivism set itself was the demonstration that in fact nothing could be verified, by the philosophy's own criteria. More than anything, "reason and right opinion" demonstrated the ultimate unprovability of language statements. Verification turned out to be a falsehood, if not a lie.

Hermes is the god of falsehood. It is interesting to conjecture that language has this character before it has the character of truth. But there is a more accurate way of looking at language. Hermes is the god of the threshold condition, the site of ambiguity between inside and outside, truth and falsity, the space between differing conditions, between meanings. Taking our lead from Wittgenstein[131] and Austin,[132] this is also the character of language. Words do not have sharp boundaries, but are always ambiguous, with multiple meanings. The meaning of a word does not reside in the fixity of some definition, but in the relationship of the word to its context, the context being formed by the words around it, the whole work, the context of culture, the situation of reading or listening, and all that has gone before—a panoply of uses and contexts in which the word has participated. As we have seen, for Wittgenstein, meaning resides in use. This is the context of the practical engagement with words in a series of concrete situations.

We can see this in the case of architectural artifacts. In part, the house gains its meaning and potency as a place of refuge and nurture from its response to the outside condition, a dependence on its spatial context in the street, the town, the countryside. House as refuge means what it does in contrast to the possibility of danger. Similarly, words gain meaning from their responses to the linguistic context. In this sense it is not just that you can deceive with language, but that language owes its potency to the threshold condition, the interaction between words and contexts, at their boundaries as it were. The less obvious phenomenon of the *homepage* similarly invokes meaning through contrast with its context. It is a place of return, a refuge, a grounding, an origin, in contrast to the intimidating territory of the Web in total. As a live metaphor it also invokes contrasts with the home in which we live, and for a designer invokes similarities and differences on which to draw for the invention of new capabilities.

A design perspective draws further attention to the threshold. The designer, the creator, the inventor, lingers on the threshold, the liminal condition, the boundary between categories: the home that is both inside and outside, the city street that is a home, the Web site that floats on an ocean of information. Design and creative endeavor seem to thrive on a consideration of the hybrid condition, the twisting and misapplication of a metaphor. The twentieth-century essayist and surrealist Walter Benjamin proffers a description of the street as home that has this character.

Streets are the dwelling place of the collective. The collective is an eternally wakeful, eternally agitated being—in the space between the building fronts—lives, experiences, understands, and invents as much as individuals do within the privacy of their own four walls. . . . glossy enameled shop signs are a wall decoration as good as, if not better than, an oil painting in the drawing room of a bourgeois. . . . walls with their "Post No Bills" are its writing desk . . . benches its bedroom furniture, and the café terrace is the balcony from which it looks down on its household.[133]

As we have seen, design invention often resorts to the hybrid condition: street as living room, house as machine, business deal as game, Web page as portal. For the designer, every metaphor is an invitation to play on the edge condition, the suggestion of what a thing both is and is not at the same time, an engagement with the game of misclassification, collecting and recombining, the art of the bricoleur.[134] Hyde does not deal with design as such but shows how the trickster function is implicated in the challenge of creative writing: "Our ideas about property and theft depend on a set of assumptions about how the world is divided up. Trickster's lies and thefts challenge those premises and in so doing reveal their artifice and suggest alternatives."[135] At the very least, the challenge to accepted categories suggests new possibilities.

Hyde draws out the mythic origins of the lie, and hence of language, a narrative that is itself fraught, the stuff of literary creativity, and that has applicability to design in the network economy. He presents meaning through the operations of the trickster: "we get the special case in which thieving and lying are in fact a necessary part of the creation of meaning."[136] A prophet tells Odysseus to carry an oar inland until he meets people who mistake the oar for a winnowing fan.[137] These are people who are so far from the coast they know nothing of the sea, or of salt, boats, or oars. You have to be a traveler (in fact or in mind) to appreciate that the meaning of the thing depends on context: "It's as if nothing is significant until it's portable; we must be able to move it, in fact or in mind, from one context to another."[138] There is no prohibition against moving the oar, so it can readily assume meaning by being moved. In the case of Hermes, the first (archetypal) liar, there is a prohibition against moving the cattle, so it is not until they are stolen that one appropriates their original meaning in the safe pasture. The thief brings out the original meaning of the cattle, by illegally moving them from their safe pasture to somewhere else, where some of them are in fact slaughtered and consumed. No one appreciates the value of safe pastures for animals more than when they have had their cattle taken from them: "Both lying and thieving multiply meanings against the grain, as it were."[139] A lie is as good as theft in this context: "Such is the mythological weight of the first lie."[140]

The ubiquity of the mass media suggests that misunderstandings about oars and fans will only arise in communities as yet untouched by the instantaneity of global communications. But the network society fosters movements across contexts, which create and sharpen meanings. We can think of the appropriation or movement of terms such as home, web, site, surf, which refine and distort meanings. There is also the incursion of the unfamiliar into our usual orbit. To search eBay[141] for fans, oars, or cattle is to cross cultural barriers and move into the unfamiliar territory of other people's classification schemes. The common practice by which some authors use a Web search engine as dictionary, thesaurus, stimulus, provocation and source of contextual cues further amplifies the portability of meanings. Navigation through global networks is implicated in the transformation and refinement of meanings.

This narrative account of the origins of meaning in the lie is richly metaphorical, a play on the edge of meaning, between truth and fiction. It also implicates travel. By this reading, the traveler, perhaps the flaneur or bricoleur, be her travels spatial or intellectual, is the best representative of interpretative practice. Odysseus carrying the oar from the edge to the interior is in the process of crossing thresholds. Such metaphorical journeyings provide a potent account of the interpretive exercise, the stuff of hermeneutics. Campbell describes the general mythic structure as such: "The hero adventures out of the land we know into darkness; there he accomplishes his adventure, or again is simply lost to us, imprisoned, or in danger; and his return is described as a coming back out of that yonder zone. Nevertheless—and here is a great key to the understanding of myth and symbol—the two kingdoms are actually one. The realm of the gods is a forgotten dimension of the world we know. And the exploration of that dimension, either willingly or unwillingly, is the whole sense of the deed of the hero."[142]

The act of interpretation has been so described, as the transformation brought about by the negotiation across a threshold, the excursion of the traveler, the alien encounter that in fact discloses something about the familiar context of the home. There is also the transformation of the home by what is outside. The movement is repetitive, involving repeated excursion and return. In interpretation there is a re-presentation and a re-creation. There are many excursions, as for Odysseus, whose restless condition involves establishing more than one home, embarking yet again, visiting and revisiting old friends, enemies, and the ghosts of his past. For interpretation, the homey aspect is the base of prejudice from which interpretation begins, an expectation of what the text, the interpretative situation, will reveal. The text in turn discloses the nature of our prejudices, which are then reinforced or modified as we return to them. We discover ourselves every time we let interpretation do its work, or at least we discover our "historical consciousness," the nature of our situation, the shared and peculiar prejudices of our time. According to Gadamer: "It is not really we ourselves who understand: it is always a past that allows us to say, 'I have understood.'"[143]

This understanding can also be seen as a process of revealing and concealing. It is not the case that everything is revealed in interpretation, as if there is a moment of enlightenment, that some pre-existing truthful condition is exposed, the Platonic or verifiable truth. The condition of understanding is more accurately described as a play along this boundary condition of revelation and concealment, exposing and masking. If we are uncomfortable with describing the lie as the beginning of meaning, then it may be easier to assert that the boundary condition captures the character of truth. Heidegger describes our condition as one in which we are "already both in the truth and untruth."[144] He also looks at truth as an issue of revealing and concealing. This is not the usual relativism that asserts that truth is always a "gray area." The boundary is agonistic, a matter of negotiation, a complex and restless condition.

Cryptography and the Occult

The revealing and concealing aspect of truth can also be examined in terms of a common etymological confusion about Hermes, that attempts to draw the process of interpretation back to a Platonic, or Neoplatonic, condition—the spurious origins of meaning in mystery and secrets.

Secrecy emerges as a key issue in the network economy. Corporations, institutions, and authors want to restrict access to information, protect intellectual property rights, and prevent the release of information that is damaging, is libelous, or diminishes one's competitive position in the marketplace. There are also those who assert the right to private communications through encryption technologies, that is, codes and techniques that make it virtually impossible for anyone other than the sender and recipient to intercept, decipher, or understand email messages or computer files. According to Ludlow, the ambition of these "crypto anarchists" is to promote commercial transactions that escape the scrutiny of traditional nation-states, their legal systems, and their tax laws. This affords hope to some of the new social systems, where "full-fledged black-market economies may emerge that will eventually become larger and more vibrant than the legitimate economies that are controlled by the nation states."[145]

This facility to deal in communications that enjoy "pretty good privacy" (PGP)[146] also raises the specter of secret societies and cults, and their right to thrive in the democracy of the network society.[147]

The desire for privacy and secrecy constitutes the other side of the open-source, freeware, and shareware ethos. Hermes occupies this ambivalent condition between concealing and revealing, PGP and open source. Hermes was a trickster, who concealed the truth. He was also a messenger, so was entrusted with faithfully communicating among the gods. Hermes traverses this space between falsity and truth, darkness and light, occupying the shadows of the threshold, an appropriate presentation of the interpretive process.

In distinction to the hermeneutical tradition, there is the hermetic tradition given extensive space in Jung's account of the transformative processes of psychoanalysis. The derivation of the word *hermetic* resides with the Renaissance revival of Hermes Trismegistus, the reputed author of occult books and traditionally the inventor of a magic seal. So an airtight seal is described as hermetic, and hermetic philosophy pertains to secrecy, and to keeping mysteries, abetted in the contemporary context by "crypto anarchy." Jung quotes Hermes Trismegistus as saying "I . . . beget the light, but the darkness too is of my nature."[148] Jung also refers to the alchemical concept of "the black sun."[149] Though Jung's appropriation of the intrigues of alchemy are provocative, they draw attention to the language of the unconscious, which has to be decoded, a philosophy to which the language of hermeneutical enquiry (of theorists such as Gadamer) is ostensibly opposed.[150]

For Jung, there is a secret inner condition, shared by all humankind, pertaining to the archetypes, that he describes as the collective unconscious, particularly implicating Hermes. Hermes the god "represents on the one hand the self and on the other the individuation process and, because of the limitless number of his names, also the collective unconscious."[151] The opposition is between inside and outside, the unconscious and the conscious. The psychoanalytical process, as when an analyst works with a patient, involves "the dialectical discussion between the conscious mind and the unconscious."[152] For Jung the objective of this discussion is not an agonistic play between opposites, but unity and wholeness. Jung's Neoplatonism is evident when he asserts that Hermes the god "is the process by which the lower and material is transformed into the higher and spiritual, and vice versa."[153] The process achieves a return to unity. There is the "mass of inborn unconscious which is to be united with consciousness."[154] For Jung, both alchemy and psychoanalysis share this pursuit of the "union of opposites," which is "a process of psychic development that expresses itself in symbols."[155] In the same way that the alchemist sought to turn base metal to gold, we are encouraged to undertake a psychic process of "refining and ennobling."[156] These Neoplatonic sentiments suggest not the agonistic play of light and dark, a celebration of the threshold condition, but the progression to illumination, abetted by secret rites and knowledges. Jung's psychoanalysis draws on such metaphors.[157] Hermes Trismegistus is the preserve of contemporary occult writing and practice, which surfaces frequently in popular and digital Web culture, but has no place at all in contemporary understandings of language. Contrary to Jung's account, the hermeneutical project runs counter to a belief in a transcendent unity, a union of opposites, a progression to a purgative condition, or the residence of this truth in mystery. The hermetic tradition does, however, reveal the limitations of a position founded on fixed distinctions: between the conscious and the unconscious, the base and the noble, ancient truths and modern understandings.

How do these reflections impinge on crypto anarchism? Whereas concepts of anarchy suggest the cynic's anti-idealism, a desire to break with totalizing structures, rules, and orders, the end of crypto anarchism is presented as participation in a new unitary condition. In his controversial declaration of the "Independence of Cyberspace," Barlow appeals to cyberspace as "the new home of Mind."[158] It is the home of a "great and gathering conversation," not the site of a marketplace of differing opinions. Echoing the familiar theme of Neoplatonic ecstasis, cyberspace is "everywhere and nowhere, but it is not where bodies live,"[159] and it is a "seamless whole."[160] May exhorts would-be crypto anarchists: "Arise, you have nothing to lose but your barbed wire fences!"[161] This unbounded condition shares with secret societies the "mystery" of oneness. Secrets point to unity among the cognoscenti, a privileged position that amounts to exclusion. Needless to say, there is no place for secrets in theories of hermeneutical inquiry. Interpretation is not so much a peeling back of layers to an inner truth as the clash, resistance between, or fusion of narratives. Such inquiry is scarcely abetted by fixation on the mystery of unity, which conceals an agenda to exclusivity, an argument not lost on its critics.[162]

Arguably, Jung's archetypes, studies of alchemy, and a freedom movement based on encrypted communications lead us to rocky ground. Negotiation can be across space, as in *The Odyssey,* the negotiation of a rocky coastline, a mountain pass. Negotiation is navigation under duress, implying resistance and danger. Negotiation of course appeals to a process by which two agents reach agreement, as in the commercial transaction, which is another metaphor for the way language works. According to Hyde: "Plato thought not only that Hermes invented language but that he did so in relation to 'bargaining,' which implies that a prime site of linguistic invention is the marketplace, another place where we are likely to meet strangers with strange goods, and, crossroads-wise, find ourselves forced to articulate newly,"[163] perhaps enabled by eBay as in the ancient agora. The negotiation of meaning in language is not so distant from the barter of the marketplace.

The Trickiness of Money

If language is tricky, then so is money. Accounting is a difficult art for some: balancing the books, living within one's means, understanding spreadsheets, tax laws, financial planning. Economics, too, presents the tricky concepts of market equilibrium, marginal utility, elasticity of demand, consumption function, control of money supply, balance of payments.[164] Adjustments to accounts and budgets are often described as tricks, as is the case of accounting with "funny money," shifting figures from one table in a ledger to another with no material transfer between accounts. Following Godwin,[165] Carlyle, and Ruskin, economics is a source of suspicion, both as a discipline and as a practice. Those who control the markets perpetuate traps and deceptions. There are the small-time confidence tricksters of the marketplace, but we need be no less suspicious of the factory and landowners, the capitalist class, or, for that matter, the consultant or theorist who supports their practices with charts and tables, reducing human endeavor to number, monetary value, and the bottom line. Through advertising, we are exhorted to buy what we do not need—in other words, to participate in the trade of vacuous signs—and the products we procure may be of dubious quality. Plato advocates laws for dealing with those who sell adulterated goods, but he observes: "Hard on the heals of tricks of adulteration come the practices of retail trade."[166] Of whatever rank, anyone will "brush aside the opportunity of modest gain in favor of insatiable profiteering."[167] The business of retail is already sullied, a tricky business throughout.

For Plato, coinage is also the bearer of deception. Citizens of one country can be wealthy with coins, but when they move to another country those same coins, as mere stones or pieces of base metal, are useless.[168] The situation with coinage is analogous to Odysseus's oar having a different meaning when moved away from the land of the coastal dwellers. For commerce, as for meaning in language, the designation of value is a matter of context. Commerce is also tricky insofar as it involves exchange at the edge, which is already the preserve of the trickster. The household is the site of comfort, but beyond, outside the gift community, lies danger and the possibility of exploitation. The edge, the domestic threshold, entails risky business.

Money finds its way into the odysseys of consumer culture in the form of payment for admission. Different thresholds require payment of differing amounts. The ability to pay is the criterion for passage. Every threshold becomes the same, in that it has an admission price. In the mythopoesis of the ancient odyssey, you may have to bribe the ferryman, but you have to steer your way past Scylla, restrain yourself from the Sirens, outsmart the Cyclops. For this narrative, each boundary condition is different and must be negotiated on its own terms, but the transformation is different at the commodified threshold, perhaps exemplified in the commercial theme park. There may be different waiting times, but all attractions are accessible if you have tickets. Commerce provides a parody, a diminished simulation, of the excursion and return of the interpretive process. Interpretation becomes a flow diagram. In fact the flow of money, number, information, data, becomes the primary model of understanding, a view abetted in no small part by the networked economy.

The Trickiness of the Network Economy

Digital commerce introduces new tricks of the trade. There are methods for extracting private information through online registration, so that the consumer can be the subject of targeted advertising at a later date. Once the registration data is held on file, the next step of inserting a credit card number is an easy transition.

Digital media lay claim to the technique of binary thresholding, another trick exploiting the on/off binary condition. With enough bits it is possible to define and manipulate a vast number of intermediate states. A row of thirty bits, which can be either on or off, yields four billion states. If we think of these as color values of a pixel on a computer screen, then we have some idea of the possibilities for image manipulation provided by computerized imaging programs. Very subtle gradations in color can be identified and mapped to alternative color schemes, exaggerating minor variations as huge threshold changes, as when a grayscale image is turned into pure black and white, the boundary being determined by the arbitrary selection of where on the scale the discrimination is to be made.

The boundary condition is not here the site of negotiation. As in the case of movement across boundary conditions on the basis of ability to pay, the ease or difficulty is in one dimension, and the threshold can be shifted along a scale. There is a revealing and a concealing, but, given the same data, the algorithm applied produces the same result every time. Image processing, of satellite data, and multispectral scanning and photography, provides a highly developed technology for disclosing and creating hitherto unseen objects and conditions, but digital thresholding provides a limited metaphor for the boundary condition in general—that is, unless we see the binary condition in relation to the interpretative context, the context of use. The identification of an edge, the discrimination between object and artifact of a process, is a skill, caught up in the hermeneutical practices of the astronomer, geographer, radiologist, and image specialist.

Internet thresholds present similar issues. The activation of a Web site's URL (uniform resource locator) offers the binary choice of being connected or not connected to a server. The threshold as a binary condition affords substantially less intrigue than the threshold to the street, the shadows of the portico, the complexity of the seashore, though practices that develop around the use of the Internet have created controversial boundary conditions: firewalls, log-in procedures, invitations to membership and the disclosure of private information, agreements, and of course opportunities for payment. There are also threshold resistances to be combated: bandwidth constraints, platform dependencies, and legal constraints. Chat rooms provide the threshold condition of the lurker, where you can monitor what is happening in a chat room without being identified as present, which is a little like having the door ajar.

There is also the potent metaphor of "virtual space," which supposedly breaks all the rules of physical space. The usual narrative is that everything is available, that anyone can cross over from one region to the next, and that boundaries are destroyed. The links from one site to another are thresholds certainly. What we previously assumed were major barriers are now porous, and in many cases boringly and uniformly so, but at the same time other threshold conditions open up, on and off the screen.

On the screen, we have new considerations of the shifting thresholds between work and play. This miniature desktop world provides access to word processing, databases, email, and computer-aided design (CAD), the paraphernalia of work. At any moment there is freedom to switch to a game world, email a friend, or indulge in idle Net surfing. The reverse is also the case; as a standard leisure device, the networked computer provides the opportunity to work from home. It is not that work and play are now blurred, but that the ways one is defined in distinction to the other change, as do the modes of transition. Of course there are those for whom the division between work and play is amplified in their attitude to digital media. One can refuse to have email access from home, or ban the computer for Internet browsing at work. These operations involve new micropractices and new exercises of the relations of power by which boundary crossings are determined.

Following the metaphor of the Internet as a vast community, space, city, global village, or marketplace, we then see that it is a city not devoid of hostility. The Internet has the character of the street, where there are those you can trust and those who are bent on exploitation. Communications technologies (the telephone) and the mass media already bring the networked world into the home, defying or rearranging the domestic threshold, but in the case of the Internet there is clearly the possibility of direct interaction, laying one vulnerable to the incursion of advertising, the offer of gifts with strings attached, the offer of dubious goods and services, the full benefits and perils of the marketplace, but proffered in the comfort of one's home and refuge. The intrusion of the commercial Internet offers the promises and dangers of the salesman with one foot in the door, the trickster with the double glazing catalogue.

With the increase in peripatetic digital devices, such as mobile phones, PDAs (personal digital assistants), laptop computers, GPSs (global positioning systems), iPods, and digital cameras, and the convergence between these, the digital world takes to the streets. Odysseus with a mobile phone can keep in constant touch with Athena. Instead of trailing a magic thread in the Labyrinth of the Minotaur, Theseus can find his way out with a GPS device. *The Odyssey* and other stories rely on for their intrigues what we now see as poor communications, a world of only local and extremely slow commerce, the passage between worlds that have only partial knowledge of one another. The gods were the repositories of a fuller knowledge. With the mass media and global communications, the god's-eye view is now within the grasp of everyone with Internet access. The invisible gods are inspecting, or pretending to inspect, the world through CCTV surveillance and webcams.[169]

This is not to say that richly material, varied, and dangerous odysseys are no longer possible. Among the many threshold conditions presented in contemporary narrative we have those created by the failure of equipment, a prominent theme of science fiction. But every day we reenact the drama of expectations dashed by technology, frustrations with the machine, a foundering on the wreck-strewn shores of digital Utopia.

The seductions of the Internet also reconfigure the threshold between commerce and the gift. This commercial world is a world of putative giving, with the ideology of free speech in the ascent. There is a communitarianism living side-by-side with, or perhaps overlaying, its pecuniary aspects, where everything is at a price.

This is a common complaint of commodification. There is the implication that we live in a commercial, and therefore inauthentic, age. If we move beyond this complaint, we cross its threshold into another area of critique, that of provocation. In the manner of a Hermes or a Diogenes, digital media disturbs the boundary condition. The trickster is the bad boy on the block, and the cynic offends. Neither of them has the role of censor.

The edge is also the site of resistance. Threshold conditions engage resistance. You have to step over, push the door, adjust your eyes to the light or dark, fumble for the password, pass inspection, linger, wait in line, pay the money, put on an overcoat. The celebration of threshold is contrary to the quest for a seamless world. Digital commerce sometimes seems to offer a barrier to design sensibility. It offers resistance to creative endeavor. But creativity flourishes under such conditions.

Conclusion

I began this book by considering the portal and the passage of information through it; then design as theft. Theft is an offense that takes place across the threshold, sometimes accomplished by breaking and entering. It involves taking something by force that belongs in one category (that which is mine) and placing it in another (someone else's things). It is the prototypical act of the trickster. Design has this character of appropriation across categories by copying, but more interestingly through the use of metaphor, an act that is provocative, transgressive, and sometimes forceful. In this respect design has the character of a gift. Something surprising, excessive, and different is offered up. In fact the designer seems to occupy this problematic space between the thief and the giver. In its own right, dealing in metaphors is an ambiguous trade. It is also the case that the application of a challenging metaphor takes place against resistance. If the network economy lays claim to being "friction free," then design certainly is not.

We examined the metaphor of the home as the initial site of the gift, and hence of design and creativity. The home is in opposition to the marketplace, across a threshold that affords resistance, brought to light in the fractious writing of the Romantics. The home is also prone to invasion. Electronic commerce serves to rob the home of its communality, by imposing the values of conspicuous consumption, challenging the dependencies of its communal structure, and threatening its security. The machine in general has this invasive propensity. The machine reduces, automates, and renders everything subject to its repetitive and mindless operations, reducing all things to a common denominator, to be considered as a potential for consumption. The machine robs objects of their "thingly" character (Heidegger). It also robs laborers of their livelihood. Machines encounter resistance, and, as Vitruvius has shown, there are machines that break down walls, that violate the threshold condition, that are implicated in the reconfiguration of spaces. Such transgressive machines appeal to the design impulse and are in the company of out-of-control machines, broken or malfunctioning machines, machines that interrupt flows, and the metaphor as machine.

The machine reputedly provides time off work for play (Smith), but we also play with machines, and machines indulge a kind of playfulness. A steam regulator (governor)[170] plays with the flow of steam to the pistons or turbines, in the manner of a steersman playing with the rudder of a boat, or a regulator of any "cybernetic" system. There are also games to be played on computing and video machines, which frequently make play on machine operations—games of control, destruction, and repetition. As well as being the site of violent machinic interactions, the threshold is also the site of play. There is safety in being able to retreat to the shadows, but there is also the play of light, the ambiguous condition, the daring that comes with being neither out nor in.

If the alliance of design with theft seems forced, then it operates in the manner of all metaphor, as a game. Games are played in the space between one metaphor and another, the institutional and the deviant. We play in the space between the safety of our imaginations, the realm of play, and what we take to be the real, with its perils and consequences. We can tell the game from reality, the ethical from the corrupt business practice, but the game is heightened by the tantalizing thought that we may be operating at the edge. In design as theft, and gift, we may be getting away with daylight robbery. Hermes, the god of the threshold, leads us off the path with his deviant trickery, or confuses us with the uncertainty as to which path to take. Such is the mischief of the game.

The safe domain of the home is defined as the preserve of the gift, with commerce taking place at the boundary. The gift can be a means of coercion, graft, and deception, with unpleasant outcomes not so far removed from theft. The gift is already transgressive in that it crosses boundaries. One tribal community passes something of its own to another community. The gift, as with stolen goods, keeps alive the idea that something that is yours was once mine, or perhaps is still mine. Theft does the same. That which was yours is now mine, taken by force or stealth. Design and invention are not always exercised with the same offense, but they can be no less transgressive, and no less tricky.

This chapter culminates my examination of the threshold condition. It shows some legacies from which to draw, and the weight of thinking about liminality. It further authorizes the metaphors through which a designer might search for stimulation and understanding: permeability, duplicity, monstrosity, rite of passage, cynic, trickster, thief. The threshold also has an impact on thinking about the home, the machine, play, and the gift in relation to the network economy. Such theorizing also neatly positions commerce and the gift as variations on a theme—namely, interaction at the threshold.

Notes

Preface

1. S. R. Hiltz and M. Turoff, *The Network Nation: Human Communication via Computer.*

2. See M. McLuhan, *The Gutenberg Galaxy: The Making of Typographic Man.*

3. M. Castells, *The Rise of the Network Society*, 62.

4. Liminality, developed as a concept within anthropology and largely attributed to Victor Turner, pertains to the condition of being at an intermediate stage in a rite of passage, a position of confusion, ambiguity, and paradox. See V. Turner, *The Forest of Symbols: Aspects of Ndembu Ritual.*

Introduction

1. Whereas the future of technology industries is uncertain, according to one report, "all content-oriented i.e. creative areas of employment will continue to show high growth rates (Web design, advertising, publishing, media, education, entertainment, etc)." See J. Reuter (ed.), *Final Report: Exploitation and Development of the Job Potential in the Cultural Sector in the Age of Digitalization.*

2. C. Crawford, *Electronic Book: The Art of Computer Game Design.* This is no more evident than in the case of computer games. See S. Kline, N. Dyer-Witheford, and G. de Peuter, *Digital Play: The Interaction of Technology, Culture and Marketing*, 98.

3. Kline, Dyer-Witheford, and de Peuter, *Digital Play: The Interaction of Technology, Culture and Marketing,* 73.

4. Ibid., 17.

5. Ibid., 21.

6. R. Burnett and P. D. Marshall, *Web Theory: An Introduction,* 86.

7. Evidence of this interstitial condition comes from the discipline of design itself, or the many disciplines of design, that incorporate their own critique into their discussions. For example, architecture, as a highly reflective design discipline, is caught between the need for a commission that pays wages and profits and the need for one that also meets the aspirational requirements of society at large, or at least of a community of users. The literature on architecture and consumerism is vast, which is not say that architects are in a comfortable position, able to integrate conflicting demands, presenting a unified, harmonious in-between synthesis. In fact, this is one of the most difficult concepts for aspiring designers and non-designers to grasp. The "space between" design and commerce is not (often) a fusion of positions, a blurring of boundaries, an open accommodation of rival positions. The space is agonistic, which is to say a contested, unresolved, and discursive realm, sustained and enhanced by continual dialogue, negotiation, contingency and provisional resolution. Edgy designers recognize it as such.

8. Turner, *The Forest of Symbols: Aspects of Ndembu Ritual,* 97.

9. B. Tschumi, *Architecture and Disjunction,* 91. This architectural affinity with the edge condition contrasts markedly with the "architecture" of the Internet as presented by Lawrence Lessig. Lessig characterizes the spatial environment as a system of constraints, a metaphor that he translates to the Internet, promoting a narrative of constraints, limits, and control that I regard as antithetical to the discourse of the threshold. See L. Lessig, *Code and Other Laws of Cyberspace.*

10. R. Koolhaas and B. Mau, "What ever happened to urbanism?," 969. This is presented in the context of a discussion about a "new urbanism," designing in and for cities, accepting the reality that no one is really in control of what happens or what gets built. Elsewhere he identifies the key to new urbanism as residing in "junkspace," which is a "fuzzy empire of blur [that] fuses high and low, public and private, straight and bent, bloated and starved to offer a seamless patchwork of the permanently disjointed." See R. Koolhaas, "Junk space," 163.

11. J. Hill, *Actions of Architecture: Architects and Creative Users,* 4.

12. N. Bourriaud, *Relational Aesthetics,* 16.

13. This is actually the dialectic "method" of the philosopher Hegel, to be discussed in chapter 2.

14. See I. Sommerville, *Software Engineering.* Note that "systems thinking" can also be deployed to indicate the converse of method, and it entails a reflective mode of research that is suspicious of the application of scientific method to complex institutions and practices. For example, see D. Russell and R. Ison, "The research-development relationship in rural communities: An opportunity for contextual science."

15. Arguably, this is always what happens in design, whatever formality is introduced to dress it up with professional rigor. As a more abstract example of the dialectic, we can consider architecture's long-time preoccupation with space, the container, the void, to be divided and partitioned in the creation of comfortable environments for human habitation and use. Space as containment perhaps brings to mind its opposite, the solid matter that occupies it and contains it, or out of which the void is carved. In this context the opposite of void (or space) is solidity. This opposition in turn brings to mind the concept of the inside, that which is contained within space, which directs one to the concept of an outside. In fact, arguably, architecture is less concerned with solid and void than the interface between inside and outside. In architectural terms this interface is the threshold, which can be an opening in a wall, a door, or a window, but it has material and social qualities worthy of scrutiny and requiring design. Much attention in architecture is expended on the nature of openings, steps, the depth of reveals, thresholds, and gaps. Arguably, architecture is all about gaps, transitions, prosceniums, frames, and between-spaces. In this particular design discipline, the idea of the gap has physical realization. But it also imbues the thinking of design. Thresholds in buildings are places of risk, where the activities of the street and the ravages of the weather may percolate in, the interface between the private (inside) and the public (outside). They are safe places into which one can retreat and keep a watchful eye, but they are also places where strangers can lurk.

16. Burnett and Marshall provide a description of the Web portal as a media type, or genre. See Burnett and Marshall, *Web Theory: An Introduction,* 81–104.

17. The term *portal* appears as one of the means of marking points of passage in theories of liminality and rites of passage. See A. van Gennep, *The Rites of Passage,* 17. The Web portal is already an invocation of liminality.

18. Cryptography embraces the various means of ensuring the security of data and communications by means of electronic codes and keys, and it raises controversies about individual liberties and governmental control. See P. Ludlow, *Crypto Anarchy, Cyberstates, and Pirate Utopias.*

19. Castells, *The Rise of the Network Society.* See also M. Poster, *What's the Matter with the Internet?*, 58.

20. See G. P. Landow and P. Delaney, "Hypertext, hypermedia and literary studies: The state of the art," and A. Tapia, "Graphic design in the digital era: The rhetoric of hypertext."

21. T. Berners-Lee, *Weaving the Web: The Past, Present and Future of the World Wide Web by its Inventor.*

22. L. Torvalds and D. Diamond, *Just for Fun: The Story of an Accidental Revolutionary.*

23. The promotion and preservation of these freedoms of necessity requires legislation, standards, and vigilance, which sometimes conflict with the freedoms themselves. Who would want to contribute to an open source project if they thought that someone else might make propriety gain from their free labors, or exercise restrictive trade practices? This would be like a neighbor walking into your house and selling off your furniture.

24. The open access ethos is prone to exploitation, in the form of invasive advertising, contamination by computer viruses, digital espionage, and theft. In addition, as commercial and professional organizations use the Web, they bring with them the culture of competition; the wish to preserve security, protect intellectual property, and maintain corporate image; and protection from libel, misrepresentation, and the charge of exclusivity. Whereas the ideals of the Web as an open access medium may persist among home computer users and hackers, those easiest to sue (corporations and institutions) are likely to exercise the most restraint and present the most severe restrictions. See V. E. Rezmierski, M. R. Seese Jr., and N. St. Clair II, "University systems security logging: Who is doing it and how far can they go?," J. Sherwood, "Security issues in today's corporate network," M. Turega, "Issues with information dissemination on global networks," and H. S. Venter, "Network security: Important issues."

25. With encryption, certain groups maintain a wall of complete privacy around their communications. See Ludlow, *Crypto Anarchy, Cyberstates, and Pirate Utopias.*

26. B. Detlor, "The corporate portal as information infrastructure: Towards a framework for portal design."

27. Such reflections may bring the designer to a realization that the portal is one meta-phor among many. Web pages are also receptacles, rooms, shops, plazas, a means of nav-igating across a sea of information, and hooks from which to string a network of associations. They offer a means of molding the amorphous Web into a particular image. Web pages are also incidental, symptoms of communicative practices (rather than re-ceptacles) constituting traces, memories and palimpsests for socially constructed narra-tives. For idealistic e-communitarians there are no portals, just the ideal of free form access. See Landow and Delaney, "Hypertext, hypermedia and literary studies: The state of the art." Community WiFi also buys into these metaphors.

28. The development of such concepts commonly falls under the heading of "user-centered security." See P. Dourish and D. Redmiles, "An approach to usable security based on event monitoring and visualization," and L. Teo G-J. Ahn, and Y. Zheng, "Dy-namic and risk-aware network access management."

29. Few authors can resist the temptation to use a Web search engine as an instant means of checking up on a "fact," exploring the usage of a word, or conjuring up an ap-propriate image?

30. K. Marx, *Karl Marx: Selected Writings,* 21. From this point we could embark on a critique of the network economy in terms of the incursion of capitalism into every area of life, and the submission of all things to the logic of the global commodity. These charges are the subject of chapter 2.

31. To steal is to take what belongs to someone else. I don't think designers knowingly engage in theft in this way. In fact they would prefer to see themselves on the side of the craft guilds, whose role it was to protect creative labors against the organized "robber barons." See Ibid., 163.

32. J. Phillips and A. Firth, *Introduction to Intellectual Property Law.*

33. See Plato, *The Republic of Plato.* Padovan provides a helpful introduction to Plato's theory of copying in the context of design. See R. Padovan, *Proportion: Science, Philosophy, Architecture,* 99–105.

34. In the practical activity of copying objects, we may also think of not just copying the entire shape and material composition of an artifact, but being selective, and identifying certain of its characteristics that we wish to copy. This is reproduction by *analogy.* That is, we identify certain features of the thing we wish to copy and ignore others. So, according to Vitruvius, the ancient architectural theorist, the column in a temple is a copy of a human

body, but it has only some of the characteristics of a body, such as its proportions, the pattern of folds in fabric worn as a garment, adornment, and so on. P. Vitruvius, *Vitruvius: The Ten Books on Architecture,* 102–105. In a similar way, a cardboard model of a building reproduces form and shape, but not dimension and materials. The wooden throne of a noble may be a copy of a monarch's solid gold throne, but in a different material. In informational terms there is a sampling process in play, a selection of attributes to be reproduced. Models of buildings and landscapes in a computer may be considered analogical in this respect. Only the coordinate geometry and surface textures of the original are reproduced, and perhaps a limited range of movements. The role of analogy is evident in the case of our notional permeable portal design, where the Web site is able to admit and exclude access in a way that bears only some of the characteristics of an opening or doorway. It is a "copy" of a doorway, but only in limited respects.

35. Aristotle, *The Poetics,* 1457b.

36. C. Desmet, "Reading the Web as fetish."

37. The rhizomic nature of language is taken up famously by Deleuze and Guattari, a theme avidly pursued by edgy designers. See G. Deleuze and F. Guattari, *A Thousand Plateaus: Capitalism and Schizophrenia.*

38. I take up this theme in full in R. Coyne, *Designing Information Technology in the Postmodern Age: From Method to Metaphor.*

39. The role of the entrepreneur has been described similarly as a task of "holding on to an anomaly and instituting the practices by which the anomaly comes into focus." See C. Spinoza, F. Flores, and H. L. Dreyfus, *Disclosing New Worlds: Entrepreneurship, Democratic Action, and the Cultivation of Solidarity,* 68. The torture of metaphors as an impetus to innovation is only partially expressed in the term *creative destruction,* given instrumental treatment by W. McKnight Lee, M. Vaaler Paul, and L. Katz Raul, *Creative Destruction: Business Survival Strategies in the Global Internet Economy.*

40. As also asserted by the Situationists. See G. Debord, *The Society of the Spectacle.*

41. See, for example, S. Plant, *Zeros and Ones: Digital Women and the New Technoculture* and M. Wertheim, *The Pearly Gates of Cyberspace: A History of Space from Dante to the Internet.*

42. Though the commission is the mainstay of design practice, and not to be despised at all, through its dealing with specifics it can be construed as sapping design of its wider instrumentality.

43. See, for example, J. Mitchell William, *City of Bits: Space, Place, and the Infobahn.*

44. M. Benedikt, *Cyberspace: First Steps.*

1 Home Economics

1. Kline and colleagues provide a helpful account of the way domestic consumption was integral to capitalism under "Fordism," named after Henry Ford whose production methods epitomized the strong relationship between labor and markets instilled by intensive factory production. Post-Fordism and globalization are less supportive of the family unit as a source of labor and markets. See Kline, Dyer-Witheford, and de Peuter, *Digital Play: The Interaction of Technology, Culture and Marketing,* 62–66.

2. See B. Gates, N. Myhrvold, and P. Rinearson, *The Road Ahead,* for examples of this kind of account of the growth of the personal computer business.

3. See Torvalds and Diamond, *Just for Fun: The Story of an Accidental Revolutionary.* See also B. Laurel, *Utopian Entrepreneur,* for an account of software development and its conflict with the world of commerce.

4. Raymond, "The cathedral and the bazaar," quoted in R. Bloor, *The Electronic Bazaar: From the Silk Road to the eRoad,* 43.

5. Hermeneutics is the study of interpretation, the means by which we make judgments, interpret and apply rules, understand a textual document, appreciate art, and so on. It is an all-embracing study and has often been contrasted with a methodological, analytical, or scientific way of looking at things, though hermeneutics often claims to embrace those modes of inquiry as well. See W. Dilthey, "The development of hermeneutics," F. Schleiermacher and A. Bowie (eds.), *Hermeneutics and Criticism: And Other Writings,* H-G. Gadamer, *Truth and Method,* H-G. Gadamer, *Gadamer in Conversation: Reflections and Commentary,* H-G. Gadamer, *Philosophical Hermeneutics,* and H-G. Gadamer, *The Enigma of Health: The Art of Healing in a Scientific Age.*

6. These enthusiasms are evident in such practical books as F. Fiore, *The Complete Idiot's Guide to Starting an Online Business.*

7. Bloor, *The Electronic Bazaar: From the Silk Road to the eRoad,* x.

8. A. Smith, *An Inquiry into the Nature and Causes of the Wealth of Nations,* 22.

9. Ibid.

10. J. Ruskin, *Unto This Last: And Other Writings,* 169. See also A. Lutz Mark, *Economics for the Common Good: Two Centuries of Economic Thought in the Humanistic Tradition,* for a critical assessment of the contribution of Ruskin and Carlyle to social economics.

11. Ruskin, *Unto This Last: And Other Writings,* 167.

12. Ibid., 212.

13. T. Carlyle, *Past and Present,* 308.

14. Ibid., 6.

15. Foucault provides a helpful account of the legacy of the stoics in our understanding restraints on the actions of the human body and sexuality. See M. Foucault, *The History of Sexuality 3: The Care of the Self.*

16. According to Lloyd, the agora had many functions, including that of marketplace, a place for litigation, political meetings, entertainment, and religious functions. The architecture of the space was very simple: an open market plaza surrounded by various stoa, single- or double-story colonnades providing shelter from the sun and the rain. See S. Lloyd, "Ancient and classical architecture," 50–53.

17. For a discussion of the ancient forum, its imputation in democracy, and its adoption as a metaphor of the Internet, see G. Graham, *The Internet: A Philosophical Inquiry,* 62–83.

18. M. Aurelius, *Meditations,* 73.

19. I canvass the sentiments pertaining to the Internet as ushering in a new, unified world order, in R. Coyne, *Technoromanticism: Digital Narrative, Holism, and the Romance of the Real.*

20. A. Smith, *The Theory of Moral Sentiments,* 289.

21. Ibid., 272.

22. Ibid., 275.

23. Ibid., 276.

24. For example, see www.newdeal.gov.uk.

25. J. Cassidy, *Dot.con: The Greatest Story Ever Told,* 321.

26. Seneca, *Dialogues and Letters,* 102.

27. Ibid. By some accounts Stoicism prepared Rome for Christianity, with evidence from Saint Augustine's references to Seneca's writing in his *Confessions.*

28. Vitruvius, *Vitruvius: The Ten Books on Architecture,* 168. For a more up-to-date account of the nature of patronage, see H. Jenkins, *Textual Poachers: Television Fans and Participatory Culture.*

29. J. Marías, *History of Philosophy,* 93

30. Vitruvius, *Vitruvius: The Ten Books on Architecture,* 5.

31. Ibid., 73.

32. Ibid., 109.

33. This architectural reserve is in contrast to the Stoic functionary, Pliny the Younger's poetic account of his own villas. See Pliny, *The Letters of the Younger Pliny.*

34. Smith, *An Inquiry into the Nature and Causes of the Wealth of Nations,* 17.

35. J. Rifkin, *The End of Work: The Decline of the Global Work-Force and the Dawn of the Post-Market Era.* In the next chapter, we will see how machine substitution features in Marx's critique of capitalism.

36. The academy was so named after a suburb of Athens and was the location of Plato's school. Plato's mentor Socrates is also associated with the stoa. So the two places are not so distant.

37. See Plato, *The Republic of Plato.* This world beyond our physical world can best be appreciated by the "higher" human faculties, such as the intellect. In many ways it would make sense to refer to the realm of the ideas as the unintelligible, as it seems always to evade comprehension.

38. Ibid.

39. The middle aspect of the soul appealed to the senses.

40. Nowhere are the conflicts of idealism more evident in design than in the attempts by architects and architectural theorists to reconcile their criticism of capitalism with the allure of the big commercial commission. See, for example, M. Tafuri, *Architecture and Utopia: Design and Capitalist Development*.

41. See Jenkins, *Textual Poachers: Television Fans and Participatory Culture*. The approach here is ethnomethodological, a scholarly approach to taste and aesthetics antithetical to idealism.

42. See C. Penly, "Brownian motion: Women, tactics, and technology." See also M. Poster, *The Second Media Age,* for an exposition on prejudice within critical theory to "low culture" in broadcast media.

43. Le Corbusier, *Towards a New Architecture,* 29.

44. Ibid., 25.

45. J. Ruskin, *The Stones of Venice,* 101.

46. Ibid., 227.

47. Ibid., 102.

48. See G. Lynn, *Animate Form,* G. Lynn, *Architecture for an Embryologic Housing,* J. Giovannini, "Building a better blob," J. Rosa, *Next Generation Architecture: Contemporary Digital Experimentation + The Radical Avant-Garde,* and N. Leach and RIBA Future Studies, *Designing for a Digital World.*

49. Ruskin, *The Stones of Venice,* 149.

50. Ibid., 153.

51. See Coyne, *Technoromanticism: Digital Narrative, Holism, and the Romance of the Real,* and R. Coyne, "The cult of the not-yet."

52. Wertheim, *The Pearly Gates of Cyberspace: A History of Space from Dante to the Internet.*

53. H. P. Moravec, *Mind Children: The Future of Robot and Human Intelligence*.

54. Epicurus, cited in J. Gaskin (ed.), *The Epicurean Philosophers*, 43.

55. Epicurus, in Ibid., 44.

56. See A. Ryan (ed.), *John Stuart Mill and Jeremy Bentham: Utilitarianism and Other Essays*.

57. See arguments outlined by D. R. Hofstadter and D. C. Dennett, *The Mind's I: Fantasies and Reflections on Self and Soul*.

58. Epicurus, in Gaskin (ed.), *The Epicurean Philosophers*, 44.

59. See Ryan, *John Stuart Mill and Jeremy Bentham: Utilitarianism and Other Essays*.

60. M. Friedman, *Capitalism and Freedom*.

61. See Foucault's famous critique of Bentham in Foucault, *Discipline and Punish: The Birth of the Prison*. The panopticon was a circular planned prison building with the warder's station at the hub. The cells were arranged around the perimeter, the intention being that the prisoners always felt as though they were under surveillance, and so behaved themselves and were reformed, whether or not the warder was on duty. See also T. Y. Levin, U. Frohne, and P. Weibel, *CTRL {SPACE}: Rhetorics of Surveillance from Bentham to Big Brother*.

62. In a helpful article aligning Marx with Aristotle, Katz asserts that "the rise of capitalism transfers the locus of the economy from the despotic household to the marketplace." See C. Katz, "The Greek matrix of Marx's critique of political economy," 245.

63. Aristotle, *The Ethics of Aristotle: The Nicomachean Ethics*, 211.

64. Ibid., 209.

65. Ibid., 211.

66. Aristotle, *The Politics*.

67. Aristotle, *The Ethics of Aristotle: The Nicomachean Ethics*, 63. See also M. Wigley, "Untitled: The housing of gender," 336, for an account of the nature of the house in

classical and renaissance society, and the legacies of privacy, surveillance, authority, and ornament.

68. Smith, *The Theory of Moral Sentiments,* 270.

69. See Gadamer, *Truth and Method,* and M. Heidegger, *Being and Time.* Domesticity also enters Heidegger's frame on the subject of language as the house of being. See M. Heidegger, "Building, dwelling, thinking."

70. See for example R. Firth (ed.), *Themes in Economic Anthropology.*

71. Of course, there are economists who have little difficulty calculating the way exchange within the family operates. See G. S. Becker, *A Treatise on the Family.*

72. M. Godelier, *The Enigma of the Gift,* 36.

73. J. Ruskin, *The Seven Lamps of Architecture,* 10.

74. Ibid.

75. Ruskin, *Unto This Last: And Other Writings,* 175.

76. See D. A. Schön, *Reflective Practitioner: How Professionals Think in Action,* and A. Snodgrass and R. Coyne, "Is designing hermeneutical?"

77. This has been stated explicitly in the case of architecture. According to the philosopher Benjamin, "architecture works necessarily within the logic of the gift." See A. Benjamin, *Architectural Philosophy,* 9.

78. We have explored some of these aspects from a technical point of view in R. Coyne et al., "Applying web-based product libraries" and R. Coyne, J. Lee, and S. Ofluoglu, "Design and the emerging e-commerce environment." See also E. Brynjolfsson and B. Kahnin, *Understanding the Digital Economy: Data, Tools, and Research.*

79. Arguably this experimentation contributed to the bullish behavior of dot-com entrepreneurs and investors. See Cassidy, *Dot.con: The Greatest Story Ever Told.*

80. Platonism also draws attention to the nature of patronage, economics under the metaphor of the mentor-student relationship, which already finds resonances with de-

sign processes. For an account of the Platonic-erotic relationship, see R. Waterfield, "Introduction."

2 Rampant Machines

1. See Cassidy, *Dot.con: The Greatest Story Ever Told*, 146.

2. This is the term used by Gates to describe the benefits of electronic business: "I used the term *friction-free capitalism* to describe how the Internet was helping to create Adam Smith's ideal marketplace, in which buyers and sellers can easily find one another without taking much time or spending much money." B. Gates and G. Hemingway, *Business @ the Speed of Thought: Using a Digital Nervous System*, 82.

3. Corbusier, *Towards a New Architecture*, 95.

4. The architectural theorist Harbison provides an interesting account of the machine in architecture, calling on its renaissance origins as an aesthetic device. See R. Harbison, *Thirteen Ways: Theoretical Investigations in Architecture*, 26–43.

5. For Terranova, the Internet updates the machine of capitalism to "cyberpunk snapshots of the immobile bodies of the hackers, electrodes like umbilical cords connecting them to the matrix, appendixes to a living, all-powerful cyberspace. Beyond the special effects bonanza, the box-office success of *The Matrix* validates the popularity of the paranoid interpretation of this mutation." T. Terranova, "Free labor: Producing culture for the digital economy," 45.

6. For example, as suggested in G. Bachelard, *The Poetics of Space*.

7. Arguable from his interest in purity and simplicity and his repetition of the motif of the sacrificial altar in his architecture. See D. Weston, "The lantern and the glass: On the themes of renewal and dwelling in Le Corbusier's early art and architecture."

8. The distinction between metaphor and metonymy is moot. A metaphor is also about the part-whole relationship insofar as it can be explained in terms of classes or sets of things. A house is a part of the set of things called machines. See R. Jakobson and M. Halle, *Fundamentals of Language*, on the roles of metaphor and metonymy. They argue that film deals in metonymy, showing parts (marching feet to stand in for the army). Romantic poetry accommodates any kind of juxtaposition, in keeping with metaphor. By extension, perhaps the computer is strictly a metaphorical medium, as it allows full

scope to the romance whereby anything can be related to anything. See also P. de Man, *Allegories of Reading: Figural Language in Rousseau, Nietzsche, Rilke.*

9. In turn, the house perhaps signifies stability, an older order, resistance, and even vulnerability.

10. For Corbusier, we are in a new machine age, but we are blinded to that fact: "Our eyes, unhappily, are unable yet to discern it." Corbusier, *Towards a New Architecture,* 87.

11. See R. Barthes, *Mythologies.*

12. See also Baudrillard, for whom consumption pertains to the production and manipulation of social signifiers rather than use and satisfaction. It is the signifiers that are being consumed, not the products. See J. Baudrillard, *Symbolic Exchange and Death,* and Poster, *The Second Media Age,* 105. See also A. Ahlava, *Architecture in Consumer Society,* for a helpful account of Baudrillard's theories in the context of architectural design.

13. J. Ruskin, *Praeterita,* quoted in J. Ruskin, *Selected Writings,* 72.

14. Echoing William Blake: "To see a world in a grain of sand and a heaven in a wild flower, hold infinity in the palm of your hand and eternity in an hour."

15. See H. Marcuse, *One-Dimensional Man: Studies in the Ideology of Advanced Industrial Society,* for a critical account of how the logical proposition serves capitalism.

16. See J. Austin, *How to Do Things with Words.*

17. R. Rorty, *Contingency, Irony, and Solidarity,* 74.

18. H. White, *Tropics of Discourse: Essays in Cultural Criticism.* Borrowing from Foucault, he asserts that in the age of metaphor, science ordered things on the basis of supposed similarity. The subsequent period emphasized metonymy, the relationship between and parallel consideration of disparate parts. There was a period of essentialism that valorized the trope of synecdoche, a variant of metonymy.

19. See Kline, Dyer-Witheford, and de Peuter, *Digital Play: The Interaction of Technology, Culture and Marketing,* 277. Terranova also notes: "Subcultural movements have stuffed the pockets of multinational capitalism for decades. Nurtured by the consumption of earlier moments, subcultures have provoked the look, style, and sounds that sell

clothes, CDs, video games, films, and advertising slots on television." See Terranova, "Free labor: producing culture for the digital economy," 39.

20. Vitruvius, *Vitruvius: The Ten Books on Architecture,* 283.

21. Ibid., 14.

22. Ibid., 283.

23. Aristotle, *Physics,* 39.

24. This is not the same as saying that the parts cause the whole, a distinction that Heidegger develops at length. For Heidegger, Aristotle is referring to a *revealing,* and the bronze and silver are not components but materials, the essences of which are revealed in the making of the artifact. For Heidegger, there is no predetermination of whether the whole brings about the parts or the parts bring the whole into being. See M. Heidegger, "The origin of the work of art."

25. Vitruvius, *Vitruvius: The Ten Books on Architecture,* 285.

26. Ibid., 282.

27. Ibid., 284.

28. The mechanical view of causation is a diminished form of Aristotle's original sense of cause, that a cause is a revealing.

29. R. Descartes, *Discourse on Method and the Meditations,* 73. Descartes says of animals: "It is nature which acts in them according to the disposition of their organs, as one sees that a clock, which is made up of only wheels and springs, can count the hours and measure time more exactly than we can with all our art" (75–76).

30. A. Wilden, *The Rules Are No Game: The Strategy of Communication.*

31. S. H. Strogatz, "Exploring complex networks."

32. Cassidy, *Dot.con: The Greatest Story Ever Told,* 320.

33. Mirowski provides a helpful account of the machine metaphor in the history of economics, including more recently the computerized automaton or cyborg. See P. Mirowski, *Machine Dreams: Economics Becomes a Cyborg Science,* 9.

34. Smith, *An Inquiry into the Nature and Causes of the Wealth of Nations,* 173.

35. M. Sahlins, *Stone Age Economics,* 79.

36. Of course, the division of labor has its limits. The cost of organization and communication increases with the number of specialized labor components. Complex, modern factory production has to be designed in a way that makes it efficient.

37. Smith, *An Inquiry into the Nature and Causes of the Wealth of Nations,* 17.

38. K. Marx, *Grundrisse,* excerpted in Marx, *Karl Marx: Selected Writings,* 379. For critical accounts of Marx's writing, see G. Lukács, *History and Class Consciousness,* and D. McLellan, *Marx After Marx: An Introduction.*

39. Rifkin, *The End of Work: The Decline of the Global Work-Force and the Dawn of the Post-Market Era.*

40. C. Alexander, *Notes on the Synthesis of Form.*

41. See, for example, Sommerville, *Software Engineering.*

42. Where he seems to adopt a more linguistic model of design. See C. Alexander, S. Ishikawa, and M. Silverstein, *A Pattern Language: Towns, Buildings, Construction.*

43. I characterized the rival approach as "edgy design" in the introductory chapter.

44. Marcuse, *One-Dimensional Man: Studies in the Ideology of Advanced Industrial Society.* See also L. Althusser and E. Balibar, *Reading Capital.*

45. See Rifkin, *The End of Work: The Decline of the Global Work-Force and the Dawn of the Post-Market Era,* and A. Feenberg, *Transforming Technology: A Critical Theory Revisited.*

46. A. M. Turing, "Computing machinery and intelligence."

47. In a similar way, Minsky's book *The Society of Mind* suggests that if we are to produce useful computers, then we need to apprehend that the mind is like a complex and

far-reaching society of communicating and negotiating individuals (agents) and clusters of individuals. The description of society that serves the computational view becomes machine-like, in its dependence on causal connections, however complex. See M. L. Minsky, *The Society of Mind*.

48. J. Ruskin, from "The Nature of Gothic," in *The Stones of Venice*, quoted in Ruskin, *Unto This Last: And Other Writings*, 87.

49. M. Weber, *The Protestant Ethic and the Spirit of Capitalism*.

50. Ibid., 281, note 105.

51. Weber says: "The Puritan wanted to work in a calling; we are forced to do so. For when asceticism was carried out of monastic cells into everyday life, and began to dominate worldly morality, it did its part in building the tremendous cosmos of the modern economic order. This order is now bound to the technical and economic conditions of machine production which today determine the lives of all individuals who are born into this mechanism, not only those directly concerned with economic acquisition, with irresistible force. Perhaps it will so determine them until the last ton of fossilized coal is burnt. In Baxter's view the care for external goods should only lie on the shoulders of the 'saint like a light cloak, which can be thrown aside at any moment.' But fate decreed that the cloak should become an iron cage." Ibid., 181.

52. The term *dystopia* was apparently first coined by John Stuart Mill.

53. G. Orwell, *1984*.

54. A. Rand, *The Fountainhead*. See also A. Saint, *The Image of the Architect*.

55. J. Derrida, "The principle of reason: the university in the eyes of its pupils."

56. Deleuze and Guattari, *A Thousand Plateaus: Capitalism and Schizophrenia*, 15.

57. Aurelius, *Meditations*, 73.

58. Smith, *The Theory of Moral Sentiments*, 289. Technically, "the universe *is like* a machine" is a simile, "the universe *is* a machine" is a metaphor, and to use a part (machine) to signify the whole (universe) is metonymy.

59. For Postman, "because of its 'universality,' the computer compels respect, even devotion, and argues for a comprehensive role in all fields of human activity." See N. Postman, *Technopoly: The Surrender of American Culture to Technology,* 119.

60. The closest Plato seems to come to an endorsement of the stoic metaphor of an interconnected network is through the metaphor of weaving, but here there is also an appeal to bureaucratic order and control. We might think of a fabric as a network of loops and knots, overlays and connections. But here weaving subjects an understanding of the social condition (of the polis) to a formal frame, an intertwining of warp and woof, measuring and dividing, marrying together dissimilar natures: the courageous and the temperate, the bold and the gentle, which are the warp and the woof of society. There is the firm texture of the warp and the looser texture of the woof. Plato says that the beneficent ruler brings the life of both components of society together, thereby "completing the most magnificent and best of all fabrics and covering with it all the other inhabitants of cities, both slave and free." See Plato, *Statesman,* 283 c.

61. Friedman, *Capitalism and Freedom,* 16.

62. Plant, *Zeros and Ones: Digital Women and the New Technoculture.*

63. Bloor, *The Electronic Bazaar: From the Silk Road to the eRoad.* This is of course counter to Ruskin's presentation of the gothic, and its purchase in the nobility of teamwork, the realm of the craft guilds.

64. See D. Ades (ed.), *Art and Power: Europe under the Dictators 1930–45 (Exhibition Catalogue to 23rd Council of Europe Exhibition).*

65. Tafuri, *Architecture and Utopia: Design and Capitalist Development,* 20–21.

66. Tschumi, *Architecture and Disjunction.* Koolhaas offers similar ironical treatment in both his writing and building. See R. Koolhaas (ed.), *The Harvard Guide to Shopping.*

67. J-F. Lyotard, *The Postmodern Condition: A Report on Knowledge.*

68. According to Marx, the idealist view of history is evident when we say things like: "'History will not be joked at . . . history has exerted its greatest efforts to . . . history has been engaged . . . what would be the purpose of history? . . . history provides the explicit proof; history proposes truths,' etc." K. Marx, "The holy family," 139.

69. As promoted by G. W. F. Hegel, *Hegel's Science of Logic.*

70. As promoted by Hegel, the development of thought is a historical process, and there are great movements in thought, each thought provoking its opposite, and in turn both are overtaken by a new thought.

71. Marx criticizes the Platonism of his contemporaries, who attach significance to categories, as opposed to the ordinary and everyday. (As he puts it they talk of fruit, as opposed to apples and oranges.) This is the ideology of the Romantics, or more precisely the German idealists, culminating in Hegel and certain of his interpreters (the so-called Young Hegelians). (Marx takes Hegel in a different direction.) From this follow positive projects: "If man is unfree in the materialist sense, i.e., is not free through the negative power to avoid this or that, but through the positive power to assert his true individuality, crime must not be punished in the individual, but the anti-social source of crime must be destroyed, and each man must be given social scope for the vital manifestation of his being. If man is shaped by his surroundings, his surroundings must be made human. If man is social by nature, he will develop his true nature only in society, and the power of his nature must be measured not by the power of separate individuals but by the power of society." Marx, "The holy family," 154.

72. Ibid., 151. See also L. Althusser, *For Marx,* for an account of Marx and the dialectic.

73. Ibid., 154. Marx also asserts: "There is no need of any great penetration to see from the teaching of materialism on the original goodness and equal intellectual endowment of men, the omnipotence of experience, habit and education, and the influences of environment on man, the great significance of industry, the justification of enjoyment, etc., how necessarily materialism is connected with communism and socialism. If man draws all his knowledge, sensation, etc., from the world of the senses and the experience gained in it, the empirical world must be arranged so that in it man experiences and gets used to what is really human and that he becomes aware of himself as man." Marx, "The holy family," 154.

74. G. Deleuze and F. Guattari, *Anti-Oedipus: Capitalism and Schizophrenia.* Poster provides an account of how Marxist theory, with its emphasis on action (labor), has undertaken a linguistic turn, with an emphasis on language and communication. See M. Poster, *The Second Media Age,* 57.

75. Vitruvius, *Vitruvius: The Ten Books on Architecture,* 283.

76. The operations of language have been described in mechanical terms as involving transformation rules. This is tantamount to a system of grammar, denigrated by Ruskin: "The sciences ceased at once to be anything more than different kinds of grammars—

grammar of language, grammar of logic, grammar of ethics, grammar of art; and the tongue, wit, and invention of the human race were supposed to have found their utmost and most divine mission in syntax and syllogism, perspective and five orders." *The Stones of Venice,* quoted in *John Ruskin: Selected Writings,* 204.

77. N. Chomsky, *Syntactic Structures.*

78. Austin, *How to Do Things with Words.*

79. Friedman, *Capitalism and Freedom,* 8.

80. K. Marx, "Grundrisse," 371.

81. Ibid.

82. Ibid., 372. He adds: "just as the despotism of the Roman emperors was the prerequisite of the free Roman civil law."

83. Ibid. He continues: "Hence the absurdity of considering free competition as being the final development of human liberty, and the negation of free competition as being the negation of individual liberty and of social production founded on individual liberty. It is only free development on a limited foundation—that of the dominion of capital" (372).

84. Ibid., 373. Furthermore, he adds: "The worker's activity, limited to a mere abstraction, is determined and regulated on all sides by the movement of the machinery, not the other way round" (374).

85. Ibid.

86. Ibid.

87. Ibid., 374.

88. Ibid., 378.

89. For example, see G. Scott and R. Scott, "Ethics and the human aspects of technological change, call centers: A case study." For a further critical view of the social impacts of information technology on work, see R. Kling, *Computerization and Controversy: Value Conflicts and Social Choices,* R. Mansell and R. Silverstone, *Communication by Design: The*

Politics of Information and Communication Technologies, and Terranova, "Free labor: Producing culture for the digital economy."

90. See K. Marx, "Theses on Feuerbach," 158, and McLellan, *Marx After Marx: An Introduction,* 2.

91. Marx presents this somewhat ironically in the context of the failure of his opponent Proudhon to develop a dialectics of political economy. It is also a criticism of Hegel, who "thinks he is constructing the world by the movement of thought, whereas he is merely reconstructing systematically and classifying by the absolute method the thoughts which are in the minds of all." K. Marx, "The poverty of philosophy," 202. Marx explains the dialectic thus: "But once it has managed to pose itself as a thesis, this thesis, this thought, opposed to itself, splits up into two contradictory thoughts—the positive and the negative, the yes and the no. The struggle between these two antagonistic elements comprised in the antithesis constitutes the dialectical movement. The yes becoming no, the no becoming yes. The struggle between these two antagonistic elements comprised in the antithesis constitutes the dialectical movement. The yes becoming no, the no becoming yes, the yes becoming both yes and no, the no becoming both no and yes, the contraries balance, neutralize, paralyse each other. The fusion of these two contradictory thoughts constitutes a new thought, which is the synthesis of them. This thought splits up once again into two contradictory thoughts, which in turn fuse into a new synthesis. Of this travail is born a group of thoughts. This group of thoughts follows the same dialectical movement as the simple category, and has a contradictory group as antithesis. Of these two groups of thoughts is born a new group of thoughts, which is the synthesis of them" (201). It would be fair to say that Marx sees the dialectics less seriously than certain of his contemporaries. It leads to no resolution and just accounts for the movement of things. It does not solve problems. It is not a method.

92. Ibid., 210.

93. Ibid., 215.

94. K. Marx follows Ricardo on many aspects of his prognosis. Ricardo highlights the hardships brought about by machine production: "The discovery and use of machinery may be attended with a diminution of gross produce; and whenever that is the case, it will be injurious to the labouring class, as some of their number will be thrown out of employment, and population will become redundant compared with the funds which are to employ it." D. Ricardo, *Principles of Political Economy and Taxation,* 272.

95. Vitruvius, *Vitruvius: The Ten Books on Architecture,* 318.

96. Hodges provides an extensive account of Turing's machines. See A. Hodges, *Alan Turing: The Enigma of Intelligence.*

97. Plant, *Zeros and Ones: Digital Women and the New Technoculture,* 26.

98. See D. E. Denning, "The future of cryptography," 87.

99. Vitruvius, *Vitruvius: The Ten Books on Architecture,* 303.

100. See Turner, *The Forest of Symbols: Aspects of Ndembu Ritual,* 106. See also M. Dorrian, "On the monstrous and the grotesque," and M. Dorrian, "The breath on the mirror: On Ruskin's theory of the grotesque."

101. M. Shelley, *Frankenstein.*

102. Insofar as modernism in architecture traded on a romance with the machine, it invoked the machine at the limits of its functionality. According to Harbison, "Modern architecture's love affair with machines often stems from and ends in a sense of drastically circumscribed possibility." Harbison, *Thirteen Ways: Theoretical Investigations in Architecture,* 43.

103. A popular computer game bears the name *Deus Ex,* and a word search on the World Wide Web reveals a large number of references to English and Latin variants of the term in page titles and in science fiction writing.

104. The ancient playwright Antiphanes was said to have railed against this technique. See M. Handley, "Shaw's response to the deus ex machina: From *The Quintessence of Ibsenism* to *Heartbreak House."*

105. Vitruvius, *Vitruvius: The Ten Books on Architecture,* 284.

106. Ibid.

107. Burnett and Marshall, *Web Theory: An Introduction.*

108. J. Ruskin, from *The Cestus of Aglaia,* 9, quoted in Ruskin, *Selected Writings,* 57.

109. Ruskin, *The Seven Lamps of Architecture,* 121.

110. J. Ruskin refers to "Switzerland defiled," in *The Queen of the Air,* quoted in Ruskin, *Selected Writings,* 118.

111. Ibid., 54.

112. J. Ruskin, from *The Cestus of Aglaia,* 9, quoted in Ruskin, *Selected Writings,* 57.

113. See E. Burke and J. Boulton (eds.), *A Philosophical Enquiry into the Origin of our Ideas of the Sublime and Beautiful,* and I. Kant, *Critique of the Power of Judgment.*

114. See Coyne, *Designing Information Technology in the Postmodern Age: From Method to Metaphor.*

115. G. Deleuze and F. Guattari, "The smooth and the striated."

3 The Lost Game

1. Smith, *An Inquiry into the Nature and Causes of the Wealth of Nations,* 17.

2. Smith, *The Theory of Moral Sentiments,* 289.

3. H. Hesse, *The Glass Bead Game.*

4. For an in-depth account of this invasion see Kline, Dyer-Witheford, and de Peuter, *Digital Play: The Interaction of Technology, Culture and Marketing.* On the subject of conspicuous consumption, according to Veblen the bourgeoisie consume leisure conspicuously and independently of any notion of need, mimicking the upper classes, who can easily demonstrate their wealth through conspicuous displays of the amount of free time they have at their disposal. See T. Veblen, *The Theory of the Leisure Class.*

5. See, for example, J. Huizinga, *Homo Ludens: A Study of the Play Element in Culture,* and R. Caillois, *Man, Play, and Games.*

6. Gadamer, *Truth and Method.* For an account of hermeneutics in the context of mass media, see T. Wilson, *Watching Television: Hermeneutics, Reception and Popular Culture.* For accounts of hermeneutics in the context of design, see Snodgrass and Coyne, "Is designing hermeneutical?," R. Coyne, H. Park, and D. Wiszniewski, "Design devices: what they reveal and conceal," and P. G. Raman and R. Coyne, "The production of architectural criticism."

7. Gadamer, *Truth and Method*, 93.

8. Huizinga, *Homo Ludens: A Study of the Play Element in Culture*, 13.

9. D. W. Winnicott, *Playing and Reality*.

10. Huizinger concurs, with a detailed analysis of the etymologies of equivalent words for play in different languages. See Huizinga, *Homo Ludens: A Study of the Play Element in Culture*, 28–45.

11. Arguably, the empiricists perpetuated this tradition and, in spite of their emphasis on the primacy of experience, never broke away from the sovereignty of the subject-object divide. Sense experience as a source of knowledge reinforces the assumption of the individual thinking being.

12. Heidegger, *Being and Time*.

13. Huizinga examines this proposition critically.

14. L. Wittgenstein, *Philosophical Investigations*, 35.

15. Huizinga advances several definitions of play, one of which is "play is a voluntary activity or occupation executed within certain fixed limits of time and place, according to rules freely accepted but absolutely binding, having its aim in itself and accompanied by a feeling of tension, joy and the consciousness that it is 'different' from 'ordinary life.'" Huizinga, *Homo Ludens: A Study of the Play Element in Culture*, 28.

16. Described in a very technical way in terms of "schemata" in D. E. Rumelhart and J. L. McClelland (eds.), *Parallel Distributed Processing: Explorations in the Microstructure of Cognition*, 20.

17. To be described at the end of the chapter. See Caillois, *Man, Play, and Games*.

18. H. L. Dreyfus, *What Computers Can't Do: The Limits of Artificial Intelligence*.

19. Huizinga begins with this proposition. See Huizinga, *Homo Ludens: A Study of the Play Element in Culture*, v.

20. J. Baudrillard, "The mirror of production," 110.

21. Huizinga, *Homo Ludens: A Study of the Play Element in Culture,* 1.

22. For the anthropologist, Gregory Bateson, play among animals is an indication of the seeds of reason. Play indicates that animals know the difference between the real fight and its simulation, a kind of meta-cognition indicative of reason. See G. Bateson, *Steps to an Ecology of Mind,* 179.

23. J. Lacan, *Écrits: A Selection.*

24. Huizinga, *Homo Ludens: A Study of the Play Element in Culture,* 143.

25. Snodgrass and Coyne, "Is designing hermeneutical?"

26. Schön, *Reflective Practitioner: How Professionals Think in Action.*

27. P. Ehn, *Work-Oriented Design of Computer Artifacts.*

28. A. Snodgrass and R. Coyne, *Interpretation in Architecture: Design as a Way of Thinking.*

29. See R. F. Woodbury, S. J. Shannon, and A. D. Radford, "Games in early design education: Playing with metaphor."

30. J. von Neumann and O. Morgenstern, *Theory of Games and Economic Behavior.*

31. See A. Newell and H. A. Simon, *Human Problem Solving.*

32. This is not the place to enter into the debates about symbolic and connectionist approaches to AI. Dreyfus presents the case for connectionism, the stochastic calculation of the microscopic interplay between neural cells, as a means of understanding cognition. See Dreyfus, *What Computers Can't Do: The Limits of Artificial Intelligence.* See also Rumelhart and McClelland, *Parallel Distributed Processing: Explorations in the Microstructure of Cognition.*

33. Kline and colleagues use the idea of the game to structure their discussion of the games industry, in terms of protagonists, competition, winners and losers. Economics is after all a game. See Kline, Dyer-Witheford, and de Peuter, *Digital Play: The Interaction of Technology, Culture and Marketing.*

34. See also J. Stallabras, *Gargantua: Manufactured Mass Culture,* 91, and J. Stallabras, "Just gaming: Allegory and economy in computer games."

35. Huizinga, *Homo Ludens: A Study of the Play Element in Culture*, 10.

36. Gadamer, *Truth and Method*, 93.

37. See S. Poole, *Trigger Happy: The Inner Life of Videogames*, for a description of most of the games mentioned in this chapter. See also L. King (ed.), *Game On: The History and Culture of Video Games*, and the critical history of video gaming provided by Kline, Dyer-Witheford, and de Peuter, *Digital Play: The Interaction of Technology, Culture and Marketing.*

38. *Doom* and *Quake* are published by Id Software.

39. *Myst III* and *Myst IV* are published by Ubisoft.

40. *Tomb Raider* is published by Eidos.

41. S. Freud, "Beyond the pleasure principle," 284–285.

42. S. Freud, "The 'uncanny.'" For an expansion of the application of the uncanny to architectural spaces, see A. Vidler, *The Architectural Uncanny: Essays in the Modern Unhomely.*

43. Vidler, *The Architectural Uncanny: Essays in the Modern Unhomely.*

44. *Myst* and *Riven* are published by Cyan. *The Sims* is published by Electronic Arts.

45. Freud, "The 'uncanny,'" 359. For Walter Benjamin, the wanderings of the *flaneur* participate in this uncanny condition. For the *flaneur*, "every street is precipitous. It leads downward—if not to the mythical Mothers, then into a past that can be all the more profound because it is not his own, not private." See W. Benjamin, *The Arcades Project*, 879–880.

46. F. W. Nietzsche, *Thus Spoke Zarathustra: A Book for Everyone and No One.* Huizinga refers to the sophistry and wordplay of Nietzsche as possibly restoring philosophy to its play origins. See Huizinga, *Homo Ludens: A Study of the Play Element in Culture*, 152. See also G. Deleuze, *Difference and Repetition*, for a detailed treatment of Nietzsche's concepts of repetition. The theme is also developed by Kierkegaard. See S. Kierkegaard, "Repetition: An essay in experimental psychology by Constantin Constantius."

47. J. Derrida, *Of Grammatology*, and J. Derrida, "Freud and the scene of writing." See also Deleuze and Guattari, *Anti-Oedipus: Capitalism and Schizophrenia.*

48. See L. Manovich, *The Language of New Media,* 272, on the subject of levels and navigation in computer games and other digital media.

49. Homer, *The Iliad.*

50. I develop the significance of this theme of transcendence for understanding digital media in Coyne, *Technoromanticism: Digital Narrative, Holism, and the Romance of the Real.* See also Wertheim, *The Pearly Gates of Cyberspace: A History of Space from Dante to the Internet,* and E. Graham, "Nietzsche gets a modem: Transhumanism and the technological sublime."

51. Hesse, *The Glass Bead Game.*

52. See the foreword by Theodore Ziolkowski, in Hesse, *The Glass Bead Game,* xi.

53. See Stallabras, *Gargantua: Manufactured Mass Culture,* 103.

54. See L. Armitt, *Theorising the Fantastic.* The computer game *American McGee's Alice* (published by Electronic Arts) is a clever parody of the *Tomb Raider* adventure game genre, but here it is a psychically deranged Alice roaming the game levels and slaughtering playing cards with a bloody carving knife.

55. P. Ricoeur, *Freud and Philosophy: An Essay in Interpretation.* Wittgenstein also advances arguments against the unconscious. See J. Bouveresse, *Wittgenstein Reads Freud: The Myth of the Unconscious.* See also R. Coyne and D. Wiszniewski, "Technical deceits: Critical theory, hermeneutics and the ethics of information technology."

56. M. Foucault, *The Archaeology of Knowledge,* 138.

57. The story presents a literal and magical take on Galileo's metaphor of the universe as a book written in a language that has to be learned and requiring interpretation. By a Lacanian reading, the story can also be interpreted as a demonstration of the basic conflict that ruptures and provokes the real, the symbolic world of language, text, assertion, and law, commonly associated with the father figure. The real resists the symbolic order. There is always something ineffable.

58. See, for example, G. Broadbent, *Design in Architecture: Architecture and the Human Sciences.*

59. Poole, *Trigger Happy: The Inner Life of Videogames.*

60. For further contemporary accounts of virtuality, realism, and digital media, see P. Lunefeld (ed.), *The Digital Dialectic: New Essays on New Media.*

61. J. H. Murray, *Hamlet on the Holodeck: The Future of Narrative in Cyberspace,* 170.

62. C. M. Turbayne, *The Myth of Metaphor.*

63. Stallabras makes this point about the derivative nature of computer games. See Stallabras, *Gargantua: Manufactured Mass Culture,* 86.

64. Manovich provides an extensive and exciting account of the computer game and other digital media in terms of a language, particularly as an extension of the language of cinema. See Manovich, *The Language of New Media,* 84–85.

65. J. D. Bolter and R. A. Grusin, *Remediation: Understanding New Media.*

66. Heidegger, *Being and Time.*

67. In the words of one of the founders of calculative economics, "the actions of men are so various and uncertain, that the best statement of tendencies, which we can make in a science of human conduct, must needs be inexact and faulty." A. Marshall, *Principles of Economics,* 32.

68. According to one game designer, the player should be able to feel the sense of "beating the designer." P. Campbell, "Designing *Tomb Raider,*" 57.

69. See Jenkins, *Textual Poachers: Television Fans and Participatory Culture,* for an account of how the interests of fans can be fed back into popular media production.

70. Kline, Dyer-Witheford, and de Peuter, *Digital Play: The Interaction of Technology, Culture and Marketing.*

71. See Jenkins, *Textual Poachers: Television Fans and Participatory Culture,* for a further account of taste and popular culture.

72. Stallabras provides a near exhaustive account of the technical, political and aesthetic failings of computer games. See Stallabras, *Gargantua: Manufactured Mass Culture,* 91.

73. Ibid., 90.

74. See Ibid., 93. See also J. Baudrillard, "The Gulf War did not take place," and K. Robins and L. Levidow, "Soldier, cyborg, citizen."

75. J. Baudrillard, "Simulacra and simulations."

76. J. Baudrillard, "Symbolic exchange and death," 149.

77. J. Baudrillard, "The perfect crime," 267.

78. Žižek, "Big brother, or, the triumph of the gaze over the eye."

79. Rawls describes social coherence in terms of the game, where a "good play of the game" is a social achievement. See J. Rawls, *A Theory of Justice,* 461. The argument advanced here derives substantially from a reading of Rorty. See R. Rorty, *Philosophy and the Mirror of Nature,* and Rorty, *Contingency, Irony, and Solidarity.*

80. For D. W. Winnicott, play in the development of the child is about developing trust. At an early stage, he writes: "The playground is a potential space between the mother and the baby or joining mother and baby. . . . The thing about playing is always the precariousness of the interplay of personal psychic reality and the experience of control of actual objects. This is the precariousness of magic itself, magic that arises in intimacy, in a relationship that is being found to be reliable. To be reliable the relationship is necessarily motivated by the mother's love, or her love-hate, or her object-relating, not by reaction-formations." Winnicott, *Playing and Reality,* 47.

81. This Freudian reading stretches Winnicott somewhat, and it assumes the alignment of the mother with the quest for unity. I have explored the tensional aspects of the unity narrative at some length in Coyne, *Technoromanticism: Digital Narrative, Holism, and the Romance of the Real.*

82. Huizinga, *Homo Ludens: A Study of the Play Element in Culture,* 61.

83. Caillois, *Man, Play, and Games.* It is worth noting that elsewhere Caillois asserts the primacy of mimicry that informed Jacques Lacan's neo-Freudian theories on the right of passage, repetition, the real, and the imaginary.

84. We have said little here about competition in the computer industry. For example, Shapiro and Varian offer advice on how to wage a "standards war," that is, how to have your own product and data formats recognized as a standard, thereby cornering the

market. See C. Shapiro and H. L. Varian, *Information Rules: A Strategic Guide to the Network Economy*, 261–296.

85. Caillois, *Man, Play, and Games*, 55.

86. It is not that we cannot tell the game from reality, the ethical from the corrupt business practice, but that the game is heightened by the tantalizing thought that we may be operating at the edge, getting away with murder.

87. Hesse describes the game: "The only way to learn the rules of this Game of games is to take the usual prescribed course, which requires many years, and none of the initiates could ever possibly have any interest in making these rules easier to learn. These rules, the sign language and grammar of the Game, constitute a kind of highly developed secret language drawing upon several sciences and arts, but especially mathematics and music (and/or musicology), and capable of expressing and establishing interrelationships between the content and conclusions of nearly all scholarly disciplines." Hesse, *The Glass Bead Game*, 14–15.

88. See Huizinga, *Homo Ludens: A Study of the Play Element in Culture*, 88. For Huizinga, the culture of Rome, with the influence of Stoicism, is less playful than that of the Greeks.

89. Plato, *The Laws*, 292.

90. As elaborated in Borges's celebrated "hypertextual" work, "The garden of the forking paths," and other playful essays. See J. L. Borges, "The garden of the forking paths."

91. The argument pertains to the complex relationship between the imaginary, the symbolic, and the real. See Lacan, *Écrits: A Selection*, and M. Bowie, *Lacan*.

92. This is Heidegger's term for a condition of being in which we cannot see ourselves as other than in company, a phenomenon prior to conceptions of our being in society. See M. Heidegger, *History of the Concept of Time: Prolegomena*, 237–243.

4   The Gift of Information

1. See M. Castells, *The Internet Galaxy: Reflections on the Internet, Business, and Society*, 39, and Berners-Lee, *Weaving the Web: The Past, Present and Future of the World Wide Web by Its Inventor*.

2. It makes good business sense to give away free samples and information "content," particularly online. See Shapiro and Varian, *Information Rules: A Strategic Guide to the Network Economy,* 85–86.

3. Castells, *The Internet Galaxy: Reflections on the Internet, Business, and Society,* 44. According to the Free Software Foundation Web site (www.gnu.org): "The Free Software Foundation (FSF), founded in 1985, is dedicated to promoting computer users' right to use, study, copy, modify, and redistribute computer programs. The FSF promotes the development and use of free (as in freedom) software —particularly the GNU operating system (used widely today in its GNU/Linux variant)—and free (as in freedom) documentation. The FSF also helps to spread awareness of the ethical and political issues of freedom in the use of software." See also www.en.wikipedia.org.

4. Most commercial computer software (e.g., a word processing program or a Web browser) is automatically converted (compiled) into an efficient machine-readable form that is virtually illegible to computer programmers, and therefore cannot be modified easily. In the case of OSI software the source code, which can be read, understood, and modified, is made available to other programmers.

5. See Torvalds and Diamond, *Just for Fun: The Story of an Accidental Revolutionary.*

6. For examples, see online articles by R. Barbrook, "The high-tech gift economy," G. Pinchot, "The gift economy," and E. Raymond, "The hacker milieu as gift culture." See also R. Barbrook and A. Cameron, "Californian ideology."

7. See Castells, *The Internet Galaxy: Reflections on the Internet, Business, and Society,* 52–55.

8. For a discussion of this phenomenon, see M. Bergquist and J. Ljungberg, "The power of gifts: Organizing social relationships in open source communities," 309.

9. I discussed the implications of McLuhan's position at length in Coyne, *Technoromanticism: Digital Narrative, Holism, and the Romance of the Real.*

10. See M. Mauss, *The Gift: The Form and Reason for Exchange in Archaic Societies,* to be elaborated on subsequently.

11. For example, Terranova argues for the "NetSlaves," who "used to work long hours and love it; now they are starting to feel the pain of being burned by digital media." See Terranova, "Free labor: Producing culture for the digital economy," 33.

12. Mauss, *The Gift: The Form and Reason for Exchange in Archaic Societies.*

13. Ibid., 105.

14. J. Derrida, *Given Time: 1. Counterfeit Money,* 122.

15. Ibid., 147.

16. Mauss, *The Gift: The Form and Reason for Exchange in Archaic Societies,* 4.

17. See J. K. Galbraith, *The Affluent Society,* 66.

18. J. K. Rowling, *Harry Potter and the Philosopher's Stone,* 121.

19. Ibid., 122.

20. The reference is to Luther's so-called tower experience, where he reputedly came to a full realization that the righteous live by faith. Luther says, "I broke though." See A. G. Dickens, *Martin Luther and the Reformation.* 24. See also C. S. Lewis, *Surprised by Joy,* for a similar attitude.

21. This is the title of the Puritan John Bunyan's autobiography. See J. Bunyan, *Grace Abounding to the Chief of Sinners.*

22. Shapiro and Varian, *Information Rules: A Strategic Guide to the Network Economy,* 6. See also J. Collins, *Architectures of Excess: Cultural Life in the Information Age.*

23. Shapiro and Varian show how software designers can take time as surplus into account in the production of software. Some people will pay more for a product that operates faster, a factor that is easy to control in the design of software. Some people will also pay more to have the product earlier rather than later. Hardback books cost more, but they come out sooner than the cheaper paperback version. Marketing strategies take advantage of the segmentation of the market according to how much people are willing to pay. See Shapiro and Varian, *Information Rules: A Strategic Guide to the Network Economy,* 55–63.

24. See Raymond, "The hacker milieu as gift culture."

25. Barbrook, "The high-tech gift economy." This could also be said of any state provision, which has been built up by the accumulated efforts and taxes of many generations,

or of literary, scientific, or artistic culture similarly built up over many years. It may simply be that the homogeneity, accessibility, and newness of the Internet promotes an exaggerated sense of its uniqueness in supporting gift culture.

26. Baudelaire's one-page essay is printed in full as an unnumbered addendum to Derrida, *Given Time: 1. Counterfeit Money.*

27. Smith nonetheless talks about benevolence, and how it is insufficient as a motive for good conduct. See Smith, *The Theory of Moral Sentiments,* 137.

28. For Smith, the determination of market price depends on free competition, but it does not take much to demonstrate that fair competition requires that buyers and sellers in any market know what is being offered and at what price.

29. Smith, *An Inquiry into the Nature and Causes of the Wealth of Nations,* 23.

30. Ibid., 203.

31. See Smith, *The Theory of Moral Sentiments,* 189.

32. W. L. Davidson, *The Stoic Creed,* 211.

33. Ibid., 205.

34. Ibid., 247.

35. Smith, *An Inquiry into the Nature and Causes of the Wealth of Nations,* 104–105.

36. Ibid., 238.

37. Ibid., 54–55.

38. F. A. Hayek, *Individualism and Economic Order,* 43.

39. Ibid., 45.

40. Hayek discusses such matters as an epistemological problem. No individual in the market has perfect knowledge, yet the whole system tends toward a condition where it would seem that the whole system has perfect knowledge.

41. Gates, Myhrvold, and Rinearson, *The Road Ahead,* 180.

42. For Georg Simmel, the economic philosopher, the use of money easily tempts us to misjudge risk. The use of money distances us from the value of our own assets, but also we easily participate in so many small, risky transactions, for example, lottery tickets and cheap bonds. See G. Simmel, *The Philosophy of Money,* 261.

43. U. Beck, *Risk Society: Towards a New Modernity.*

44. In the case of modern-day risk, it seems that the probability of something going wrong (explosions at a power station, release of mutant organisms) is extremely low, but the consequences could be globally catastrophic if they do. The difficulty is that with all this uncertainty, we still have to make the crucial decisions. See Žižek, *The Ticklish Subject: The Absent Centre of Political Ontology.*

45. Or hacking, illegally breaking into other people's systems.

46. See A. Ross, "Hacking away at counterculture."

47. See Castells, *The Internet Galaxy: Reflections on the Internet, Business, and Society,* 80.

48. See P. Coggan, *The Money Machine: How the City Works.*

49. See Castells, *The Internet Galaxy: Reflections on the Internet, Business, and Society,* 81.

50. Shapiro and Varian counsel software developers to shift the risk of their product failing onto "big players," such as the government or a regulated monopoly, if possible. This means the developers should enlist the big players as main customers. Others will buy the product thinking that if the developer goes under, then the government will back them up. See Shapiro and Varian, *Information Rules: A Strategic Guide to the Network Economy,* 244.

51. See Cassidy, *Dot.con: The Greatest Story Ever Told.*

52. Castells, *The Internet Galaxy: Reflections on the Internet, Business, and Society,* 87.

53. See J. Gleick, *Chaos: Making a New Science.*

54. R. Thom, *Structural Stability and Morphogenesis.*

55. According to Shapiro and Varian, the software developer should garner support from "natural allies." This involves being "prepared to offer special deals to early supporters: with positive feedback, a few visible early supporters can be enough to tip expectations in your favour, making it easier to attract more allies over time." Shapiro and Varian, *Information Rules: A Strategic Guide to the Network Economy,* 259.

56. R. Axelrod, *The Evolution of Co-operation.* Also see O. Stark, *Altruism and Beyond: An Economic Analysis of Transfers and Exchanges within Families and Groups,* for an alternative, calculative theory of altruism.

57. The gift economy of the Internet is unusual in that the giver and receiver often do not know each other. An individual emails a user group, or posts a message on a notice board, for free advice on some topic. According to certain studies, this activity is caught up in a socialization process. The new contributor to this community (newbie) learns how to behave, how best to contribute to and benefit from the gift community, and how to enhance one's reputation. See Bergquist and Ljungberg,"The power of gifts: Organizing social relationships in open source communities." See also D. Zeitlyn, "Gift economies in the development of open source software: Anthropological reflections."

58. Torvalds and Diamond, *Just for Fun: The Story of an Accidental Revolutionary,* 122.

59. See M. Castells, *The Internet Galaxy: Reflections on the Internet, Business, and Society.*

60. Ryan, *John Stuart Mill and Jeremy Bentham: Utilitarianism and Other Essays,* 65.

61. Ruskin, *The Seven Lamps of Architecture,* 149.

62. Ibid., 27.

63. Ibid., 158.

64. Ruskin's is far from the last word on ornament in design and in architecture. See, for example, J. Bloomer, "D'or," for some of the debate on structure and ornament, particularly as it invokes the masculine and the feminine.

65. Ruskin, *Unto This Last: And Other Writings,* 175.

66. M. Boden, *The Creative Mind: Myths and Mechanisms,* 237.

67. Hesiod, *Theogony and Works and Days,* 5.

68. J. T. Godbout, *The World of the Gift*.

69. Ibid., 165.

70. L. Hyde, *Imagination and the Erotic Life of Property*.

71. Torvalds and Diamond, *Just for Fun: The Story of an Accidental Revolutionary*, 205.

72. Coyne, *Technoromanticism: Digital Narrative, Holism, and the Romance of the Real*.

73. Castells, *The Internet Galaxy: Reflections on the Internet, Business, and Society*, 57.

74. Or a fore-having, a fore-sight, and a fore-conception. See Heidegger, *Being and Time*, 191.

75. We discussed the issue of prejudice, and its role in interpretation and play, in chapter 3.

76. E. Bloch, *The Principle of Hope*.

77. In utilitarian mode, Shapiro and Varian counsel effective "expectation management," as a principle of good business: "Your goal is to convince customers and complementors that you will emerge as the victor; such expectations can easily become a self-fulfilling prophecy. To manage expectations, you should engage in aggressive marketing, make early announcements of new products, assemble allies, and make visible commitments to your technology." Shapiro and Varian, *Information Rules: A Strategic Guide to the Network Economy*, 296.

78. Here we use technology in the most general sense, as promoted by Heidegger. We are in a technological condition; we see the world technologically, particularly in terms of causal, machinic relationships. See M. Heidegger, *The Question Concerning Technology and Other Essays*.

79. Sahlins, *Stone Age Economics*.

80. Or conversely saturate us with spectacle. See Debord, *The Society of the Spectacle*.

81. M. Heidegger, "The thing." See also A. Borgmann, *Technology and the Character of Contemporary Life: A Philosophical Inquiry*.

82. See Heidegger, *The Question Concerning Technology and Other Essays.*

83. Mauss, *The Gift: The Form and Reason for Exchange in Archaic Societies.* Mauss makes no overt appeal to Heidegger or phenomenology in this essay.

84. Ibid., 7.

85. Ibid., 16.

86. Ibid.

87. Godbout, *The World of the Gift,* 188.

88. Freud's theories have come under criticism, refinement, and revision from various quarters in the context of a discussion of the gift. See P. Berry, "Kristeva's feminist re-figuring of the gift."

89. Expanding on Freud through Lacan, and Žižek. See Žižek, *Looking Awry: An Intro-duction to Jacques Lacan through Popular Culture.*

90. Leaving aside the complex question of objects as symbols, which seems central to Freud, but is peripheral to Heidegger.

91. Godbout, *The World of the Gift,* 134. See also his discussion of the themes of return (p. 97) and reciprocation (p. 188).

92. Ranging from the gift of feces to the gift of a baby.

93. For apparently allowing her castration.

94. S. Freud, "Infantile sexuality," 103–104.

95. S. Freud, "On transformations of instinct as exemplified in anal eroticism," 301.

96. Evidence for the association between excrement and money comes through terms such as "filthy lucre," the equation of gold with feces. See S. Freud, "Character and anal eroticism," 214.

97. See H. Marcuse, *Eros and Civilisation: A Philosophical Inquiry into Freud* and Deleuze and Guattari, *Anti-Oedipus: Capitalism and Schizophrenia.*

98. Torvalds and Diamond, *Just for Fun: The Story of an Accidental Revolutionary,* 75. Gates presents a similar nerdy persona though with less self-effacing charm than Torvalds, and with greater claim to the realm of filthy lucre. See B. Gates, N. Myhrvold, and P. Rinearson, *The Road Ahead.*

99. Apparently the term *nerd* originates in the Dr. Seuss children's book *If I Ran the Zoo.* The fantasy creature resembles the computer devotee hunched over a terminal.

100. Torvalds and Diamond, *Just for Fun: The Story of an Accidental Revolutionary,* 26.

101. According to Freud, if a patient vehemently denies that the character in a dream is his mother, then the analyst can be certain that it is. See S. Freud, "Negation."

102. Mauss, *The Gift: The Form and Reason for Exchange in Archaic Societies.* Mauss's writing on the theme of the potlatch has intrigued theorists of consumer culture—notably, Bataille and Baudrillard. See F. Botting and S. Wilson (eds.), *The Bataille Reader,* and Baudrillard, "Symbolic exchange and death."

103. Godbout, *The World of the Gift,* 47.

104. Mauss, *The Gift: The Form and Reason for Exchange in Archaic Societies,* 20.

105. Ibid., 53.

106. Note that for certain theorists, the agonistic, competitive approach to the gift accords with a male response to giving. A man might give and return to restore the balance of power. On the other hand, the woman "gives without a thought of return." See T. Moi, *Sexual/Textual Politics: Feminist Literary Theory,* 112, for a summary of this position.

107. See F. Botting and S. Wilson, *Bataille,* for an account of Bataille's work.

108. Botting and Wilson (eds.), *The Bataille Reader,* 201, 196.

109. Ibid., 172.

110. Ibid., 176.

111. Ibid., 177.

112. Galbraith, *The Affluent Society,* 74.

113. Ibid., 115.

114. Debord, *The Society of the Spectacle,* 29.

115. See Baudrillard, "Symbolic exchange and death."

116. Botting and Wilson, *The Bataille Reader,* 173. We can look to Freud for the genesis of such a pessimistic account.

117. See D. A. F. de Sade, *120 Days of Sodom and Other Writings.*

118. M. Griffiths, "Sex on the Internet: Issues, concerns, and implications," 279.

119. Ibid., 278.

120. K. Marx, "Capital," 435–443.

121. Desmet, "Reading the Web as fetish."

122. S. Freud, "Three essays on the theory of sexuality," 65–68.

123. Castells, *The Rise of the Network Society,* 428.

124. See F. Jameson, "Future city," R. Koolhaas and B. Mau, "Generic city," Koolhaas, "Junk space," and M. Augé, *Non-places: Introduction to an Anthropology of Supermodernity.*

125. Harris provides a fascinating account of the complex relationship between money and the earth in Aztec mining communities. See O. Harris, "The earth and the state: The sources and meanings of money in Northern Potosí, Bolivia." The earth (the chthonic) features prominently in mythic accounts of origins. See D. Ø. Endsjø, "To lock up Eleusis: A question of liminal space." Lévi-Strauss outlines rival theories of origins in terms of procreation by two parents, and autochthony, born from one, the earth. See C. Lévi-Strauss, *Structural Anthropology 1,* 215–217.

126. Vitruvius, *Vitruvius: The Ten Books on Architecture,* 26.

127. This theory is elaborated by A. Snodgrass, *Architecture, Time and Eternity: Studies in the Stellar and Temporal Symbolism of Traditional Buildings, Volumes I and II.* See also Augé, *Non-places: Introduction to an Anthropology of Supermodernity,* 57.

128. G. Semper, *The Four Elements of Architecture and Other Writings.*

129. Hesiod, *Theogony and Works and Days,* 6.

130. Carlyle, *Past and Present,* 174.

131. Including in the area of agricultural economics. For an innovative account, see R. Ison and D. Russell (eds.), *Agricultural Extension and Rural Development: Breaking Out of Traditions.*

132. T. R. Malthus, *An Essay on the Principle of Population,* 152.

133. Godbout, *The World of the Gift,* 133.

134. Ibid.

135. Heidegger also develops the concept of "the given." The philosophical tradition treats certain concepts, such as the self or the "I," as gifts, as already "given." See Heidegger, *Being and Time,* 151. The given is a fundamental, an essence, an appeal to solid ground.

136. Botting and Wilson (eds.), *The Bataille Reader,* 189. For Bataille, excess is also associated with death: "life is the luxury of which death is the highest degree" (246). Baudrillard further develops the theme of death and excess in his *Symbolic Exchange and Death,* 154–156. See also Poster, *The Second Media Age,* 104–116, for an invaluable summary and assessment of Baudrillard's complex and evolving thoughts on economics, the gift, and death.

137. See Heidegger, "The origin of the work of art."

138. The context is a discussion of how truth is revealed in a work of art.

139. See M. E. Zimmerman, *Heidegger's Confrontation with Modernity: Technology, Politics, Art.*

140. *Encarta® World English Dictionary* (North American Edition) © & (P) 2001 Microsoft Corporation. All rights reserved. Developed for Microsoft by Bloomsbury Publishing Plc.

141. N. Negroponte, *Being Digital,* 6.

142. Which by no means exempts the Internet as a major medium for the sale of real estate, and the circulation of interactive maps, travel planners and guides. As a further rarefaction, popular economic theory appropriates a mechanized view of nature, of biology, implicating concepts of survival, system, and complexity. Darwin's *Origin of Species* provides the model. This engenders a faith in the machine as a means of not only simulating and creating life, but also defining a new problematic, that of the new cyborg identity, and its supposed challenge to the economic order. See D. J. Haraway, *Simians, Cyborgs, and Women: The Reinvention of Nature*. Of course, the abrogation of locality takes on a negative cast. It furthers the Cartesian view of the world. Global communications make everywhere the same. Space is further homogenized and even commodified.

143. The community of strangers goes beyond, but is perhaps well exemplified by, Internet chat rooms, where participants enjoy sociability, but under circumstances of controlled anonymity.

144. For an account of globalization, see A. Giddens, *Runaway World: How Globalization Is Shaping Our Lives,* and W. Hutton and A. Giddens, *On the Edge: Living with Global Capitalism.*

145. Gay and other cohesive but ostensibly marginalized groups also benefit from anonymity and interaction. See D. I. Snyder, "'I don't go by Sean Patrick': On-line/off-line/out identity and SeanPatrickLive.com."

146. Veblen, *The Theory of the Leisure Class.* See Baudrillard, *Symbolic Exchange and Death,* for an advance on Veblen into the realms of signification. For Baudrillard, Veblen is referring to a "classical configuration where signs constitute a distinct material having a finality and are used for prestige, status and social differentiation" (57). Baudrillard effects a linguistic turn in this argument, showing how conspicuous consumption is supplanted by the notion that it is symbols that are being exchanged, not commodities.

147. Veblen, *The Theory of the Leisure Class,* 253.

148. See Freud, "Beyond the pleasure principle."

149. The cultural theorist Giroux identifies this film as exemplifying the worst of capitalist consumption, in the guise of radical critique. See H. A. Giroux, *Public Spaces, Private Lives: Beyond the Culture of Cynicism.*

150. For one account of the problematic of gender and consumption in the domestic sphere, see C. M. Goldstein, "From service to sales: Home economics in light and power 1920–1940."

151. Godbout summarizes the anthropological account: "The gift abhors equality. It seeks alternating inequality [and is characterized by a] reciprocal indebtedness" (93). Godbout, *The World of the Gift*, 33, 179.

152. This account is derived from Godbout, *The World of the Gift*, 123.

153. Castells, *The Internet Galaxy: Reflections on the Internet, Business, and Society* 39. For a summary of the more pessimistic prognoses of information technology developments and globalization, see P. Golding, "Global village or cultural pillage? The unequal inheritance of the communications revolution." See also H. Menzies, "Challenging capitalism: The information highway, the postindustrial economy, and people."

154. H. Rheingold, *The Virtual Community: Homesteading on the Electronic Frontier.*

155. Castells, *The Internet Galaxy: Reflections on the Internet, Business, and Society*, 60.

156. Godbout, *The World of the Gift*, 165.

157. Žižek further problematizes the concept of sacrifice in Žižek, *The Puppet and the Dwarf: The Perverse Core of Christianity.*

158. Derrida, *Given Time: 1. Counterfeit Money*, 44.

159. The debate in economic theory on how governments should intervene is summarized by T. G. Buchholz, *New Ideas from Dead Economists: An Introduction to Modern Economic Thought.*

160. J. M. Keynes, *The General Theory of Employment, Interest and Money.*

161. For Godbout, in the modern economy, "What circulates no longer carries social ties with it. It is dissociated from them; it is freed from the gift." Godbout, *The World of the Gift*, 155.

162. Ibid., 152–153.

163. These transgressive characteristics of the gift constitute surprise, a shock to the fair dealing of free enterprise.

164. Derrida, *Given Time: 1. Counterfeit Money,* 123.

165. In fact his target is all who promote metaphysics, the inescapable belief in underlying causes, foundations, fundamentals, and unifying schemas, including the beliefs of those who most vehemently ague against such a position, including Heidegger.

166. Marshall, *Principles of Economics,* 16.

167. Marshall's example is that of choosing between a cigar and taking a carriage home.

168. Or that it is essential that the gift involves the passage of something from one person to another, but that a gift should be reciprocated is accidental (supplemental). It is not always the case that gifts are returned in kind. In fact the surprise element, the trade in excess and the imbalance engendered by the gift, could each be considered as supplemental, rather than essential, to what constitutes a gift. Alternatively we could be trying to assert a tripartite essence of the gift (in surprise, excess and different), with everything else as incidental.

169. Derrida draws attention to the political motivation in this kind of operation, as in the case of Mauss's valorization of the gift as an attempt to denigrate the economic imperatives of capitalism, and of Marxism.

170. See Heidegger, *Being and Time.* See also R. Coyne, "Cyberspace and Heidegger's pragmatics."

171. For Bataille, it seems that the potlatch would suffice as the proto-gift.

172. Derrida, *Given Time: 1. Counterfeit Money,* 6–7.

173. Ibid., 12.

174. Deleuze and Guattari advance a provocative argument that the gift actually bears "the power of the inexchangeable." See C. V. Boundas, "Exchange, gift, and theft."

175. Derrida, *Given Time: 1. Counterfeit Money,* 14.

176. Ibid., 81.

177. Godbout, *The World of the Gift*, 35.

178. Žižek also recounts the character of the Event. See Žižek, *The Puppet and the Dwarf: The Perverse Core of Christianity*, 135–136.

179. Tschumi, *Architecture and Disjunction*, 256.

180. In the manner of a Foucauldian archaeological narrative, as opposed to a history.

181. Without referring to the gift explicitly, Miller and Slater offer a helpful account of how gift culture operates in a particular community. See D. Miller and D. Slater, *The Internet: An Ethnographic Approach*, 164–168.

182. See A. Currah, "The virtual geographies of retail display."

183. See M. Nesbit, "In the absence of the Parisienne . . ." for a critical account of the early department store as entertainment.

184. Castells, *The Internet Galaxy: Reflections on the Internet, Business, and Society*, 101. See also J. Camp, "Sustainable open source software business models."

185. The celebrated example is the erotic adaptation of the *Star Trek* characters by certain groups. For arguments for and against, see Jenkins, *Textual Poachers: Television Fans and Participatory Culture*. Kline et al provide an account of appropriation among games enthusiasts. See Kline, Dyer-Witheford, and de Peuter, *Digital Play: The Interaction of Technology, Culture and Marketing*.

186. And other forms of "crypto anarchy." See T. C. May, "Crypto anarchy and virtual communities."

187. As suggested by Kline, Dyer-Witheford, and de Peuter, *Digital Play: The Interaction of Technology, Culture and Marketing*, 215–217.

188. As does the concept of the commodity fetish.

189. This is called "visceral democracy." See K. Best, "Beating them at their own game: The cultural politics of the open software movement and the gift economy," 455.

5 Liminal Computing

1. Marshall, *Principles of Economics.* This is the so-called law of diminishing returns.

2. T. R. Malthus, *An Essay on the Principle of Population,* 28.

3. According to the *Oxford English Dictionary.* Liminality is developed in anthropological study by van Gennep, who discusses the role of the threshold in rites of passage. See van Gennep, *The Rites of Passage.* See also Turner, *The Forest of Symbols: Aspects of Ndembu Ritual.*

4. Rumelhart and McClelland (eds.), *Parallel Distributed Processing: Explorations in the Microstructure of Cognition.*

5. According to the *Oxford English Dictionary.*

6. See Freud, "Three essays on the theory of sexuality," 163.

7. See Brian Charles Clarke, "Thresholding."

8. Lyotard, *The Postmodern Condition: A Report on Knowledge,* 78.

9. Ibid. Mosco provides an account of the technological sublime from the point of view of cyberspace myths. See V. Mosco, *The Digital Sublime: Myth, Power, and Cyberspace,* 22–25. I am indebted to a fulsome account of the sublime in science and technology by I. Greig, "The aesthetics of the sublime in twentieth century physics."

10. Aristotle, *The Politics,* 1252.

11. See Bergquist and Ljungberg, "The power of gifts: Organizing social relationships in open source communities," and Zeitlyn, "Gift economies in the development of open source software: Anthropological reflections."

12. The anthropologist Mary Douglas provides an extensive account of the boundary condition, the threshold, and sacrificial rites. See M. Douglas, *Purity and Danger: An Analysis of Concepts of Pollution and Taboo.*

13. See Godbout, *The World of the Gift,* and Hyde, *Imagination and the Erotic Life of Property.*

14. See Turner, *The Forest of Symbols: Aspects of Ndembu Ritual,* and Endsjø, "To lock up Eleusis: A question of liminal space." Elsewhere, Derrida writes about the *arrivant.*

15. See Homer, *The Odyssey.*

16. See "Janus in myth," *Mythography,* available online at www.loggia.com, for the entry.

17. See R. Graves, *The Greek Myths: Volume 1,* 120.

18. J. Campbell, *The Hero with a Thousand Faces,* 92.

19. Hyde, *Imagination and the Erotic Life of Property,* 115.

20. Aristotle, *The Politics,* 87. See also M. Bloch and J. Parry, "Introduction: Money and the morality of exchange," for a critical examination of this Aristotelian legacy.

21. Hyde, *Imagination and the Erotic Life of Property,* 128.

22. See Coggan, *The Money Machine: How the City Works.*

23. Derrida, *Given Time: 1. Counterfeit Money.*

24. Homer, *The Odyssey,* 207.

25. L. Diogenes, *The Lives and Opinions of Eminent Philosophers,* 241. For a general account of Diogenes' life and teaching, see F. Sayre, *Diogenes of Sinope: A Study of Greek Cynicism.*

26. Diogenes, *The Lives and Opinions of Eminent Philosophers,* 234. D. Dudley, *A History of Cynicism: From Diogenes to the 6th Century AD,* 201.

27. Simmel identifies the contemporary capitalist cynic with the cynic of ancient Greece. For both, the Platonic/Socratic hierarchy is upturned. In the contemporary condition everything is rendered qualitatively indistinguishable by the same measure, namely, money. See Simmel, *The Philosophy of Money,* 255.

28. See P. Radin, *The Trickster: A Study in American Indian Mythology.*

29. Katz aligns Aristotle's reference to the petty trader as the huckster or cheat in the marketplace. See Katz, "The Greek matrix of Marx's critique of political economy," 241.

30. L. Hyde, *Trickster Makes This World: Mischief, Myth and Art,* 296.

31. See Mosco, *The Digital Sublime: Myth, Power, and Cyberspace,* 46–49.

32. Marx, "The holy family," 136.

33. See C. Douglas, "The historical context of analytical psychology."

34. C. G. Jung, *Four Archetypes: Mother, Rebirth, Spirit, Trickster,* 4.

35. Ibid., 17.

36. Ibid., 128.

37. C. G. Jung, *Psychological Types.*

38. See S. Salman, "The creative psyche: Jung's major contribution," 57.

39. Management technique at times resorts to the Myers-Briggs system of personality type classification—a system based on various polarities: introverted/extroverted, intuitive/logical, thinking/feeling and judging/experiencing—to produce sixteen personality categories.

40. D. Bell, *An Introduction to Cybercultures.*

41. S. Turkle, *Life on the Screen: Identity in the Age of the Internet.*

42. Bell, *An Introduction to Cybercultures,* 179.

43. Campbell, *The Hero with a Thousand Faces,* 30.

44. M. V. Adams, "The archetypal school," 103.

45. J. Russo, "A Jungian analysis of Homer's *Odysseus,*" 241.

46. Adams, "The archetypal school," 242.

47. Haraway, *Simians, Cyborgs, and Women: The Reinvention of Nature.*

48. In fact, on this subject the relationship between Freud and his student Jung is telling. See D. A. Davis, "Freud, Jung, and psychoanalysis."

49. Coyne, *Technoromanticism: Digital Narrative, Holism, and the Romance of the Real.*

50. Jung, *Four Archetypes: Mother, Rebirth, Spirit, Trickster,* 26.

51. Ibid., 92. He adds: "The invisibility of this source is frequently emphasized by the fact that it consists simply of an authoritative voice which passes final judgement. Mostly it is the figure of a wise old man who symbolises the spiritual factor."

52. Lacan, *Écrits: A Selection.*

53. In fact, thinking of Bataille, Lacan, and Derrida, one speculates that it could be the cunning of the philosopher that accomplishes the role of trickster, in subverting otherwise stable categories.

54. Among a wealth of metaphors on the theme of ornament, Bloomer identifies the door with gold, the gift, and the feminine. See Bloomer, "D'or," 164.

55. See Bell, *An Introduction to Cybercultures,* 117–118.

56. Odysseus is known as Ulysses in Latin translations.

57. James Joyce sees Ulysses as the everyman, as the main character in his colorful story of a prosaic day in the life of a Dubliner. Joyce's *Ulysses* famously parallels the episodes in Homer's *Odyssey.* See J. Joyce, *Ulysses.*

58. Russo, "A Jungian analysis of Homer's *Odysseus,*" 247.

59. Among his many ruses, Odysseus tells the Cyclops that his name is Oudeis, which means "nobody." So the blinded Cyclops gives chase to Odysseus declaring to his countrymen that *nobody* is to blame for his condition. See R. Graves, *The Greek Myths, Volume 2,* 356–357.

60. Athena was born from the head of Zeus, after he swallowed the maiden Metis. Metis disguised herself in various forms in order to evade his advances. See Graves, *The Greek Myths, Volume 1,* 46.

61. Homer, *The Odyssey,* 210.

62. Hermes is also known as Mercury, or Mercurius, from Latin translations.

63. The complete text of "The Homeric Hymn to Hermes" is to be found in Hyde, *Trickster Makes This World: Mischief, Myth and Art*, 317–331.

64. Ibid., 317.

65. Ibid., 320.

66. Hesiod, *Theogony and Works and Days*, 19–20. Nietzsche elevates Prometheus' thieving as indicating that even sacrilege can have dignity. See F. W. Nietzsche, *The Gay Science: With a Prelude in German Rhymes and an Appendix of Songs*, 125.

67. Russo, "A Jungian analysis of Homer's *Odysseus*," 248.

68. Ibid.

69. C. G. Jung, *Alchemical Studies: The Collected Works of C. G. Jung.* Vol. 13, 237.

70. Ibid.

71. Ibid.

72. Hyde, *Trickster Makes This World: Mischief, Myth and Art*, 6.

73. Ibid., 7. The reference to "gray-haired baby" invokes the assertion that Hermes was scarcely one day old when he conducted his cattle-stealing. This list recalls Ruskin's company of the poor and imaginative: "the irregularly and impulsively wicked, the clumsy knave, the open thief . . ." Ruskin, *Unto This Last: And Other Writings*, 212. One of the paradoxes of the trickster is that whereas he is a source of great enjoyment as a literary or fictional character, people are much less happy to be within his orbit, to be the butt of his jokes, the victim of his pranks. Plato is critical of the implication in Homer that justice is somehow equated with the craft of stealing. See Plato, *The Republic of Plato*, 334b, 979.

74. Hyde, *Trickster Makes This World: Mischief, Myth and Art*, 7–8. The role of trickster has also been assigned with that of women. See Bloomer, "D'or," and Wigley, "Untitled: The housing of gender." Wigley invokes Greek and Renaissance architectural texts that consign the woman to the inner reaches of the house, while the man belongs in the public arena. At the same time woman will not be constrained, and "she endlessly disrupts the boundaries of others, that is men, disturbing their identity, if not calling it into question" (335).

75. Nietzsche, *The Gay Science: With a Prelude in German Rhymes and an Appendix of Songs*.

76. See Mosco, *The Digital Sublime: Myth, Power, and Cyberspace*, 46–49.

77. D. Haraway, "The actors are cyborgs, nature is coyote, and the geography is everywhere: Postscript to 'cyborgs are at large.'"

78. Jung, *Four Archetypes: Mother, Rebirth, Spirit, Trickster*, 94.

79. Ibid.

80. Diogenes, *The Lives and Opinions of Eminent Philosophers*, 235. Yet he would assume the upper hand. A belligerent citizen once said to him, "If you can persuade me, I will give you something," to which Diogenes replied, "If I could persuade you, I would beg you to hang yourself" (239).

81. As raised in chapter 4 on the Freudian "denial."

82. Or "Cease to shade me from the sun." Diogenes, *The Lives and Opinions of Eminent Philosophers*, 230.

83. Ibid., 224.

84. Ibid. Dudley, *A History of Cynicism: From Diogenes to the 6th Century AD*, 28.

85. See Coggan, *The Money Machine: How the City Works*, 12–16.

86. Dudley, *A History of Cynicism: From Diogenes to the 6th Century AD*, 28.

87. P. Marshall, *Demanding the Impossible: A History of Anarchism*, 69.

88. Dudley, *A History of Cynicism: From Diogenes to the 6th Century AD*, 212. See P. A. Kropotkin and M. Shatz, *The Conquest of Bread and Other Writings*.

89. Ibid.

90. See Ludlow, *Crypto Anarchy, Cyberstates, and Pirate Utopias*. The cynic and the anarchist also resonate with the Anabaptists, "who opposed all constituted authority, and regarded the state as inherently evil." Dudley, *A History of Cynicism: From Diogenes to the 6th Century AD*, 211.

91. See Marshall, *Demanding the Impossible: A History of Anarchism.*

92. Apple Computer Inc. used "think different" as a slogan, advancing a poem on its Web site: "Here's to the crazy ones. The misfits. The rebels. The troublemakers. The round pegs in the square holes. The ones who see things differently. They're not fond of rules. And they have no respect for the status quo. You can praise them, disagree with them, quote them, disbelieve them, glorify or vilify them. About the only thing you can't do is ignore them. Because they change things. They invent. They imagine. They heal. They explore. They create. They inspire. They push the human race forward. Maybe they have to be crazy. How else can you stare at an empty canvas and see a work of art? Or sit in silence and hear a song that's never been written? Or gaze at a red planet and see a laboratory on wheels? We make tools for these kinds of people. While some see them as the crazy ones, we see genius. Because the people who are crazy enough to think they can change the world, are the ones who do." Available online at www.apple.com/thinkdifferent/.

93. Haraway, *Simians, Cyborgs, and Women: The Reinvention of Nature.*

94. May, "Crypto anarchy and virtual communities," 69.

95. For a compilation of design manifestos see R. Banham, *Theory and Design in the First Machine Age.* See also E. Hughes, "The cypherpunk's manifesto."

96. Marinetti's 1909 *Futurist Manifesto* is available online at www.unknown.nu/futurism/.

97. Diogenes, *The Lives and Opinions of Eminent Philosophers,* 228.

98. Dudley, *A History of Cynicism: From Diogenes to the 6th Century AD,* 37.

99. Ibid., 5.

100. Diogenes, *The Lives and Opinions of Eminent Philosophers,* 239. He parodied his own dog-like condition. When people at a banquet threw bones at him as if he were a dog, he cocked up his leg against them before leaving (234).

101. See Hyde, *Trickster Makes This World: Mischief, Myth and Art,* for an exposition of the coyote myths. The werewolf has a similar characterization. According to Agamben: "What had to remain in the collective unconscious as a monstrous hybrid of human and animal, divided between the forest and the city—the werewolf—is, therefore, in its

origin the figure of the man who has been banned from the city." G. Agamben, *Homo Sacer: Sovereign Power and Bare Life,* 105. Agamben relates this figure to the bandit, the condemned man, who is subject to capital punishment. In such a role the bandit becomes "sacred man" and tests the claims of sovereign power and the rights of individual sovereignty.

102. Hyde, *Trickster Makes This World: Mischief, Myth and Art,* 18. According to Hyde, this cunning is also derived from the coyote's propensity to fall into traps. He is all the smarter for being the trap's victim.

103. See, for example, www.disney.co.uk.

104. Arguably the digital corollary of Baudrillard, "Simulacra and simulations."

105. Diogenes, *The Lives and Opinions of Eminent Philosophers,* 225, and Dudley, *A History of Cynicism: From Diogenes to the 6th Century AD,* 36.

106. Diogenes, *The Lives and Opinions of Eminent Philosophers,* 225, Dudley, *A History of Cynicism: From Diogenes to the 6th Century AD,* 33.

107. Dudley, *A History of Cynicism: From Diogenes to the 6th Century AD,* 209.

108. Ibid., 211.

109. Diogenes, *The Lives and Opinions of Eminent Philosophers,* 217.

110. See Bell, *An Introduction to Cybercultures,* 140–142.

111. Dudley, *A History of Cynicism: From Diogenes to the 6th Century AD,* 27.

112. Diogenes, *The Lives and Opinions of Eminent Philosophers,* 229.

113. Ibid., 244.

114. He said: "Young men ought not to marry yet, and old men never ought to marry at all." See Ibid., 237. He said that all women "ought to be possessed in common" and that "marriage was a nullity" (244).

115. Jung, *Psychological Types,* 40.

116. Ibid.

117. Ibid., 41. As discussed in chapter 2, Karl Marx was so aligned with the anti-idealists, and thus indirectly with cynicism.

118. Diogenes, *The Lives and Opinions of Eminent Philosophers,* 226.

119. Ibid., 225.

120. Ibid., 245.

121. The historian Diogenes Laërtius, from whom we derive most of our understanding of Diogenes the cynic, is thought to have been of the Epicurean school. See the preface to Ibid.

122. Ibid., 227.

123. Jung, *Psychological Types,* 39.

124. Dudley, *A History of Cynicism: From Diogenes to the 6th Century AD,* 43.

125. Crates is not recorded as being a beggar. See Ibid., 43–44.

126. Plato, "Letter VII," 342e, 1660.

127. Plato, "Cratylus," 408a, 126.

128. Ibid., 408c, 126.

129. Plato, "Letter VII," 342c, 1660.

130. See L. Wittgenstein, *Tractatus Logico Philosophicus.*

131. Wittgenstein, *Philosophical Investigations.*

132. Austin, *How to do Things with Words.*

133. Benjamin, *The Arcades Project,* 879.

134. Hypertext has been presented in this light, as a process of collage-writing. See G. P. Landow, "Hypertext as collage-writing."

135. Hyde, *Trickster Makes This World: Mischief, Myth and Art,* 72.

136. Ibid., 64.

137. Homer, *The Odyssey,* 130.

138. Hyde, *Trickster Makes This World: Mischief, Myth and Art,* 65.

139. Ibid.

140. Ibid., 66. Hyde also relates meaning to the body's dealing with hunger, with filling the belly as a recurrent theme of the trickster. Travelers tell lies until their stomachs are full: "Trickster lies because he has a belly, the stories say; expect truth only from those whose belly is full or those who have escaped the belly altogether." Hyde, *Trickster Makes This World: Mischief, Myth and Art,* 77.

141. A popular Internet site where individuals can auction secondhand goods. See www.Ebay.com.

142. Campbell, *The Hero with a Thousand Faces,* 217. See also A. Snodgrass, "Travel in a different world makes a world of difference," A. Snodgrass, "Random thoughts on the way: The architecture of excursion and return," and A. Snodgrass, "Asian studies and the fusion of horizons."

143. Gadamer and David, *Philosophical Hermeneutics,* 58. See also A. Snodgrass, "Design amnesia and remembering history in the design studio."

144. Heidegger, *Being and Time,* 265.

145. P. Ludlow, "New foundations: On the emergence of sovereign cyberstates and their governance structures," 5.

146. Ibid., 4.

147. See D. Frissell, "Re: Denning's crypto anarchy," and H. Bey, "The temporary autonomous zone."

148. C. G. Jung, *Psychology and Alchemy. The Collected Works of C. G. Jung. Vol. 12*, 105.

149. Ibid., 106.

150. See Ricoeur, *Freud and Philosophy: An Essay in Interpretation.*

151. Jung, *Alchemical Studies: The Collected Works of C. G. Jung. Vol. 13*, 237.

152. Jung, *Psychology and Alchemy. The Collected Works of C. G. Jung. Vol. 12*, 4.

153. Jung, *Alchemical Studies: The Collected Works of C. G. Jung. Vol. 13*, 237.

154. Jung, *Psychology and Alchemy. The Collected Works of C. G. Jung. Vol. 12*, 137.

155. Jung, *Alchemical Studies: The Collected Works of C. G. Jung. Vol. 13*, 21.

156. Ibid., 24.

157. See Douglas, "The historical context of analytical psychology," 30, for an account of Jung's interest in Gnosticism and other occult systems.

158. J. P. Barlow, "A declaration of the independence of cyberspace," 28.

159. Ibid.

160. Ibid., 29.

161. T. C. May, "A crypto anarchist's manifesto," 63.

162. Ludlow provides a helpful summary of the debates for and against encryption technologies. See P. Ludlow, "New foundations: On the emergence of sovereign cyberstates and their governance structures."

163. Hyde, *Trickster Makes This World: Mischief, Myth and Art*, 299.

164. See H. R. Heller, *The Economic System.*

165. W. Godwin, *Enquiry Concerning Political Justice.*

166. Plato, "Laws," 918a, 1571.

167. Ibid., 918d, 1572.

168. Plato, "Eryxias" 400a, 1726.

169. See Žižek, "Big Brother, or, the triumph of the gaze over the eye."

170. James Watt's flyball governor.

References

Adams, Michael Vannoy. 1997. "The archetypal school." In P. Young-Eisendrath, and T. Dawson (eds.), *The Cambridge Companion to Jung:* 101–118. Cambridge: Cambridge University Press.

Ades, Dawn (ed.). 1995. *Art and Power: Europe under the Dictators 1930–45 (exhibition catalogue to 23rd Council of Europe Exhibition).* London: Hayward Gallery.

Agamben, Giorgio. 1998. *Homo Sacer: Sovereign Power and Bare Life.* Trans. D. Heller-Roazen. Stanford: Stanford University Press.

Ahlava, Antti. 2002. *Architecture in Consumer Society.* Helsinki: Ilmari.

Alexander, Christopher. 1964. *Notes on the Synthesis of Form.* Cambridge, Mass.: Harvard University Press.

Alexander, Christopher, Sara Ishikawa, and Murray Silverstein. 1977. *A Pattern Language: Towns, Buildings, Construction.* New York: Oxford University Press.

Althusser, Louis. 1990. *For Marx.* Trans. B. Brewster. London: Verso.

Althusser, Louis, and Étienne Balibar. 1997. *Reading Capital.* Trans. B. Brewster. London: Verso. First published in French in 1968.

Anonymous. 2004. "Janus in myth." *Mythography,* February 6, 2005. Available online at http://www.loggia.com/myth/janus.html.

Anonymous. 2005. "Here's to the crazy ones." *Apple Web Site,* February 6, 2005. Available online at http://www.apple.com/thinkdifferent/.

Aristotle. 1968. *The Poetics.* Trans. D. W. Lucas. Oxford: Oxford University Press.

Aristotle. 1976. *The Ethics of Aristotle: The Nicomachean Ethics.* Trans. J. A. K. Thomson. London: Penguin. Written ca. 334–323 BC.

Aristotle. 1981. *The Politics.* Trans. T. A. Sinclair. London: Penguin.

Aristotle. 1996. *Physics.* Trans. R. Waterfield. Oxford: Oxford University Press.

Armitt, Lucy. 1996. *Theorising the Fantastic.* London: Arnold.

Augé, M. 1995. *Non-places: Introduction to an Anthropology of Supermodernity.* Trans. J. Howe. London: Verso.

Aurelius, Marcus. 1964. *Meditations.* Trans. M. Staniforth. London: Penguin. Manuscript from the second century AD.

Austin, John. 1966. *How to do Things with Words.* Cambridge, Mass.: Harvard University Press.

Axelrod, Robert. 1990. *The Evolution of Co-operation.* London: Penguin.

Bachelard, Gaston. 1964. *The Poetics of Space.* New York: Orion Press.

Banham, Reyner. 1960. *Theory and Design in the First Machine Age.* London: Architectural Press.

Barbrook, Richard. 1998. "The high-tech gift economy." *FirstMonday,* February 5, 2005. Available online at http://www.firstmonday.rg/issues/issue3_12/barbrook/index.html.

Barbrook, Richard, and Andy Cameron. 2001. "Californian ideology." In P. Ludlow (ed.), *Crypto Anarchy, Cyberstates, and Pirate Utopias,* 363–387. Cambridge, Mass.: MIT Press.

Barlow, John Perry. 2001. "A declaration of the independence of cyberspace." In P. Ludlow (ed.), *Crypto Anarchy, Cyberstates, and Pirate Utopias,* 27–30. Cambridge, Mass.: MIT Press.

Barthes, Roland. 1973. *Mythologies.* Trans. A. Lavers. London: Paladin.

Bateson, Gregory. 2000. *Steps to an Ecology of Mind.* Chicago: University of Chicago Press.

Baudrillard, Jean. 1993. *Symbolic Exchange and Death.* Trans. I. H. Grant. London: Sage.

Baudrillard, Jean. 2001a. "The Gulf War did not take place." In M. Poster (ed.), *Selected Writings,* 231–253. Cambridge: Polity.

Baudrillard, Jean. 2001b. "The mirror of production." In M. Poster (ed.), *Selected Writings,* 101–121. Cambridge: Polity.

Baudrillard, Jean. 2001c. "The perfect crime." In M. Poster (ed.), *Selected Writings,* 266–275. Cambridge: Polity.

Baudrillard, Jean. 2001d. "Simulacra and simulations." In M. Poster (ed.), *Selected Writings,* 169–187. Cambridge: Polity.

Baudrillard, Jean. 2001e. "Symbolic exchange and death." In M. Poster (ed.), *Selected Writings,* 122–151. Cambridge: Polity.

Beck, Ulrich. 1992. *Risk Society: Towards a New Modernity.* Trans. M. Ritter. London: Sage.

Becker, Gary S. 1981. *A Treatise on the Family.* Cambridge, Mass.: Harvard University Press.

Bell, David. 2001. *An Introduction to Cybercultures.* London: Routledge.

Benedikt, Michael. 1994. *Cyberspace: First Steps.* Cambridge, Mass.: MIT Press.

Benjamin, Andrew. 2000. *Architectural Philosophy.* London: Athlone.

Benjamin, Walter. 2000. *The Arcades Project.* Trans. H. Eiland and K. McLaughlin. Cambridge, Mass.: Harvard University Press.

Bergquist, Magnus, and Jan Ljungberg. 2001. "The power of gifts: Organizing social relationships in open source communities." *Information Systems Journal* 11: 305–320.

Berners-Lee, Tim. 1999. *Weaving the Web: The Past, Present and Future of the World Wide Web by Its Inventor.* London: Texere.

Berry, Phillipe. 1995. "Kristeva's feminist refiguring of the gift." *Paragraph* 18(3): 223–238.

Best, Kirsty. 2003. "Beating them at their own game: The cultural politics of the open software movement and the gift economy." *International Journal of Cultural Studies* 6(4): 449–470.

Bey, Hakim. 2001. "The temporary autonomous zone." In P. Ludlow (ed.), *Crypto Anarchy, Cyberstates, and Pirate Utopias,* 401–434. Cambridge, Mass.: MIT Press.

Bloch, Ernst. 1986. *The Principle of Hope.* Oxford: Blackwell.

Bloch, Maurice, and Jonathan Parry. 1989. "Introduction: Money and the morality of exchange." In J. Parry and M. Bloch (eds.), *Money and the Morality of Exchange,* 1–32. Cambridge: Cambridge University Press.

Bloomer, Jennifer. 1992. "D'or." In B. Colomina (ed.), *Sexuality and Space,* 163–183. Princeton, N.J.: Princeton University Press.

Bloor, Robin. 2000. *The Electronic Bazaar: From the Silk Road to the eRoad.* London: Nicholas Brealey.

Boden, Margaret. 1990. *The Creative Mind: Myths and Mechanisms.* London: Abacus.

Bolter, J. David, and Richard A. Grusin. 1999. *Remediation: Understanding New Media.* Cambridge, Mass.: MIT Press.

Borges, Jorg Luis. 1970. "The garden of the forking paths." In *Labyrinths,* 44–54. London: Penguin.

Borgmann, Albert. 1984. *Technology and the Character of Contemporary Life: A Philosophical Inquiry.* Chicago: University of Chicago Press.

Botting, Fred, and Scott Wilson. 2001. *Bataille.* Basingstoke, Hampshire: Palgrave.

Botting, Fred, and Scott Wilson (eds.). 1997. *The Bataille Reader.* Oxford: Blackwell.

Boundas, Constantin, V. 2001. "Exchange, gift, and theft." *Angelaki: Journal of Theoretical Humanities* 6(2): 101–112.

Bourriaud, Nicolas. 2002. *Relational Aesthetics.* Trans. S. Pleasance, F. Woods, and M. Copeland. Dijon, France: Les Presses du Réel.

Bouveresse, Jacques. 1995. *Wittgenstein Reads Freud: The Myth of the Unconscious.* Princeton, N.J.: Princeton University Press.

Bowie, Malcolm. 1991. *Lacan.* London: Fontana.

Broadbent, Geoffrey. 1973. *Design in Architecture: Architecture and the Human Sciences.* New York: Wiley.

Brynjolfsson, Erik, and Brian Kahnin. 2000. *Understanding the Digital Economy: Data, Tools, and Research.* Cambridge, Mass.: MIT Press.

Buchholz, Todd G. 1999. *New Ideas from Dead Economists: An Introduction to Modern Economic Thought.* London: Penguin.

Bunyan, John. 1987. *Grace Abounding to the Chief of Sinners.* London: Penguin. First published in 1666.

Burke, Edmund, and James Boulton (eds.). 1958. *A Philosophical Enquiry into the Origin of Our Ideas of the Sublime and Beautiful.* Notre Dame, Ind.: University of Notre Dame Press.

Burnett, Robert, and P. David Marshall. 2003. *Web Theory: An Introduction.* London: Routledge.

Caillois, Roger. 1961. *Man, Play, and Games.* New York: The Free Press of Glencoe.

Camp, Jean. 2001. "Sustainable open source software business models." In L. W. McKnight, P. M. Vaaler, and P. L. Katz (eds.), *Creative Destruction: Business Survival Strategies in the Global Internet Economy,* 228–213. Cambridge, Mass.: MIT Press.

Campbell, Joseph. 1993. *The Hero with a Thousand Faces.* London: Fontana. First published in 1949.

Campbell, Philip. 2000. "Designing *Tomb Raider.*" In *Tomb Raider Level Editor: Tutorial and Manual,* 56–60. London: Core Design Ltd. and Eidos Interactive.

Carlyle, Thomas. 1984. *Past and Present.* Ed. Takaaki Tanizaki. Tokyo: Yamagushi Shoten.

Cassidy, John. 2002. *Dot.con: The Greatest Story Ever Told.* London: Penguin.

Castells, Manuel. 1996. *The Rise of the Network Society.* Malden, Mass.: Blackwell Publishers.

Castells, Manuel. 2001. *The Internet Galaxy: Reflections on the Internet, Business, and Society.* Oxford: Oxford University Press.

Chomsky, Noam. 2002. *Syntactic Structures.* Berlin: Mouton de Gruyter.

Clarke, Brian Charles. 2000. "Thresholding." *Scriptorium Sagittaire,* February 6, 2005. Available online at http://www.wdog.com/brian/Scriptorium/sublime_etym.htm.

Coggan, Philip. 2002. *The Money Machine: How the City Works.* London: Penguin.

Collins, Jim. 1995. *Architectures of Excess: Cultural Life in the Information Age.* London: Routledge.

Corbusier, Le. 1931. *Towards a New Architecture.* Trans. F. Etchells. New York: Dover. First published as *Vers une Architecture* in 1923.

Coyne, Richard. 1995. *Designing Information Technology in the Postmodern Age: From Method to Metaphor.* Cambridge, Mass.: MIT Press.

Coyne, Richard. 1998. "Cyberspace and Heidegger's pragmatics." *Information Technology and People (Special Issue: Heidegger and Information Technology)* 11(4): 338–350.

Coyne, Richard. 1999. *Technoromanticism: Digital Narrative, Holism, and the Romance of the Real.* Cambridge, Mass.: MIT Press.

Coyne, Richard. 2002. "The cult of the not-yet." In N. Leach (ed.), *Designing for a Digital World,* 45–48. London: Wiley-Academic.

Coyne, Richard, John Lee, David Duncan, and Salih Ofluoglu. 2001. "Applying Web-based product libraries. *Automation in Construction* 10: 549–559.

Coyne, Richard, John Lee, and Salih Ofluoglu. 2000. "Design and the emerging e-commerce environment." In R. Coyne, J. Lee, and K. Zreik (eds.), *Proc. Design and the Emerging E-Commerce Environment* (November 14–15): 39–52. Edinburgh: EUROPIA Productions, Paris.

Coyne, Richard, Hoon Park, and Dorian Wiszniewski. 2000. "Design devices: What they reveal and conceal." *Kritische Berichte: Zeitschrift für Kunst- und Kulturwissenschaften* 3: 55–69.

Coyne, Richard, and Dorian Wiszniewski. 2000. "Technical deceits: Critical theory, hermeneutics and the ethics of information technology." *International Journal of Design Sciences and Technology* 8(1): 9–18.

Crawford, Chris. 1982. *Electronic Book: The Art of Computer Game Design.* Vancouver: Washington State University. February 5, 2005. Available online at http://www.vancouver.wsu.edu/fac/peabody/game-book/Coverpage.html.

Currah, Andrew. 2003. "The virtual geographies of retail display." *Journal of Consumer Culture* 3(1): 5–37.

Davidson, William L. 1979. *The Stoic Creed.* New York: Arno Press.

Davis, D. A. 1997. Freud, Jung, and Psychoanalysis. In P. Young-Eisendrath and T. Dawson (eds.), *The Cambridge Companion to Jung,* 35–51. Cambridge: Cambridge University Press.

de Man, Paul. 1979. *Allegories of Reading: Figural Language in Rousseau, Nietzsche, Rilke.* New Haven: Yale University Press.

de Sade, Donatien Alphonse François. 1966. *120 Days of Sodom and Other Writings.* Trans. S. de Beauvoir, P. Klossowski, R. Seaver, and A. Wainhouse. New York: Grove Press.

Debord, Guy. 1983. *The Society of the Spectacle.* Detroit, Mich.: Black and Red.

Deleuze, Gilles. 1994. *Difference and Repetition.* Trans. P. Patton. London: Athlone Press.

Deleuze, Gilles, and Felix Guattari. 1977. *Anti-Oedipus: Capitalism and Schizophrenia.* New York: Viking Press.

Deleuze, Gilles, and Felix Guattari. 1988. The smooth and the striated. *A Thousand Plateaus: Capitalism and Schizophrenia,* 474–500. London: Athlone Press.

Deleuze, Gilles, and Felix Guattari. 1988. *A Thousand Plateaus: Capitalism and Schizophrenia.* Trans. B. Massumi. London: Athlone Press.

Denning, Dorothy E. 2001. "The future of cryptography." In P. Ludlow (ed.), *Crypto Anarchy, Cyberstates, and Pirate Utopias,* 85–101. Cambridge, Mass.: MIT Press.

Derrida, Jacques. 1976. *Of Grammatology.* Trans. G. C. Spivak. Baltimore, Md.: Johns Hopkins University Press.

Derrida, Jacques. 1978. "Freud and the scene of writing." In *Writing and Difference,* 196–231. Chicago: University of Chicago Press.

Derrida, Jacques. 1983. "The principle of reason: The university in the eyes of its pupils." *Diacritics* 13: 3–20.

Derrida, Jacques. 1992. *Given Time: 1. Counterfeit Money.* Trans. P. Kamuf. Chicago: University of Chicago Press.

Descartes, René. 1968. *Discourse on Method and the Meditations.* Trans. F. E. Sutcliffe. Harmondsworth, Middlesex: Penguin.

Desmet, Christy. 2001. "Reading the Web as fetish." *Computers and Composition* 18: 55–72.

Detlor, B. 2000. "The corporate portal as information infrastructure: Towards a framework for portal design." *International Journal of Information Management* 20(2): 91–101.

Dickens, A. G. 1967. *Martin Luther and the Reformation.* London: Hodder and Stoughton.

Dilthey, Wilhelm. 1976. "The development of hermeneutics." In H. P. Rickman (ed.), *W. Dilthey: Selected Writings,* 246–263. Cambridge: Cambridge University Press.

Diogenes, Laërtius. 1853. *The Lives and Opinions of Eminent Philosophers.* Trans. C. D. Yonge. London: Henry G. Bohn. Originally written ca. AD 200.

Dorrian, Mark. 2000. "On the monstrous and the grotesque." *Word & Image* 16(3): 310–317.

Dorrian, Mark. 2003. "The breath on the mirror: On Ruskin's theory of the grotesque." In A. Perez-Gomez and S. Parcell (eds.), *Chora: Intervals in the Philosophy of Architecture 4*: 25–48. Montreal: McGill-Queens Press.

Douglas, Claire. 1997. The historical context of analytical psychology. In P. Young-Eisendrath and T. Dawson (eds.), *The Cambridge Companion to Jung,* 17–34. Cambridge: Cambridge University Press.

Douglas, Mary. 1966. *Purity and Danger: An Analysis of Concepts of Pollution and Taboo.* London: Routledge and Kegan Paul.

Dourish, Paul, and David Redmiles. 2002. "An approach to usable security based on event monitoring and visualization." In *Proc. New Security Paradigms Workshop '02, September 23–26,* 75–81. Virginia Beach, Va.: ACM.

Dreyfus, Hubert L. 1972. *What Computers Can't Do: The Limits of Artificial Intelligence.* New York: Harper and Row.

Dudley, Donald. 1967. *A History of Cynicism: From Diogenes to the 6th Century AD.* Hildesheim, Germany: Georg Olms Verlagsbuchhandlung.

Ehn, Pelle. 1988. *Work-Oriented Design of Computer Artifacts.* Stockholm: Arbetslivscentrum.

Endsjø, Dag Øistein. 2000. "To lock up Eleusis: A question of liminal space." *Numen* 47: 351–386.

Feenberg, A. 2002. *Transforming Technology: A Critical Theory Revisited.* Oxford: Oxford University Press.

Fiore, Frank. 2000. *The Complete Idiot's Guide to Starting an Online Business.* Indianapolis, Ind.: Macmillan.

Firth, Raymond (ed.). 1970. *Themes in Economic Anthropology.* London: Tavistock.

Foucault, Michel. 1972. *The Archaeology of Knowledge.* Trans. A. M. Sheridan Smith. London: Tavistock.

Foucault, Michel. 1977. *Discipline and Punish: The Birth of the Prison.* London: Penguin.

Foucault, Michel. 1988. *The History of Sexuality 3: The Care of the Self.* Trans. R. Hurley. London: Penguin.

Freud, Sigmund. 1990. "Beyond the pleasure principle." In A. Richards (ed.), *The Penguin Freud Library, Volume 11: On Metapsychology,* 269–338. Harmondsworth, Middlesex: Penguin.

Freud, Sigmund. 1990. "The 'uncanny.'" In A. Dickson (ed.), *The Penguin Freud Library, Volume 14: Art and Literature,* 335–376. Harmondsworth, Middlesex: Penguin.

Freud, Sigmund. 1991a. "Character and anal eroticism." In A. Richards (ed.), *The Penguin Freud Library, Volume 7: On Sexuality,* 205–215. Harmondsworth, Middlesex: Penguin.

Freud, Sigmund. 1991b. "Infantile sexuality." In A. Richards (ed.), *The Penguin Freud Library, Volume 7: On Sexuality,* 88–126. Harmondsworth, Middlesex: Penguin.

Freud, Sigmund. 1991c. "Negation." In *The Penguin Freud Library, Volume 11: On Metapsychologyy,* 435–442. Harmondsworth, Middlesex: Penguin.

Freud, Sigmund. 1991d. "On transformations of instinct as exemplified in anal eroticism." In A. Richards (ed.), *The Penguin Freud Library, Volume 7: On Sexuality,* 293–302. Harmondsworth, Middlesex: Penguin.

Freud, Sigmund. 1991e. "Three essays on the theory of sexuality." In A. Richards (ed.), *The Penguin Freud Library, Volume 7: On Sexuality,* 31–169. Harmondsworth, Middlesex: Penguin.

Freud, Sigmund. 1991f. "Infantile sexuality." In A. Richards (ed.), *The Penguin Freud Library, Volume 7: On Sexuality,* 88–126. Harmondsworth, Middlesex: Penguin.

Friedman, Milton. 1962. *Capitalism and Freedom.* Chicago, Ill.: University of Chicago Press.

Frissell, Duncan. 2001. "Re: Denning's crypto anarchy." In P. Ludlow (ed.), *Crypto Anarchy, Cyberstates, and Pirate Utopias,* 105–114. Cambridge, Mass.: MIT Press.

Gadamer, Hans-Georg. 1975. *Truth and Method.* New York: Seabury Press.

Gadamer, Hans-Georg. 1976. *Philosophical Hermeneutics.* Ed. and trans. David Edward Linge. Berkeley: University of California Press.

Gadamer, Hans-Georg. 1996. *The Enigma of Health: The Art of Healing in a Scientific Age.* Trans. J. Gaiger and N. Walker. Cambridge: Polity.

Gadamer, Hans-Georg. 2001. *Gadamer in Conversation: Reflections and Commentary.* Ed. and trans. Richard E. Palmer. New Haven: Yale University Press.

Galbraith, John Kenneth. 1998. *The Affluent Society.* London: Penguin. First published in 1958.

Gaskin, John (ed.). 1995. *The Epicurean Philosophers.* London: Everyman.

Gates, Bill, and Collins Hemingway. 1999. *Business @ the Speed of Thought: Using a Digital Nervous System.* London: Penguin.

Gates, Bill, Nathan Myhrvold, and Peter Rinearson. 1995. *The Road Ahead.* London: Viking.

Giddens, Anthony. 1999. *Runaway World: How Globalization Is Shaping Our Lives.* London: Profile Books.

Giovannini, J. 2000. "Building a better blob." *Architecture* 89(9): 126–129.

Giroux, Henry A. 2001. *Public Spaces, Private Lives: Beyond the Culture of Cynicism.* Lanham, Md.: Rowman & Littlefield.

Gleick, James. 1988. *Chaos: Making a New Science.* London: Heinemann.

Godbout, Jacques T. 1998. *The World of the Gift.* Trans. D. Winkler. Montreal: McGill-Queen's University Press.

Godelier, Maurice. 1999. *The Enigma of the Gift.* Trans. N. Scott. Cambridge: Polity Press.

Godwin, William. 1976. *Enquiry Concerning Political Justice.* London: Penguin. First published in 1793.

Golding, Peter. 1998. "Global village or cultural pillage? The unequal inheritance of the communications revolution." In R. W. McChesney, E. M. Wood, and J. B. Foster (eds.), *Capitalism and the Information Age: The Political Economy of the Global Communication Revolution,* 69–86. New York: Monthly Review Press.

Goldstein, Carolyn M. 1997. "From service to sales: Home economics in light and power 1920–1940." *Technology and Culture* 38(1): 121–152.

Graham, Elaine. 2002. "Nietzsche gets a modem: Transhumanism and the technological sublime." *Literature and Theology* 16(1): 65–80.

Graham, Gordon. 1999. *The Internet: A Philosophical Inquiry.* London: Routledge.

Graves, Robert. 1960a. *The Greek Myths: Volume 1.* London: Penguin.

Graves, Robert. 1960b. *The Greek Myths: Volume 2.* London: Penguin.

Greig, Ian. 2002. "The aesthetics of the sublime in twentieth century physics." Ph.D. thesis, South Australian School of Art, Division of Education, Arts and Social Sciences, University of South Australia.

Griffiths, Mark. 2003. "Sex on the Internet: Issues, concerns, and implications." In J. Turow and A. L. Kavanaugh (eds.), *The Wired Homestead: An MIT Press Sourcebook on the Internet and the Family,* 261–281. Cambridge, Mass.: MIT.

Handley, Miriam. 2000. "Shaw's response to the deus ex machina: From *The Quintessence of Ibsenism* to *Heartbreak House.*" In L. Hardwick (ed.), *Theatre: Ancient and Modern,* 54–67. Milton Keynes: The Open University Press.

Haraway, Donna. 1991. "The actors are cyborgs, nature is coyote, and the geography is everywhere: Postscript to 'Cyborgs are at large.'" In C. Penley and A. Ross (eds.), *Technoculture,* 21–26. Minneapolis: University of Minnesota Press.

Haraway, Donna J. 1991. *Simians, Cyborgs, and Women: The Reinvention of Nature.* London: FAb.

Harbison, Robert. 1997. *Thirteen Ways: Theoretical Investigations in Architecture.* Cambridge, Mass.: MIT Press.

Harris, Olivia. 1989. "The earth and the state: The sources and meanings of money in Northern Potosí, Bolivia." In J. Parry and M. Bloch (eds.), *Money and the Morality of Exchange,* 232–268. Cambridge: Cambridge University Press.

Hayek, Friedrich A. 1948. *Individualism and Economic Order.* Chicago: University of Chicago Press.

Hegel, Georg Wilhelm Friedrich. 1969. *Hegel's Science of Logic.* London: Allen & Unwin.

Heidegger, Martin. 1962. *Being and Time.* Trans. J. Macquarrie and E. Robinson. London: SCM Press.

Heidegger, Martin. 1971a. "Building, dwelling, thinking." In *Poetry, Language, Thought,* 143–161. New York: Harper and Rowe.

Heidegger, Martin. 1971b. "The origin of the work of art." In *Poetry, Language, Thought,* 15–87. New York: Harper and Rowe.

Heidegger, Martin. 1971c. "The thing." In *Poetry, Language, Thought,* 165–186. New York: Harper and Row.

Heidegger, Martin. 1977. *The Question Concerning Technology and Other Essays.* Trans. W. Lovitt. New York: Harper and Row.

Heidegger, Martin. 1992. *History of the Concept of Time: Prolegomena.* Trans. T. Kisiel. Bloomington: Indiana University Press.

Heller, H. Robert. 1972. *The Economic System.* New York: Macmillan.

Hesiod. 1988. *Theogony and Works and Days.* Trans. M. L. West. Oxford: Oxford University Press. Written ca. 8 BC.

Hesse, Hermann. 1990. *The Glass Bead Game.* Trans. R. Winston and C. Winston. New York: Henry Holt and Company. First published in German in 1943.

Hill, Jonathan. 2003. *Actions of Architecture: Architects and Creative Users.* London: Routledge.

Hiltz, Starr Roxanne, and Murray Turoff. 1993. *The Network Nation: Human Communication via Computer.* Cambridge, Mass.: MIT Press.

Hodges, Andrew. 1985. *Alan Turing: The Enigma of Intelligence.* London: Unwin Paperbacks.

Hofstadter, Douglas R., and Daniel C. Dennett. 1981. *The Mind's I: Fantasies and Reflections on Self and Soul.* Brighton: Harvester Press.

Homer. 1980. *The Odyssey.* Trans. W. Shewring. Oxford: Oxford University Press. Written ca. 750 BC.

Homer. 1998. *The Iliad.* Trans. R. Fitzgerald. Oxford: Oxford University Press. Written ca. 750 BC.

Hughes, Eric. 2001. The cypherpunk's manifesto. In P. Ludlow (ed.), *Crypto Anarchy, Cyberstates, and Pirate Utopias,* 81–83. Cambridge, Mass.: MIT Press.

Huizinga, Johan. 1955. *Homo Ludens: A Study of the Play Element in Culture.* Boston: Beacon Press.

Hutton, Will, and Anthony Giddens. 2001. *On the Edge: Living with Global Capitalism.* London: Vintage.

Hyde, Lewis. 1983. *Imagination and the Erotic Life of Property.* New York: Random House.

Hyde, Lewis. 1998. *Trickster Makes This World: Mischief, Myth and Art.* New York: North Point Press.

Ison, Ray, and David Russell (eds.). 1999. *Agricultural Extension and Rural Development: Breaking Out of Traditions.* Cambridge: Cambridge University Press.

Jakobson, Roman, and Morris Halle. 1956. *Fundamentals of Language.* The Hague, Holland: Mouton.

Jameson, Fredric. 2003. "Future city." *New Left Review* 21: 65–79.

Jenkins, Henry. 1992. *Textual Poachers: Television Fans and Participatory Culture.* New York: Routledge.

Joyce, James. 1992. *Ulysses.* London: Penguin.

Jung, Carl G. 1944. *Psychological Types.* Trans. H. Godwin Baynes. London: Kegan Paul.

Jung, Carl G. 1953. *Psychology and Alchemy. The Collected Works of C. G. Jung. Vol. 12.* Trans. R. F. C. Hull. London: Routledge.

Jung, Carl G. 1967. *Alchemical Studies: The Collected Works of C. G. Jung. Vol. 13.* Trans. R. F. C. Hull. Princeton, N.J.: Princeton University Press.

Jung, Carl G. 1986. *Four Archetypes: Mother, Rebirth, Spirit, Trickster.* London: Ark. First published in German in 1934–1956.

Kant, Immanuel. 2000. *Critique of the Power of Judgment*. Ed. and trans. Paul Guyer and Allen W. Wood. Cambridge: Cambridge University Press.

Katz, Claudio. 1994. "The Greek matrix of Marx's critique of political economy." *History of Political Thought* 15(2): 229–248.

Keynes, John Maynard. 1997. *The General Theory of Employment, Interest and Money*. Amherst, New York: Prometheus. First published in 1936.

Kierkegaard, Soren. 2001. "Repetition: An essay in experimental psychology by Constantin Constantius." In J. Chamberlain and J. Rée (eds.), *The Kierkegard Reader*, 115–150. London: Blackwell.

King, Lucien (ed.). 2002. *Game On: The History and Culture of Video Games*. London: Laurence King.

Kline, Stephen, Nick Dyer-Witheford, and Greig de Peuter. 2003. *Digital Play: The Interaction of Technology, Culture and Marketing*. Montreal: McGill-Queen's University Press.

Kling, R. 1996. *Computerization and Controversy: Value Conflicts and Social Choices*. Academic Press: San Diego.

Koolhaas, Rem. 2004. "Junk space." In R. Koolhaas, AMO, and OMA (eds.), *Content*, 162–171. Köln: Taschen.

Koolhaas, Rem (ed.). 2001. *The Harvard Guide to Shopping*. Köln: Benedikt Taschen Verlag.

Koolhaas, Rem, and B. Mau. 1997a. "Generic city." In R. Koolhaas and B. Mau (eds.), *S, M, L, XL*, 1239–1264. Rotterdam: 010 Publishers.

Koolhaas, Rem, and B. Mau. 1997b. "What ever happened to urbanism?" In R. Koolhaas and B. Mau (eds.), *S, M, L, XL*, 959–971. Rotterdam: 010 Publishers.

Kropotkin, Peter Alekseevich, and Marshall Shatz. 1995. *The Conquest of Bread and Other Writings*. New York: Cambridge University Press.

Lacan, Jacques. 1977. *Écrits: A Selection*. Trans. A. Sheridan. London: Routledge. First published in French in 1966.

Landow, George P. 1994. "Hypertext as collage-writing." In P. Delany and G. P. Landow (eds.), *Hypermedia and Literary Studies,* 150–170. Cambridge, Mass.: MIT Press.

Landow, George P., and Paul Delany. 1994. "Hypertext, hypermedia and literary studies: The state of the art." In P. Delany and G. P. Landow (eds.), *Hypermedia and Literary Studies,* 3–50. Cambridge, Mass.: MIT Press.

Laurel, Brenda. 2001. *Utopian Entrepreneur.* Cambridge, Mass.: MIT Press.

Leach, Neil, and RIBA Future Studies. 2002. *Designing for a Digital World.* Chichester: Wiley.

Lessig, Lawrence. 1999. *Code and Other Laws of Cyberspace.* New York: Basic Books.

Lévi-Strauss, Claude. 1963. *Structural Anthropology 1.* London: Penguin.

Levin, Thomas Y., Ursula Frohne, and Peter Weibel. 2002. *CTRL {SPACE}: Rhetorics of Surveillance from Bentham to Big Brother.* Cambridge, Mass.: MIT Press.

Lewis, C. S. 1977. *Surprised by Joy.* London: Fount.

Lloyd, Seton. 1963. Ancient and classical architecture. In T. Copplestone (ed.), *World Architecture: An Illustrated History,* 15–80. London: Hamlyn.

Ludlow, Peter. 2001a. *Crypto Anarchy, Cyberstates, and Pirate Utopias.* Cambridge, Mass.: MIT Press.

Ludlow, Peter. 2001b. "New foundations: On the emergence of sovereign cyberstates and their governance structures." In P. Ludlow (ed.), *Crypto Anarchy, Cyberstates, and Pirate Utopias,* 1–23. Cambridge, Mass.: MIT Press.

Lukács, Georg. 1971. *History and Class Consciousness.* Trans. R. Livingstone. London: Merlin. Essays first published in French between 1918 and 1930.

Lunefeld, Peter (ed.). 1999. *The Digital Dialectic: New Essays on New Media.* Cambridge Mass.: MIT Press.

Lutz, Mark, A. 1998. *Economics for the Common Good: Two Centuries of Economic Thought in the Humanistic Tradition.* London: Routledge.

Lynn, Greg. 1999. *Animate Form.* New York: Princeton Architectural Press.

Lynn, Greg. 2002. *Architecture for an Embryologic Housing.* Berlin: Birkhauser Verlag AG.

Lyotard, Jean-François. 1986. *The Postmodern Condition: A Report on Knowledge.* Manchester: Manchester University Press.

Malthus, Thomas Robert. 1992. *An Essay on the Principle of Population.* Cambridge: Cambridge University Press. First published in 1798.

Malthus, Thomas Robert. 1993. *An Essay on the Principle of Population.* Oxford: Oxford University Press. First published in 1798.

Manovich, Lev. 2002. *The Language of New Media.* Cambridge, Mass.: MIT Press.

Mansell, R., and R. Silverstone. 1995. *Communication by Design: The Politics of Information and Communication Technologies.* Oxford: Oxford University Press.

Marcuse, Herbert. 1987. *Eros and Civilization: A Philosophical Inquiry into Freud.* London: Routledge and Kegan Paul.

Marcuse, Herbert. 1991. *One-Dimensional Man: Studies in the Ideology of Advanced Industrial Society.* London: Routledge.

Marías, Julián. 1967. *History of Philosophy.* Trans. C. C. Strowbridge and S. Appelbaum. New York: Dover Publications.

Marinetti Filippo, Tommaso. 1909. "Manifesto of futurism." In K. Scarborough (ed.), *Futurism,* February 6, 2005. Available online at http://www.unknown.nu/futurism/manifesto.html.

Marshall, Alfred. 1997. *Principles of Economics.* Amherst, N.Y.: Prometheus. First published in 1890.

Marshall, Peter. 1992. *Demanding the Impossible: A History of Anarchism.* London: Fontana.

Marx, Karl. 1977a. "Capital." In D. McLellan (ed.), *Karl Marx: Selected Writings,* 415–507. Oxford: Oxford University Press.

Marx, Karl. 1977b. "Grundrisse." In D. McClellan (ed.), *Karl Marx: Selected Writings*, 245–387. Oxford: Oxford University Press.

Marx, Karl. 1977c. "The holy family." In D. McClellan (ed.), *Karl Marx: Selected Writings*, 131–155. Oxford: Oxford University Press.

Marx, Karl. 1977d. *Karl Marx: Selected Writings*. Oxford: Oxford University Press.

Marx, Karl. 1977e. "The poverty of philosophy." In D. McClellan (ed.), *Karl Marx: Selected Writings*, 195–215. Oxford: Oxford University Press.

Marx, Karl. 1977f. "Theses on Feuerbach." In D. McClellan (ed.), *Karl Marx: Selected Writings*, 156–158. Oxford: Oxford University Press.

Mauss, Marcel. 1990. *The Gift: The Form and Reason for Exchange in Archaic Societies*. Trans. W. D. Halls. New York: W. W. Norton. First published in French in 1925.

May, Timothy C. 2001a. "A crypto anarchist's manifesto." In P. Ludlow (ed.), *Crypto Anarchy, Cyberstates, and Pirate Utopias*, 61–63. Cambridge, Mass.: MIT Press.

May, Timothy C. 2001b. "Crypto anarchy and virtual communities." In P. Ludlow (ed.), *Crypto Anarchy, Cyberstates, and Pirate Utopias*, 65–79. Cambridge, Mass.: MIT Press.

McKnight Lee, W., M. Vaaler Paul, and Luciano Katz Raul. 2001. *Creative Destruction: Business Survival Strategies in the Global Internet Economy*. Cambridge, Mass.: MIT Press.

McLellan, David. 1977. *Marx After Marx: An Introduction*. London: MacMillan.

McLuhan, Marshall. 1962. *The Gutenberg Galaxy: The Making of Typographic Man*. Toronto: University of Toronto Press.

Menzies, Heather. 1998. "Challenging capitalism: The information highway, the postindustrial economy, and people." In R. W. McChesney, E. M. Wood, and J. B. Foster (eds.), *Capitalism and the Information Age: The Political Economy of the Global Communication Revolution*, 87–98. New York: Monthly Review Press.

Miller, Daniel, and Don Don Slater. 2000. *The Internet: An Ethnographic Approach*. Oxford: Berg.

Minsky, Marvin Lee. 1986. *The Society of Mind*. New York: Simon and Schuster.

Mirowski, Philip. 2002. *Machine Dreams: Economics Becomes a Cyborg Science.* Cambridge: Cambridge University Press.

Mitchell William, J. 1995. *City of Bits: Space, Place, and the Infobahn.* Cambridge, Mass.: MIT Press.

Moi, Toril. 1985. *Sexual/Textual Politics: Feminist Literary Theory.* London: Methuen.

Moravec, Hans P. 1988. *Mind Children: The Future of Robot and Human Intelligence.* Cambridge, Mass.: Harvard University Press.

Mosco, Vincent. 2004. *The Digital Sublime: Myth, Power, and Cyberspace.* Cambridge, Mass.: MIT Press.

Murray, Janet H. 1999. *Hamlet on the Holodeck: The Future of Narrative in Cyberspace.* Cambridge, Mass.: MIT Press.

Negroponte, Nicholas. 1995. *Being Digital.* London: Hodder and Stoughton.

Nesbit, Molly. 1992. "In the absence of the Parisienne . . ." In B. Colomina (ed.), *Sexuality and Space,* 307–325. Princeton, N.J.: Princeton University Press.

Neumann, J. von, and O. Morgenstern. 1947. *Theory of Games and Economic Behavior.* Princeton, N.J.: Princeton University Press.

Newell, A., and H. A. Simon. 1972. *Human Problem Solving.* Englewood Cliffs, N.J.: Prentice-Hall.

Nietzsche, Friedrich Wilhelm. 1961. *Thus Spoke Zarathustra: A Book for Everyone and No One.* Trans. R. J. Hollingdale. London: Penguin Books. First published in German in 1892.

Nietzsche, Friedrich Wilhelm. 2001. *The Gay Science: With a Prelude in German Rhymes and an Appendix of Songs.* Trans. J. Nauckhoff. Cambridge: Cambridge University Press.

Orwell, George. 1984. *1984.* Oxford: Clarendon Press. First published in 1949.

Padovan, Richard. 1999. *Proportion: Science, Philosophy, Architecture.* London: Spon.

Penly, Constance. 1991. "Brownian motion: Women, tactics, and technology." In C. Penley and A. Ross (eds.), *Technoculture,* 135–161. Minneapolis: University of Minnesota Press.

Phillips, Jeremy, and Alison Firth. 2001. *Introduction to Intellectual Property Law.* London: Butterworths.

Pinchot, Gifford. 1995. "The gift economy." *Context: A Quarterly of Humane Sustainable Culture,* February 5, 2005. Available online at http://www.context.org/ICLIB/IC41/:PinchotG.htm.

Plant, Sadie. 1998. *Zeros and Ones: Digital Women and the New Technoculture.* London: Fourth Estate.

Plato. 1941. *The Republic of Plato.* Trans. F. M. Cornford. London: Oxford University Press.

Plato. 1975. *The Laws.* Trans. T. J. Saunders. London: Penguin.

Plato. 1997a. "Cratylus." In J. M. Cooper (ed.), *Complete Works,* 101–156. Indianapolis, Ind.: Hackett.

Plato. 1997b. "Eryxias." In J. M. Cooper (ed.), *Complete Works,* 1718–1733. Indianapolis, Ind.: Hackett.

Plato. 1997c. "Laws." In J. M. Cooper (ed.), *Complete Works,* 1318–1616. Indianapolis, Ind.: Hackett.

Plato. 1997d. "Letter VII." In J. M. Cooper (ed.), *Complete Works,* 1646–1667. Indianapolis, Ind.: Hackett.

Plato. 1999. *Statesman.* Trans. C. J. Rowe. Indianapolis, Ind.: Hackett. Originally written ca. 360 BC.

Pliny, (The Younger). 1963. *The Letters of the Younger Pliny.* Trans. B. Radice. London: Penguin. Written ca. AD 80–113.

Poole, Steven. 2000. *Trigger Happy: The Inner Life of Videogames.* London: Fourth Estate.

Poster, Mark. 1995. *The Second Media Age.* Oxford: Blackwell.

Poster, Mark. 2001. *What's the Matter with the Internet?* Minneapolis, Minn.: University of Minnesota Press.

Postman, N. 1992. *Technopoly: The Surrender of American Culture to Technology.* New York: Alfred A. Knopf.

Radin, Paul. 1956. *The Trickster: A Study in American Indian Mythology.* London: Routledge and Kegan Paul.

Raman, Pattabi G., and Richard Coyne. 2000. The production of architectural criticism. *Architectural Theory Review* 5(1): 83–103.

Rand, Ayn. 1972. *The Fountainhead.* London: Grafton.

Rawls, John. 1999. *A Theory of Justice.* Oxford: Oxford University Press. First published in 1971.

Raymond, Eric. 2001. "The hacker milieu as gift culture." *Future Positive.* February 9, 2005. Available online at http://futurepositive.synearth.net/stories/storyReader$223.

Reuter, Jochen (ed.). 2001. *Final Report: Exploitation and Development of the Job Potential in the Cultural Sector in the Age of Digitalization.* Munich: European Commission DG Employment and Social Affairs, MKW Wirtschaftsforschung GmbH.

Rezmierski, V. E., M. R. Seese Jr., and N. St. Clair II. 2002. "University systems security logging: Who is doing it and how far can they go?" *Computers and Security* 21(6): 557–564.

Rheingold, Howard. 1993. *The Virtual Community: Homesteading on the Electronic Frontier.* Reading, Mass.: Addison-Wesley.

Ricardo, David. 1996. *Principles of Political Economy and Taxation.* Amherst, N.Y.: Prometheus. First published in 1817.

Ricoeur, Paul. 1970. *Freud and Philosophy: An Essay in Interpretation.* Trans. D. Savage. New Haven: Yale University Press.

Rifkin, Jeremy. 2000. *The End of Work: The Decline of the Global Work-Force and the Dawn of the Post-Market Era.* London: Penguin.

Robins, Kevin, and Les Levidow. 1995. "Soldier, cyborg, citizen." In J. Brook and I. A. Boal (eds.), *Resisting the Virtual Life: The Culture and Politics of Information,* 131–143. San Francisco: City Lights.

Rorty, Richard. 1980. *Philosophy and the Mirror of Nature.* Oxford: Basil Blackwell.

Rorty, Richard. 1989. *Contingency, Irony, and Solidarity.* Cambridge: Cambridge University Press.

Rosa, Joseph. 2003. *Next Generation Architecture: Contemporary Digital Experimentation + The Radical Avant-Garde.* London: Thames and Hudson.

Ross, Andrew. 1991. "Hacking away at counterculture." In C. Penley and A. Ross (eds.), *Technoculture,* 107–134. Minneapolis: University of Minnesota Press.

Rowling, J. K. 1997. *Harry Potter and the Philosopher's Stone.* London: Bloomsbury.

Rumelhart, D. E., and J. L. McClelland (eds.). 1987. *Parallel Distributed Processing: Explorations in the Microstructure of Cognition.* Cambridge, Mass.: MIT Press.

Ruskin, John. 1956. *The Seven Lamps of Architecture.* London: Everyman's Library. First published in 1849.

Ruskin, John. 1960. *The Stones of Venice.* Ed. J. G. Links. New York: Da Capo Press. First published in 1853.

Ruskin, John. 1985. *Unto This Last: And Other Writings.* Ed. Clive Wilmer. London: Penguin. First published in 1862–1871.

Ruskin, John. 1995. *John Ruskin: Selected Writings.* Ed. Philip Davis. London: Everyman.

Russell, David, and Ray Ison. 1999. "The research-development relationship in rural communities: An opportunity for contextual science." In R. Ison and D. Russell (eds.), *Agricultural Extension and Rural Development: Breaking Out of Traditions,* 10–31. Cambridge: Cambridge University Press.

Russo, Joseph. 1997. "A Jungian analysis of Homer's *Odysseus.*" In P. Young-Eisendrath and T. Dawson (eds.), *The Cambridge Companion to Jung,* 240–254. Cambridge: Cambridge University Press.

Ryan, Alan (ed.). 1987. *John Stuart Mill and Jeremy Bentham: Utilitarianism and Other Essays*. London: Penguin.

Sahlins, Marshall. 1974. *Stone Age Economics*. London: Tavistock.

Saint, Andrew. 1983. *The Image of the Architect*. New Haven: Yale University Press.

Salman, Sherry. 1997. "The creative psyche: Jung's major contribution." In P. Young-Eisendrath and T. Dawson (eds.), *The Cambridge Companion to Jung,* 52–70. Cambridge: Cambridge University Press.

Sayre, Farrand. 1938. *Diogenes of Sinope*. Baltimore: J. H. Furst Company.

Schleiermacher, Freidrich, and Andrew Bowie (ed.). 1998. *Hermeneutics and Criticism: And Other Writings*. Trans. A. Bowie. Cambridge: Cambridge University Press. Written in 1805–1833.

Schön, Donald A. 1983. *Reflective Practitioner: How Professionals Think in Action*. London: Temple Smith.

Scott, R., and Scott G. 2000. Ethics and the human aspects of technological change — Call centres: A case study. *The International Journal of Design Science* 8(1): 25–35.

Semper, Gottfried. 1989. *The Four Elements of Architecture and Other Writings*. Trans. F. Mallgrave and W. Hermann. New York: Cambridge University Press.

Seneca. 1997. *Dialogues and Letters*. Trans. C. D. N. Costa. London: Penguin. Written in the first century AD.

Shapiro, Carl, and Hal R. Varian. 1999. *Information Rules: A Strategic Guide to the Network Economy*. Boston: Harvard Business School Press.

Shelley, Mary. 1992. *Frankenstein*. Basingstoke: MacMillan.

Sherwood, J. 1997. "Security issues in today's corporate network." *Information Security Technical Report* 2(3): 8–17.

Simmel, Georg. 1990. *The Philosophy of Money*. Trans. T. Bottomore and D. Frisby. London: Routledge. First published in German in 1907.

Smith, Adam. 1984. *The Theory of Moral Sentiments.* Indianapolis, Ind.: Liberty Fund. First published in 1759.

Smith, Adam. 1998. *An Inquiry into the Nature and Causes of the Wealth of Nations.* Oxford: Oxford University Press. First published in 1776.

Snodgrass, Adrian. 1992. "Asian studies and the fusion of horizons." *Asian Studies Review* 15(3): 81–95.

Snodgrass, Adrian. 2001. "Random thoughts on the way: The architecture of excursion and return." *Architectural Theory Review* 6(1): 1–15.

Snodgrass, Adrian. 2002. "Travel in a different world makes a world of difference." *Architectural Theory Review* 7(1): 85–100.

Snodgrass, Adrian. 2004. "Design amnesia and remembering history in the design studio." *Design Theory Review* 8(2): 1–16.

Snodgrass, Adrian. 1990. *Architecture, Time and Eternity: Studies in the Stellar and Temporal Symbolism of Traditional Buildings, Volumes I and II.* New Delhi, India: Aditya Prakashan.

Snodgrass, Adrian, and Richard Coyne. 1997. "Is designing hermeneutical?" *Architectural Theory Review* 2(1): 65–97.

Snodgrass, Adrian, and Richard Coyne. 2005. *Interpretation in Architecture: Design as a Way of Thinking.* London: Routledge.

Snyder, D. I. 2002. "'I don't go by Sean Patrick.' On-line/off-line/out identity and SeanPatrickLive.com." *International Journal of Sexuality and Gender Studies* 7(2–3): 177–195.

Sommerville, Ian. 2001. *Software Engineering.* Harlow, England: Addison-Wesley.

Spinoza, Charles, Fernando Flores, and Hubert L. Dreyfus. 1997. *Disclosing New Worlds: Entrepreneurship, Democratic Action, and the Cultivation of Solidarity.* Cambridge, Mass.: MIT Press.

Stallabras, Julian. 1993. "Just gaming: Allegory and economy in computer games." *New Left Review* 198: 83–106.

Stallabras, Julian. 1996. *Gargantua: Manufactured Mass Culture*. London: Verso.

Stark, Oded. 1995. *Altruism and Beyond: An Economic Analysis of Transfers and Exchanges within Families and Groups*. Cambridge: Cambridge University Press.

Strogatz, Steven H. 2001. "Exploring complex networks." *Nature* 410: 268–276.

Tafuri, Manfredo. 1996. *Architecture and Utopia: Design and Capitalist Development*. Trans. B. L. La Penta. Cambridge, Mass.: MIT Press. First published in Italian in 1973.

Tapia, Alejandro. 2003. "Graphic design in the digital era: The rhetoric of hypertext." *Design Issues* 19(1): 5–24.

Teo, Lawrence, Gail-Joon Ahn, and Yuliang Zheng. 2003. "Dynamic and risk-aware network access management." In *Proc. SACMAT'03:* 217–230. Como, Italy: ACM.

Terranova, Tiziana. 2000. "Free labor: Producing culture for the digital economy." *Social Text* 18(2): 33–58.

Thom, René. 1975. *Structural Stability and Morphogenesis*. Trans. H. Fowler. Reading, Mass.: W. A. Benjamin.

Torvalds, Linus, and David Diamond. 2000. *Just for Fun: The Story of an Accidental Revolutionary*. New York: Texere.

Tschumi, Bernard. 1994. *Architecture and Disjunction*. Cambridge, Mass.: MIT Press.

Turbayne, Colin M. 1970. *The Myth of Metaphor*. Columbia: University of South Carolina Press.

Turega, M. 2000. "Issues with information dissemination on global networks." *Information Management & Computer Security* 8(5): 244–248.

Turing, Alan M. 1995. "Computing machinery and intelligence." In E. A. Feigenbaum and J. Feldman (eds.), *Computers and Thought,* 11–35. Cambridge, Mass.: MIT Press.

Turkle, Sherry. 1995. *Life on the Screen: Identity in the Age of the Internet*. London: Weidenfeld and Nicolson.

Turner, Victor. 1967. *The Forest of Symbols: Aspects of Ndembu Ritual.* Ithaca, N.Y.: Cornell University Press.

van Gennep, Arnold. 1960. *The Rites of Passage.* Trans. M. B. Vizedom and G. L. Caffee. London: Routledge and Kegan Paul.

Veblen, Thorstein. 1998. *The Theory of the Leisure Class.* Amherst, N.Y.: Prometheus. First published in 1899.

Venter, H. S. 2000. "Network security: Important issues." *Network Security* 6: 12–16.

Vidler, Anthony. 1995. *The Architectural Uncanny: Essays in the Modern Unhomely.* Cambridge, Mass.: MIT Press.

Vitruvius, Pollio. 1960. *Vitruvius: The Ten Books on Architecture.* Trans. M. H. Morgan. New York: Dover Publications. Written ca. AD 50.

Waterfield, Robin. 1994. "Introduction." In R. Waterfield (ed.), *Plato's Symposium,* xi–xl. Oxford: Oxford University Press.

Weber, Max. 1992. *The Protestant Ethic and the Spirit of Capitalism.* Trans. T. Parsons. London: Routledge. First published in German in 1904–1905.

Wertheim, Margaret. 1999. *The Pearly Gates of Cyberspace: A History of Space from Dante to the Internet.* London: Virago.

Weston, Dagmar. 2003. "The lantern and the glass: On the themes of renewal and dwelling in Le Corbusier's early art and architecture." In I. B. Whyte (ed.), *Spirituality and the City,* 146–177. London: Routledge.

White, Hayden. 1978. *Tropics of Discourse: Essays in Cultural Criticism.* Baltimore, Md.: Johns Hopkins University Press.

Wigley, Mark. 1992. "Untitled: The housing of gender." In B. Colomina (ed.), *Sexuality and Space,* 327–389. Princeton, N.J.: Princeton University Press.

Wilden, Anthony. 1987. *The Rules Are No Game: The Strategy of Communication.* London: Routledge and Kegan Paul.

Wilson, Tony. 1993. *Watching Television: Hermeneutics, Reception and Popular Culture.* Cambridge: Polity.

Winnicott, D. W. 1991. *Playing and Reality.* London: Routledge. First published in 1971.

Wittgenstein, Ludwig. 1922. *Tractatus Logico Philosophicus.* Trans. C. K. Ogden. London: Routledge and Kegan Paul.

Wittgenstein, Ludwig. 1953. *Philosophical Investigations.* Trans. G. E. M. Anscombe. Oxford: Blackwell.

Woodbury, R. F., S. J. Shannon, and A. D. Radford. 2001. "Games in early design education: Playing with metaphor." In B. de Vries, J. van Leeuwen, and H. Achten (eds.), *Proceedings of CAAD Futures 2001:* 201–214. Bordrecht, The Netherlands: Kluwer Academic.

Zeitlyn, David. 2003. "Gift economies in the development of open source software: Anthropological reflections." *Research Policy* 32: 1287–1291.

Zimmerman, M. E. 1990. *Heidegger's Confrontation with Modernity: Technology, Politics, Art.* Bloomington: Indiana University Press.

Žižek, Slavoj. 1991. *Looking Awry: An Introduction to Jacques Lacan through Popular Culture.* Cambridge, Mass.: MIT Press.

Žižek, Slavoj. 1999. *The Ticklish Subject: The Absent Centre of Political Ontology.* London: Verso.

Žižek, Slavoj. 2002. "Big Brother, or, the triumph of the gaze over the eye." In T. Y. Levin, U. Frohne, and P. Weibel (eds.), *CTRL {SPACE}: Rhetorics of Surveillance from Bentham to Big Brother,* 224–227. Cambridge, Mass.: MIT Press.

Žižek, Slavoj. 2003. *The Puppet and the Dwarf: The Perverse Core of Christianity.* Cambridge, Mass.: MIT Press.

Index

Index

Index